A
GREATER
PERSPECTIVE

Secrets of Success from the Sermon on the Mount
MARK HUGHES

A GREATER PERSPECTIVE
Copyright © 2022 by Mark Hughes

All rights reserved. Neither this publication nor any part of this publication may be reproduced or transmitted in any form or by any means, electronic or mechanical, including photocopying, recording or any information storage and retrieval system, without permission in writing from the author.

In some instances, names, dates, locations, and other identifying details have been changed to protect the identities and privacy of those mentioned in this book.

The mountain symbol ▲▲ has been included to highlight the Scripture verses that are part of the Sermon on the Mount.

Unless otherwise noted, all Scripture quotations are taken from the New King James Version. Copyright © 1982 by Thomas Nelson, Inc. Used by permission. All rights reserved. Scripture quotations marked ESV are from the ESV® Bible (The Holy Bible, English Standard Version®), copyright © 2001 by Crossway, a publishing ministry of Good News Publishers. Used by permission. All rights reserved. Scripture quotations marked KJV are from the King James Version. Scripture quotations marked MSG are taken from The Message, copyright © 1993, 2002, 2018 by Eugene H. Peterson. Used by permission of NavPress. All rights reserved. Represented by Tyndale House Publishers. Scripture quotations marked NASB taken from the (NASB®) New American Standard Bible®, Copyright © 1960, 1971, 1977, 1995, 2020 by The Lockman Foundation. Used by permission. All rights reserved. www.lockman.org" Scripture quotations marked NIV are from THE HOLY BIBLE, NEW INTERNATIONAL VERSION®, NIV® Copyright © 1973, 1978, 1984, 2011 by Biblica, Inc.™ Used by permission. All rights reserved worldwide. Scripture marked *Voice* taken from The Voice™. Copyright © 2008 by Ecclesia Bible Society. Used by permission. All rights reserved.

In the following pages, the form L*ORD*, in quotations from the Bible, represents the Hebrew *Yahweh*, while *Lord* represents *Adonai*, in accordance with the Bible version used.

Print ISBN: 978-0-9948601-4-9
eBook ISBN: 978-0-9948601-5-6

Printed in Canada

Contents

Introduction - Welcome to Opposite Day	1
1. The Stairway to Heaven	9
2. The Joy of Sorrow	21
3. Don't Worry, Be Happy	29
4. The Last Shall Be First	45
5. The Way Up Is Down	55
6. From the Inside Out	63
7. Messing with Moses	81
8. The Inverted Law	91
9. The Titanium Rule	107
10. For the Love of Pete	117
11. The F-Bomb	127
12. A Woke Nightmare	141
13. Mercy over Justice	153
14. Off Broadway	163
15. Knock, Knock! Who's There?	183
16. Rock around the Clock	211
Conclusion - Light in Darkness	221
Notes	231

Introduction

Welcome to Opposite Day

I do not believe there is a problem in this country or the world today which could not be settled if approached through the teaching of the Sermon on the Mount.

—Harry S. Truman

FOR MY SIXTIETH birthday, Kathy bought us tickets to see Jerry Seinfeld in person for his one and only visit to the great city of Winnipeg. He will probably never be back. It was the middle of January and it was -32°C outside—he wondered out loud if he had arrived at the North Pole. None of the 10,000 fans that packed the arena that night even noticed the temperature. Almost every face in the crowd was exclusively from my age demographic, a generation for whom Jerry Seinfeld had been a weekly staple. We had some of the best seats in the house, just five rows back from front and dead centre, so we could clearly see every wry facial expression throughout the 70-minute set of non-stop laughs. For most of us that night it was a dream come true. For me it was the best gift ever!

Jerry Seinfeld's iconic TV show of the 1990s was brilliant because it addressed all the funny little idiosyncrasies of modern life without being overly rude or perverse like so many shows are today. Many fans appreciated Seinfeld's ethic that you did not have to use profanity to be funny. One of my favourite episodes was called "The Opposite." In it, the hapless underachieving George Costanza concludes that he has been a failure because every choice he has ever made in life has been the wrong one.

> George: It's not working, Jerry. It's just not working.
>
> Jerry: What is it that isn't working?
>
> George: Why did it all turn out like this for me? I had so much promise. I was personable, I was bright. Oh, maybe not academically speaking, but… I was perceptive. I always know when someone's uncomfortable at a party. It became very clear to me sitting out there today, that every decision I've ever made, in my entire life, has been wrong. My life is the opposite of everything I want it to be. Every instinct I have, in every aspect of life, be it something to wear, something to eat… It's all been wrong.
>
> Jerry: If every instinct you have is wrong, then the opposite would have to be right.
>
> George: Yes, I will do the opposite. I used to sit here and do nothing, and regret it for the rest of the day, so now I will do the opposite, and I will do something![1]

George decides to take Jerry's advice to start doing the opposite of what he would normally have done and, wouldn't you know it, everything starts working for him. He stops shaving, starts confronting rude people in public and begins practising a new boldness with women. He immediately gets a date with a gal who is clearly out of his league, and she sets up a job interview for him with the New York Yankees baseball club. While walking out of the initial meeting, he bumps into team owner, George Steinbrenner. Acting contrary to his normal instincts, he criticizes the big man's management practices which, in ironic form, lands him the job of

Assistant to the Traveling Secretary. Buoyed with confidence and against his better judgment, he moves out of his parents' house. Enraptured with his success, he comes to regard "the opposite" as his new personal philosophy. Unfortunately for George, his newfound strategy only lasts a single episode (anything else would spoil the comedic premise of his character).

> What if some (or even many) of the choices that we make everyday are actually wrong and we don't even know it?

Fortunately for us, few of us have judgment as poor as George Costanza's. We generally don't need to do exactly the opposite for every single decision, but what if some (or even many) of the choices that we make everyday are actually wrong and we don't even know it?

The Sermon on the Mount (Matthew 5:1 to Matthew 7:29 ⛰) will forever be considered the greatest speech ever delivered. It has been universally praised—by leaders of world religions and atheists alike—for its meaningful and profound content. And yet, what Jesus teaches flies almost completely in the face of conventional wisdom. It is counterintuitive and antithetical from beginning to end: the first shall be last and the last shall be first; the way up is down, and the way down is up; less is more, more is less; the poor are blessed; the meek inherit the earth; it is good to be persecuted and bad to be praised; we should love our enemies and do good to people who hate us. In other words, Jesus teaches us to do… the opposite.

The Sermon on the Mount is also, without question, the single most significant teaching in the entire Bible and, arguably, from any literary source. Even non-Christians, who would otherwise disregard the rest of Scripture, highly praise the brilliance of Jesus' most famous words. The Hindu leader Mahatma Gandhi was absolutely infatuated with it. He said of it, "Christ's Sermon on the Mount fills me with bliss even today. Its sweet verses have even today the power to quench my agony of soul."[2] He admitted that if his faith was based solely on this one teaching alone he would be considered a Christian: "If then I had to face only the Sermon on the Mount and my own interpretation of it, I should not hesitate to say, 'Oh yes, I am a Christian.'"[3]

Jesus delivered this sermon in His home region of Galilee very early on in His ministry. He starts off with a bang, offering up the most radical, controversial and pragmatic advice (arguably commandments) on how religious faith is to be lived out. He repeatedly addresses the generally accepted interpretation of Old Testament theology only in terms of turning it on its head.

> *You have heard that it was said, "An eye for an eye and a tooth for a tooth." But I tell you not to resist an evil person. But whoever slaps you on your right cheek, turn the other to him also.*
>
> —Matthew 5:38–39 ▲

Jews in Jesus' day would have commonly understood the reference from Exodus 21 to mean that if someone harmed you, it was within your rights to repay them in kind. Even today, many gun rights proponents claim the same thing. They would say that if someone comes onto my property to harm me or my family, then I have the right to take out my gun and shoot them dead. However, Jesus claims the right thing to do is actually "the opposite"—we need to turn the other cheek. One could make a compelling argument for why this is a bad idea. But that doesn't change the fact that Jesus said it.

One of the little-known secrets of the Sermon on the Mount is that it does not contain any doctrine or statements of what Christians should believe.[4] We generally draw from the epistles of Paul and others to construct a New Testament theology. Jesus, on the other hand, concerns Himself here only with how we should live. What the Sermon on the Mount really is… (are you ready for this—it's deep) … a sermon!

Sermons are, by nature, meant to inspire people to the higher objectives of spiritual life. They are not typically theological treatises. When I preach, my unstated goal is not to try to fill people's heads with profound theological concepts but to try to communicate *one single truth* that might help them get through the next week. For me, that is a win. Neither do I have any delusions that I could possibly transform an entire crowd of peoples' lives in one single lesson. Jesus, on the other hand, accomplishes exactly that in one sermon. If the Sermon on the Mount came with a money-back guarantee—i.e. that if reading and studying it did not dramatically revolutionize your life for the better, you would get your money back—no one would ever get a refund! Nor would anyone want one!

If that sounds like hyperbole, it is intentional. The concepts within this sermon are nothing short of transformative; they have the potential to dramatically alter your life with every encounter. The words of the text can and should affect the hearer at a visceral level, which probably explains why Jesus shared it in a sermon form. Even as He concluded the discourse, the audience expressed amazement. In today's vernacular we would say they were "blown away!"

> *And so it was, when Jesus had ended these sayings, that the people were astonished at His teaching, for He taught them as one having authority, and not as the scribes.*
>
> —Matthew 7:26–27 ⛰

During the months I spent writing this book, virtually every day I experienced an epiphany on one level or another as I worked through the text. Many times, I had to cease from my writing to deal with bad attitudes, misgivings toward another person, forgiveness for someone that I had forgotten all about, or incorrect perspectives on living out my faith. Some days were painful. I pensively kept wondering why I was putting myself through such torment. But in fact, it was glorious, as I was experiencing the power of the written Word.

> *For the word of God is living and powerful, and sharper than any two-edged sword, piercing even to the division of soul and spirit, and of joints and marrow, and is a discerner of the thoughts and intents of the heart.*
>
> —Hebrews 4:12

I was being constantly reminded that the Sermon on the Mount had to apply to me personally before I was ever to be equipped to instruct another. It was an amazing experience, and even if I never sell a single copy the journey alone will still have been worth the effort.

Thousands of books have been written on the Sermon on the Mount. The majority systematically move through the discourse exegetically from beginning to end. It is an ambitious task, as Jesus touches on so many aspects of the Christian life that it is easy to get bogged down in it all. A complete treatment of the sermon might require dozens of volumes. Hence, many authors have chosen to cover only selected portions of the sermon like the Beatitudes or the Lord's Prayer.

The approach here, however, is unique. *A Greater Perspective* is essentially a crash course, covering the material in Jesus' sermon thematically rather than chronologically. As we examine each of the remarkable themes, we will look first at "putting it into perspective" and then gradually morph into a practical application of "putting it into practice." By the time we are done we will have, in one way or another, covered much of the Sermon on the Mount, hopefully in an accessible and applicable way—after all, it was always meant to be a practical guide for how we are to live as Christians.

We do not want to let it escape our notice that, within the Sermon on the Mount, Jesus reveals the true nature of God to us. He contrasts this with our own fallen and deficient nature, exposing where we have failed to measure up. He discloses why we make mistakes and yield to temptation, why we become bitter, sick and impoverished. He holds up a mirror to show us how selfish, petty and unforgiving we are. But most importantly, He reveals how much better we can be, teaching us how to pray, behave righteously and overcome evil. He describes how we can find joy and purpose in life. Jesus explains the meaning of true prosperity and happiness and how we can share it with others. He divulges the mysteries of the kingdom of heaven and how we can tap into little-known spiritual principles that will allow us to live a life that transcends the ordinary.

Virtually everything Jesus asks us to do flies in the face of convention and feels contrary to human nature. Though not quite as counterintuitive as George Costanza's "opposite day," the Sermon on the Mount does require a certain conviction on our part to do the *right thing* rather than the *easy thing*.

Throughout the following chapters, we will dive into these themes and break them down one at a time. The process of applying these truths to daily life will result in our lives being truly transformed as we discover the *greater perspective*.

Chapter One

The Stairway to Heaven

The fact that there's a Highway to Hell and only a Stairway to Heaven says a lot about anticipated traffic numbers.

—Darynda Jones

Around AD 600, John Climacus was a scholar monk at the monastery on Mount Sinai. He wrote a treatise for what later became the Eastern Orthodox Church. His document is called *The Ladder of Divine Ascent*. In its description it resembled a ladder that led from earth to heaven. There were thirty steps leading upward through things like meekness, forgiveness, holiness, honesty, prayer and so forth.[1] In many ways there is a resemblance to the themes found in the Beatitudes, which serve as Jesus' confounding introduction to the Sermon on the Mount. The Beatitudes are also best understood as a ladder or set of steps on what I am whimsically referring to in this chapter as the Stairway to Heaven. Each successive Beatitude progressively builds on the previous one.

> *Blessed are the poor in spirit,*
> *For theirs is the kingdom of heaven.*
> *Blessed are those who mourn,*
> *For they shall be comforted.*
> *Blessed are the meek,*
> *For they shall inherit the earth.*
> *Blessed are those who hunger and thirst after righteousness,*

For they shall be filled.
Blessed are the merciful,
For they shall obtain mercy.
Blessed are the pure in heart,
For they shall see God.
Blessed are the peacemakers
For they shall be called the sons of God.
Blessed are those who are persecuted for righteousness' sake,
For theirs is the kingdom of heaven.

—Matthew 5:3–10 ▲

As the introduction to the Sermon on the Mount, Jesus just throws the Beatitudes out there and makes no attempt to explain them. Our first response is likely to just read them and think, "You've got to be kidding!" The more astute reader may recognize them as a prelude to the rest of the sermon. The meek, the mournful and the poor in spirt are exactly the kind of people who will be the forgiving, loving, generous, truthful, prayerful types that He validates throughout the rest of His discourse. Here Jesus is establishing the overarching presuppositions that are the basis for the difficult "rules for life" in the rest of the sermon. There is no question that the Sermon on the Mount is challenging the listener to live a life of exceptional conduct, but such a thing is virtually impossible without first developing excellence in character. If conduct is what you do, character is who you are. One cannot consistently live in a manner inconsistent with their true character.

> *Even so, every good tree bears good fruit, but a bad tree bears bad fruit. A good tree cannot bear bad fruit, nor can a bad tree bear good fruit.*
>
> —Matthew 7:17–18 ▲

Anyone can feign good behaviour temporarily, but ultimately our true inner character will always be revealed. Some call it the toothpaste test—when the pressure is on, what's on the inside comes out. (We will discuss this in more detail in Chapter Six.)

In simple terms, Jesus is placing character before conduct. Attitude before action. Perspective before practice. It is amazing how this nuanced principle eludes so many adherents of the Christian faith. We often place far too much value on outward appearances and grossly underemphasize character. If we could be successful in developing unimpeachable character, we wouldn't have to give appropriate conduct a second thought. What "we do" would be an inevitable by-product of "who we are."

The Beatitudes, therefore, deal exclusively with the condition of the heart. These thoughts introduce potential followers of Jesus to the *greater perspective* of true Christianity, a perspective so foreign to our modern world that our most deeply held values stand in stark contrast to theirs. Tony Campolo is famous for saying, "If we were to set out to establish a religion in polar opposition to the Beatitudes Jesus taught, it would look strikingly similar to the pop Christianity that has taken over the airwaves of North America."[2] It is therefore intriguing that the very first step on the Stairway to Heaven is the renunciation of the world—becoming poor in this world and therefore poor in spirit.

In the 1970s Robert Plant spent much of his time answering questions about the lyrics he wrote for the song "Stairway to Heaven." The song was not only Led Zeppelin's greatest hit but is generally regarded as the greatest song of all time—at least by rock 'n' roll junkies. When asked why the song was so popular, he said it could be its "abstraction," adding, "Depending on what day it is, I still interpret the song a different way—and I wrote the lyrics."[3] In other words, he has no idea and was probably high when he wrote it.

Frankly, the lyrics are kind of all over the place, but the beginning of the song is about a woman who accumulates money only to find out the hard way that her life had no meaning and will not get her into heaven. This is the only part Plant would really explain, as he said it was "a woman getting everything she wanted without giving anything back."[4]

Eventually Plant came to hate his iconic song. It is one of the reasons he refused to reunite with his surviving Led Zeppelin bandmates for a world tour: "No amount of money is worth having to sing 'Stairway to Heaven' like you mean it, night after night, after night, after night...."[5] You have to appreciate his conviction, but no song should ever be given this kind of reverence. After all, the idea of a stairway to heaven did not originate with Led Zeppelin. That credit should be reserved for the Beatitudes.

The preaching of the kingdom of heaven always starts with a call to repent of worldly sin. John the Baptist, Jesus and Peter all began their ministries with the word "repent" (Matthew 3:2, 4:17, Acts 2:38). The point is, it really doesn't matter who we are or what we have accomplished already in life, God is only interested in us humbling ourselves and starting at the very lowest rung. The Beatitudes are not in random order but in a careful slow upward progression. But to be sure, they start at the very bottom—the very lowest rung.

Jesus tells a parable about two men who went up to the temple to pray. One was a Pharisee and the other, a tax collector. *"The Pharisee stood and prayed thus with himself, 'God, I thank You that I am not like other men—extortioners, unjust, adulterers, or even as this tax collector. I fast twice a week; I give tithes of all that I possess'"* (Luke 18:11–12). It was a proud prayer, to say the least. The Pharisee is just glad he is not like that wretched tax collector who, on the other hand, *"... stood afar off and would not so much as raise his eyes to heaven but beat his breast, saying, 'God, be merciful to me a sinner!'"* (Luke 18:13). Jesus commends the tax collector and concludes the parable with the words, *"... for everyone who exalts himself will be humbled, and he who humbles himself will be exalted"* (Luke 18:14).

Here's a point we don't want to miss: both men were rich, but only one of them was poor in spirit. Being "poor" and being "poor in spirit" are not exactly the same thing. One can be rich and still be poor in spirit. Like with the rest of the Sermon on the Mount, it has everything to do with the condition of the heart.

Solomon said it best in Proverbs:

> *"The poor plead for mercy, but the rich answer harshly."*
> —Proverbs 18:23 NIV

The backstory of this verse is very likely based on a story about his father, David, that Solomon would have known well from his youth. When David was a young man fleeing from his disapproving father-in-law, King Saul, he came near the lands of a very rich man named Nabal. Nabal owned huge tracts of land, had many servants and possessed thousands of goats and sheep. Since David had been protecting Nabal's people from harm, it seemed only reasonable to send a few men to Nabal to request provisions for his company.

> *David sent ten young men; and David said to the young men, "Go up to Carmel, go to Nabal, and greet him in my name. And thus you shall say to him who lives in prosperity: 'Peace be to you, peace to your house, and peace to all that you have!'"*
> —1 Samuel 25:5–6

Instead of offering assistance, Nabal answered harshly and basically insulted David by saying, *"Who is this David? Who does this son of Jesse think he is? I'm not giving anything to this man I don't even know!"* (1 Samuel 25:10).[6]

David, having his own pride issues, reacted and readied 400 men to attack Nabal's household and take what he needed by force. The only reasonable person in the entire story was Nabal's wife Abigail. Knowing that her husband was a recalcitrant scoundrel and having heard an attack was imminent, she secretly arranged to bring grain, wine, figs, five sheep and 200 loaves of bread for David and his men. She met him on the road and bowed before him, begging for mercy. David relented from his anger and pronounced blessing upon Abigail instead. Ten days later, Nabal died of a heart attack. David then proposed to Abigail and she became one of his wives.

Plot twists and turns aside, the evidence of this woman's virtue was clear. Abigail was not poor, but unlike her former husband, she was poor in spirit.

Being "poor" and being "poor in spirit" are not exactly the same thing. One can be rich and still be poor in spirit.

If the spirit of the poor is humility, the spirit of the rich is pride. The rich have power, influence and the wherewithal to procure anything they want. It is uncommon for the very wealthy to be humble. They can do what they want, say what they want and there is not really anything anyone can do about it. For example, people are entertained by the brashness of *Dragon's Den/Shark Tank's* Kevin O'Leary or Mark Cuban. They can be rude and even cruel when they think a presenter has a bad idea or did a poor job. O'Leary will use the expression "You're dead to me,"[7] which has reduced many a fledgling entrepreneur to tears. Viewers all think it is just part of his shtick, but insiders are adamant that it is no act and he really is a jerk.[8]

Of course, you don't have to be rich to have the spirit of the rich and be a jerk. Anyone who is proud and arrogant has nicely settled into this role, and most of us know a few of these as well.

The poor, by contrast, have no clout, no political power, no authority or standing in the community. They find themselves in the place where they must rely on the kindness of others, so they approach others more carefully. They are rarely brash. They know better. God loves the "poor in spirit" because He is looking for people that are contrite, humble and willing to submit themselves under the mighty hand of God.

Likely all of us have had a "rich man" moment, where our sense of entitlement kicked in and we acted in a way unbecoming of our faith. Unfortunately, I have had many. In the late '90s, our church was growing at an unprecedented rate. Over the course of a couple of years, we had grown from single to double to triple and quadruple services. We started services at 8:15 a.m. and finished at 8:15 p.m. on Sunday evening. Success was not my friend, as I made more mistakes during that season than any other. Sure, I was physically and emotionally exhausting myself, but that is never an excuse for bad behaviour.

It was in that season that we bought our first building. It was in a fantastic, highly visible location. The only problem was that we did not have sufficient parking for all the cars. We had a Canadian Tire store right next door with a parking lot that remained empty on Sunday until they opened at noon. I went and visited Carl, the store manager, and approached him as the poor man I was—I had a need, and he had the resources to solve my problem. I asked nicely and humbly and made a grand promise that our congregation would be patronizing the store on the way home from church. He graciously granted my request with the one caveat that the cars would be gone by noon. I assured him that they would, and we had a deal.

Everything worked swimmingly while we had one service that was dismissed before noon. But as time went by and we added services, the Canadian Tire parking lot remained full most of the day. Carl sent a few messages over, asking that we would deal with it. I reminded the congregation, but we had not provided any alternatives to them so they just kept parking in Carl's lot.

One Sunday he had enough, and he tagged every car with a note that the next time they parked there they would be towed at their own expense. Carl had every right to do what he did, but I flipped out anyway. Instead of praying or making him an offer to pay for parking or something… I put my "rich man" hat on and went over and ripped him a good one. I let him know what poor PR it was and what a short-sighted businessman he was that he would chase away potential customers instead of finding a way to reach them. After I had sufficiently "answered roughly" I turned on my heel and walked away.

I was no sooner past the door than I realized what I had done. I thought, "Have I completely lost my mind?" I realized I had acted in such an unseemly way that I had brought reproach on the church and perhaps the gospel. Maybe I was the only encounter Carl had ever had with a Christian pastor. What was he to now think of God and His people?

Feeling justifiably humiliated, I returned the next day as a "poor man" and I begged for mercy. Oh, and to clarify, my goal was not so we could keep parking there—I had burned that bridge. At this point I was just trying to salvage the reputation of Christ and His church. I told Carl I had acted in an unforgivable fashion, and I apologized profusely. I could see this made him more uncomfortable than my outburst the day before. It turned out Carl was a better man than me, and he immediately forgave me. Then, in a surprising twist of favour, he offered another way to make it work. He suggested we use his parking lot exclusively for the first service and leave our lot open for the second service. We took up the offer and it ended up working well, with very few people parking in their lot at noon when they opened.

We often learn more from our failures than our successes and that was certainly the case that day. I will not say I never acted like a "rich man" again, but I certainly became cognizant of its folly and have since worked very hard to remember that a Christ follower is blessed only when he or she is poor in spirit.

The COVID-19 global pandemic became one of the greatest tests that I (and every other pastor I know) ever had to face in my forty years of ministry. Adversity is always a better teacher than success. In our province of Manitoba, Canada, we faced more restrictions and lockdowns than almost any other jurisdiction. Our church was fortunate in that, because we had twenty-five years of television production and broadcast experience, taking our services online was a very quick pivot and the model was quite successful. However, over the course of the first two years of the pandemic, our buildings were closed to the public more than they were open. Each time we emerged from lockdown, less people ventured back to the church in person. If that wasn't frustrating enough, the regulations were changing weekly and, on occasion, almost daily. Many times, the new restrictions would roll out on a Friday and we needed to figure out how to both enact them and communicate them to our congregations by Sunday.

Most pastors found themselves in a no-win situation. We no longer had any sense of self-determination. We were at the mercy of health professionals who had been given extraordinary power to influence public policy. They essentially defaulted to focusing on the medical concerns of keeping the hospitals from overflowing and most Canadians, by nature being a pretty compliant bunch, understood they were doing the best they could, as everyone was in uncharted territory. Still, many factors did not seem well considered, like economic, constitutional and psychological concerns.

As the months dragged on, people became, understandably, more and more grumpy. I started getting calls and emails criticizing me for being weak, compliant or even cowardly (I have been called a lot of things before but never these). Some wanted me to make a defiant stand for our constitutional rights. Others thought it was time for civil disobedience. On the other side of the continuum, there were those that were mad that I was not using my influence to implore all church members to get the vaccine. Just like many others, I had strong opinions on COVID-19, lockdowns, vaccines and vaccine mandates. But they were just that—opinions. They had no power to change anything. My job was to try to navigate the situation with prudence, keep people safe and make sure we emerged from the pandemic with our reputation as a church intact. Some churches defied the health orders, and a few local pastors became household names as they made the news on a regular basis. There were court cases that ensued, and these churches and pastors lost every single time.

As I prayed about how to respond, an old idiom kept coming to mind: "You catch more flies with honey than vinegar." I knew exactly what it meant. I was to take on the posture of the "poor man" and avoid being the fist-waving acerbic personality that I am clearly capable of being. I had several personal relationships within the Manitoba Legislative Assembly, including the Premier. These leaders were in a really difficult place, where on balance they couldn't make anybody happy. I kept the lines of communication open and encouraged these men and women instead of attacking them. Then one day I got the call to come down to the Premier's office and pray for him. Instead of giving him my advice—which I had plenty of, by the way—I prayed for him to have God's wisdom as he wrestled with making the hard decisions he was facing every day.

At the end of the meeting, which included two other pastors, the Premier asked us if we would meet with the Chief Medical Officer, Dr. Roussin, who was the main spokesperson and framer of the provincial health orders. By this point in the pandemic, this man was easily the most publicly recognizable face in our city; he was either loved or loathed, depending on one's perspective as to how these things should have been handled. As we met with Dr. Roussin, we gave him our best arguments in favour of keeping the churches open, and then I put on my "poor man" hat and begged for mercy—I literally said, "We are begging you not to shut us down again." In response, he actually admitted out loud that we had certainly been a lot kinder in our approach to him than anybody else he had met with that week.

Two days later, he announced new highly restrictive health orders, but the ones for the churches were exactly what we had recommended to him. Honestly, we could barely believe the outcome. We had lost virtually every battle up until that point, and finally, a win. When many church leaders were clamouring on about how the church was being singled out and the subject of religious persecution, in effect, it was the exact opposite. We had gained incredible favour with the powers-that-be and were the last public gathering place to remain open.

> *Blessed are* the poor in spirit,
> For theirs is the *kingdom of heaven.*
>
> —Matthew 5:3 ▲

Chapter Two

The Joy of Sorrow

You can't be happy unless you're unhappy sometimes.
—Lauren Oliver

THE WORD "BLESSED" found in the Beatitudes could be more accurately translated as "happy." This is a contradiction of terms that should not be lost on us. How can you be happy when you are poor, mournful, meek and hungry (Matthew 5:3–7 ▲)? If you ask people what they want out of life, nine times out of ten they will say happiness. The American dream has been based on it for 300 years: "Life, Liberty and the pursuit of Happiness."[1] If this is the case, then why is it that only 33% of Americans claim that they are happy with their life?[2] Statistics vary, but there may be as many people struggling with depression or anxiety as there are people who report being happy.

Something seems out of whack. Why are so many people unhappy, or at least not happy? Maybe we have put unrealistic expectations on what happiness is. If it means having money, things, perfect health and ideal relationships, it is going to be a moving target at best. As soon as something goes out of place, we will be unhappy.

As the second step up the Stairway to Heaven, Jesus tells us we can be happy—not despite being mournful, but because of it. How can that be? Because it is during those moments that He will comfort us. "*Blessed are those who mourn, / For they shall be comforted*"

(Matthew 5:4 ▲). This comfort is a divine intervention more powerful than any negativity or adversity the world can throw at us.

> *Sorrow is better than laughter,*
> *For by a sad countenance the heart is made better.*
> *The heart of the wise is in the house of mourning,*
> *But the heart of fools is in the house of mirth."*
>
> —Ecclesiastes 7:3–4

There is an old story[3] about a man that was so depressed that he decided to walk to the Brooklyn Bridge and throw himself into the Hudson River to end it all. On his way to the bridge, he passed a stone mason who was on the sidewalk, fashioning a stone with his chisel. He looked up at the adjacent building and could not see where the stone would go, as the building looked complete. Even though the man had better (worse) things to do, his curiosity got the best of him and he asked the mason where the stone was going. The mason pointed up to the pinnacle of the facade and said, "Do you see that opening way up there? I am shaping the stone down here so it will fit in up there."

As the man carried on his way to the bridge, those words, "I am shaping the stone down here so it will fit in up there," ran over and over in his head. Suddenly, he gained a *greater perspective*; God was shaping him down here so he would fit in up there. He returned to his home with a new reason to live.

The heart cannot change if it never knows pain. C. S. Lewis, in his book *The Problem of Pain*, describes the value of pain this way: "God whispers to us in our pleasures, speaks in our conscience, but shouts in our pains: it is His megaphone to rouse a deaf world."[4]

In Western culture, we have been taught to avoid sorrow at any cost. We have failed to see its value and have often seen it as a sign of weakness, which, categorically, it is not. The benefits of sorrow, though not always apparent, are an essential part of spiritual life. First, sorrow helps us recognize happiness when it arrives, but more importantly, it puts things into a *greater perspective*. Even a rose garden has its thorns, and a bowl of cherry still has its pits. It's just life; it goes with the territory.

Jesus made one of the "worst" promises ever when He said, *"in the world you will have tribulation; but be of good cheer, for I have overcome the world"* (John 16:33). Indeed, we need to look past the promise of trouble to the reward of having good cheer. It is a two-edged sword. Nobody, and I mean nobody, gets a free ride. It would be ridiculous to think that we could just sail through life all happy-clappy every single day. Too many have bought into the big lie that if we just had fame, fortune, talent, influence or love, then all our troubles would be over. If this was even remotely true, why would the likes of Earnest Hemmingway or Robin Williams, wildly successful celebrities who possessed all those things, take their own lives? The world did not make them happy enough to want to live even one more day in it.

In 1978 two marketing researchers stumbled on an interesting human phenomenon. They had conducted an experiment where a group of children were shown two advertisements for a new toy while a control group was not shown any ads. The two groups were then offered the choice to play with the new toy with a not-so-nice boy or play with a different toy with a nice boy. Overwhelmingly, the children who had seen the ad chose to play with the not-so-nice boy. The control group, which did not see the ad, chose to play with the nice boy rather than the new toy.[5] The researchers were surprised that TV ads had the power to convince even children to prefer an inanimate lump of plastic over human kindness.

Advertisers have been capitalizing on this human weakness ever since. Today, the average North American sees up to 10,000 advertisements a day, [6] which costs the advertisers approximately $300 billion per year.[7] They do it for one reason and one reason alone—it works! These ads seem to be able to convince us that we cannot possibly be happy in life if we do not have the latest cell phone, the most luxurious car or the most powerful laundry detergent. We are truly a bunch of suckers.

In the 1980s, psychology professor Tim Kassar began doing meta-analysis on this subject, to determine whether this level of consumerism and materialism made people happier. His survey of twenty-two different studies determined that the outcome was the exact opposite: the more materialistic a person was, the more likely they were to be depressed or suffer from anxiety.[8] Kassar claims, not only do materialistic people pay a very high price with their wellbeing but they are also less happy, less satisfied in life, and more likely to suffer from physical ailments than their less materialistic counterparts.[9] Even worse, these same people tend to affect other peoples' wellbeing in that they are more selfish, more narcissistic and more likely to manipulate others for their own interests.[10]

> Maybe we need to rethink what it is to be happy. Maybe happiness was never meant to be a life of continuous mirth and celebration. Maybe we were never meant to go from mountaintop to mountaintop and avoid the valleys in between.

Martin Luther King Jr. decried the cultural brokenness of materialism decades ago. He believed that it was the bedfellow of racism and militarism and that none of these problems would ever be resolved until we had a radical shift in cultural values. In one of the last speeches of his life, just days before he was assassinated, he implored Americans with these words:

> I am convinced that if we are to get on the right side of the world revolution, we as a nation must undergo a radical revolution of values. We must rapidly begin…we must rapidly begin the shift from a thing-oriented society to a person-oriented society. When machines and computers, profit motives and property rights, are considered more important than people, the giant triplets of racism, extreme materialism, and militarism are incapable of being conquered.[11]

Clearly, that revolution never happened and we just carried on down the path of becoming an even greater things-oriented society. The challenge was then, and still is today, that we cannot just one day become less selfish and more altruistic. Worldly values must be replaced with something else—something higher, better and more meaningful—which is precisely what the Sermon on the Mount is capable of providing.

I have always argued that the pursuit of worldly happiness is an emotional rollercoaster that no one should be on.[12] What we really should be pursuing is joy. This is because, generally, happiness is based on external circumstances while joy comes from within.[13] Nevertheless, the word that Jesus uses in the Sermon on the Mount is "happy." Eight times He specifically uses the Greek word *makarios*, which when properly translated can only mean "happy."[14] Maybe we need to rethink what it is to be happy. Maybe happiness was never meant to be a life of continuous mirth and celebration. Maybe we were never meant to go from mountaintop to mountaintop and avoid the valleys in between. Maybe this is why only one third of people can describe themselves as happy. Another third are sad and the other third somewhere in between, as they are currently on their way up or the way down the mountainside of happiness.

Personally, I have always struggled a bit with the mountaintop analogy. For one thing, as a snow skier I am always happier when I am going down the mountain than up. Hmm?

What if we could learn to be happy irrespective of what end of the slope we are on? Frankly, that is exactly what the Beatitudes are suggesting. After all, life is a journey to be enjoyed, not a destination to be reached. It doesn't matter who you are—unless you are a Tibetan monk, you will not be living on the mountain top. And who would even want to, anyway? I've been to the Himalayas; they don't even have running water up there, let alone internet access.

The Sermon on the Mount, specifically in the Beatitudes, redefines happiness. We are taught that we can be and should be happy when we are poor, mournful, meek, hungry, etc. How can this possibly be true?

Again, Tim Kassar's research gives us some incredible insight into a paradigm of happiness that is lost on most people. It at least in part explains the values of the Sermon on the Mount.

Kassar articulates two types of motivations in life: extrinsic goals and intrinsic goals.[15] Extrinsic goals relate to external influences such as money, fame, status, or anything that requires validation from others. Intrinsic goals relate to yourself—personal growth, health and relationships with yourself and others.

Unfortunately, people in our culture are trained at a very young age to pursue extrinsic goals. The average three-year-old can already identify 200 name brands. By the time they enter grade school they have learned the importance of wearing the "right" clothes and owning the "right" Nike basketball shoes, even though they do not play basketball. There is no internal or intrinsic motivation behind this; it is solely to receive validation from others. This bankrupt and shallow extrinsic motivation continues as they age, and the accoutrements just get more expensive as they take on the form of cars, boats and houses.

Our fascination with the excessive lifestyles of movie stars, sports icons and rap artists only feeds the insatiable monster of desire. Kassar's research shows that, on average, these celebrities are much more miserable than those who are not encumbered by excessive things.

Intrinsic goals do not require external validation. They include things like (but not limited to) playing the piano in an empty family room for your own enjoyment, painting a watercolour of a sunset, reading a book, going for a jog, having a picnic under a tree, hanging out with family, enjoying a long conversation with friend, praying to the God of heaven, worshipping in a church service, serving a meal to the homeless, going on a short term mission trip… and so on. The simplest way to find happiness is the do more things that are intrinsically motivated and less things that are extrinsically motivated.

Orville Kelly was a US Army commander sent to the Bikini Atolls in the South Pacific in 1957.[16] Those were the days when the Americans were experimenting with atomic bombs, blowing the "useless" atolls out of the water and sending gigantic radioactive clouds drifting aimlessly across the Pacific. Kelly witnessed the testing of twenty-two separate atomic explosions. There was no way of knowing for sure how much radioactive exposure he received, but it was significant. In 1973 he was diagnosed with terminal lymphatic cancer and given three to six months to live. The US Army, in their inimitable fashion, would not admit the connection to the nuclear testing and disavowed any compensation.

Kelly was miserable, depressed and dying. One day he read *"Blessed are they that mourn: for they shall be comforted"* (Matthew 5:4 KJV ▲). He read it over again and realized it was for him. He turned the Beatitude into a prayer and prayed it continually. Soon after, Kelly had an epiphany that we are all terminal. He came to grips with the fact that everybody dies—some people just know when. He concluded there was no benefit in lamenting that fact and forfeiting living the days he still had left. He decided to host a big party and told the guests, "This is a cancer party. I have been told I have terminal cancer. But my wife and I realized we are all terminal. We decided to start a new organization: MTC. Make Today Count. You are all charter members."[17]

From that day forward, he decided to inspire people to live every day like it was important, love life and make a difference. His new purpose captured the imagination of thousands of others who decided to *make today count* as well. The initial three months came and went, and Orville was still here. The outside-chance six months came and went, and he was still going strong. Twelve months arrived and there was no sign of departure. Then two years, then three years and then four. Orville Kelly lived an astonishing seven years after he was diagnosed and accomplished more with his life during that time than he had in all the years before.

What would happen if, instead of loathing our difficult and painful moments of life, we, too, embraced them as an opportunity to grow? People who have discovered a *greater perspective* on life do precisely that.

Chapter Three

Don't Worry, Be Happy

In every life we have some trouble.
But when you worry you make it double.

—Bobby McFerrin

IN 1988 WHEN Bobby McFerrin released the borderline nursery rhyme "Don't Worry, Be Happy," it quickly rose to number one on the charts. With its Jamaican beat, the song became an unofficial anthem in Jamaica after Hurricane Gilbert struck the island in September 1988, causing months of hardship.[1] At the Grammys the following year it won Song of the Year, Record of the Year and Best Male Pop Vocal Performance. Never mind that it had no instrumentals whatsoever and was sung entirely a cappella. The chorus goes, "(Ooh, ooh ooh ooh oo-ooh ooh oo-ooh) don't worry. (Ooh, ooh ooh ooh oo-ooh ooh oo-ooh) be happy" over and over again!

The song's insipid message somehow struck a chord (pun intended) with a North American audience that, after a bitter economic recession in the early 1980s, was now experiencing the longest period of economic growth since WWII. Grumpy comedian George Carlin opined it "was exactly the kind of mindless philosophy that Americans would respond to."[2] *Blender* magazine was even less kind when it wrote, "It's difficult to think of a song more likely to plunge you into suicidal despondency than this."[3]

Be that as it may, the advice echoes exactly what Jesus gave to His listeners on that Galilean hillside 2,000 years ago in the Sermon on the Mount. However, Jesus did it in reverse order by first telling His audience to "be happy" repeatedly in the Beatitudes and then saying "don't worry" in the following discourse. And then He makes a compelling case for why worry doesn't work anyway.

> *Therefore I say to you, do not worry about your life, what you will eat or what you will drink; nor about your body, what you will put on. Is not life more than food and the body more than clothing? Look at the birds of the air, for they neither sow nor reap nor gather into barns; yet your heavenly Father feeds them. Are you not of more value than they? Which of you by worrying can add one cubit to his stature?*
>
> *So why do you worry about clothing? Consider the lilies of the field, how they grow: they neither toil nor spin; and yet I say to you that even Solomon in all his glory was not arrayed like one of these. Now if God so clothes the grass of the field, which today is, and tomorrow is thrown into the oven, will He not much more clothe you, O you of little faith?*
>
> *Therefore do not worry, saying, 'What shall we eat?' or 'What shall we drink?' or 'What shall we wear?' For after all these things the Gentiles seek. For your heavenly Father knows that you need all these things. But seek first the kingdom of God and His righteousness, and all these things shall be added to you. Therefore do not worry about tomorrow, for tomorrow will worry about its own things. Sufficient for the day is its own trouble.*
>
> —Matthew 6:25–34 ▲

In light of the fact that humans are the only species that even have the capacity to worry, it is interesting that Jesus keeps comparing us to birds, flowers and grass. Lions, for example, don't pace back and forth in their caves worrying about whether little Simba is going to get into a good college or not. (Although animals do suffer from anxiety and can get under extreme stress.[4]) Still, it seems like a bit of an unfair comparison, since birds don't have mortgages to pay, flowers don't buy their clothes on maxed-out credit cards and who knows what grass thinks about. (Not much, me thinks.)

However, if there is one line that should stand out to us in this didactic it is where He says, *"O you of little faith"* (Matthew 6:30 ⛰). That is the nub of the real problem. Worry is a sign that we lack faith, that we really don't trust God to take care of our every need like He said He would.

Jesus had a lot of patience with His twelve disciples but He did seem to indicate a certain frustration with them when they lacked faith. He mostly connected that deficiency with their fear and worry. When they were caught in the storm on the Sea of Galilee, they woke Jesus from a much-needed nap and said, *"Do you not care that we are perishing?"* After He calmed the winds and waves, He rebuked them: *"Why are you so fearful? How is it that you have no faith?"* (Mark 4:38–40). It is doubtful that Jesus was just grumpy from being aroused from his *meddachschlop*.[5] Fear and worry are the opposite of faith.

We often imagine unbelief to be the opposite of faith—and it is a major detriment—but fear is much more than that, fear is the real faith killer. Fear is negative faith. Whereas faith expects something good is going to happen, fear expects something negative to happen.

When we read through the book of Job it is hard not to feel sorry for the poor slob, as it just doesn't look like any of his calamity was self-inflicted. It seemed like God made a bet with Satan that Job would never flinch in his faith no matter what he threw at him (Job 2:3–7). Or, as Alan Arkin told his grandchildren in the movie *Joshua, Then and Now*, "The Book of Job is much more than a gambling story with a happy ending."[6] For the most part, the Bible describes

Job's character as unimpeachable. But then we stumble on this little revealing line that comes out of his mouth, *"For the thing I greatly feared has come upon me, and what I dreaded has happened to me"* (Job 3:25). Clearly there was some level of culpability on Job's part. He carried certain fears regarding his children and sure enough, they came to pass. This is the problem with fear and worry; it has the potential to produce significant results, just like faith—only very negative ones.

In 1948 Columbia University Professor of Sociology Robert K. Merton coined the term "self-fulfilling prophecy." The idea was that if someone predicted or deeply believed that something was going to happen, they would act into its eventuality and it would actually happen. His most famous example was the story of the fictious "Last National Bank." Rumours began to spread around the town of Millingville that the bank was going to file for bankruptcy. Because of this fear, which had no root in reality, the townsfolk rushed down to the bank and began closing their accounts for cash all at once. Because banks do not hold cash reserves anywhere near the level of their deposits, the bank suspended withdrawals. This further convinced the account holders that the bank was insolvent, and the situation escalated to the point of Cartwright Millingville, the bank owner, declaring bankruptcy.[7]

This phenomenon has taken on different nomenclatures over the years: the "Oedipus effect," "bootstrapped induction" and "Barnesian performativity," but they are really just other names for what I often call the Fear Factor. Over the years we have seen it manifest in stock market crashes, oil shortages, and my personal favourite, toilet paper shortages. It seems that in North American culture we have this irrational fear of running out of toilet paper. In December of 1973, during what was dubbed the "oil crisis" in the US, Johnny Carson joked one night in his monologue that what he was really worried

Don't Worry, Be Happy

about was a toilet paper shortage. The next day people began to hoard the rolls and, sure enough, created a shortage.[8] It happened again in 2020 during the early days of the COVID-19 pandemic. News reports were warning that supply issues might affect groceries, gas and other essentials, and given the bizarre nature of humanity, people stocked up on toilet paper. I comforted our congregation by reminding them that if there really was a food shortage coming, they wouldn't need toilet paper—do the math!

One of the most tragic but instructive examples of the Fear Factor is that of Karl Wallenda. He grew up in Germany as part of a family circus act that went by the name The Great Wallendas. They were a high wire act that innovated with new and dangerous stunts. Their signature move was the four-man pyramid. In 1928 the family moved to the USA, becoming known as The Flying Wallendas, and Karl took the act to a new level with the seven-man high wire pyramid.

The Wallendas were no strangers to tragedy, as in 1962, after a decade of performing the pyramid, something went wrong and the team fell to the ground. Two family members were killed and one of the uncles was paralyzed from the waist down. Karl broke his ribs during the fall but still managed to catch one of the performers with his legs, saving his life.[9] In 2017 the team once again crashed to the ground. and although no one died, Karl's great-granddaughter Lijana broke every bone in her face. It required seventy-three screws to put her back together and she now breathes threw a tracheal hole in her neck and talks without being able to move her jaw. It is truly sad to watch her struggle to communicate.

Karl's end was just as inglorious. In 1978 the then seventy-three-year-old was in San Juan, Puerto Rico, attempting to walk a wire stretched between two towers of the ten-story Condado Plaza Hotel. Spectators filled the streets and television cameras were recording the event. This was something Karl could almost do in his sleep; even at his age he had great balance and composure. Halfway across, he lost his balance and fell to his death when he struck the ground 37 metres below. Many speculated what had gone wrong, but his widow said this: "All Karl thought about for three straight months prior to the accident was falling. I believe he fell because he expected to fall."[10]

The short list of what we worry about usually includes our money, our health, our family and our job. When I poll audiences on this, most people are four for four. And of course, these are exactly the things Jesus told us not to worry about in the Sermon on the Mount. Different schools of thought vary slightly on how fear progresses, but in general, *worry* is phase one; *anxiety*, phase two; and *terror* is the full-blown expression of dread.[11]

WORRY tends to reside in the mind, occurring when we think about the possible negative outcomes of specific situations. This was Jesus' accusation of Martha when she was busy making lunch and her lazy-butt sister Mary wouldn't help: *"Martha, Martha, you are worried and troubled about many things"* (Luke 10:41).

ANXIETY is visceral and is experienced deeper, more at a gut level. Often people are not even sure what they are anxious about. In the book of Daniel we learn that King Nebuchadnezzar had a dream that he couldn't even remember. He was greatly vexed and full of anxiety about it: *"I have had a dream, and my spirit is anxious to know the dream"* (Daniel 2:3).

TERROR is experienced externally. It is not an imagined or hypothetical threat but a life-threatening event, producing a mental, emotional and physical reaction. When the disciples were in a boat that was filling with water and about to sink to the bottom of the Sea of Galilee, the boys were understandably fearful. They spent every day on that body of water, so if they said, *"Do You not care that we are perishing?* (Mark 4:38) they weren't just whistling Dixie—they were actually in danger of perishing.

Interestingly, Jesus was not sympathetic toward their terror. From His perspective, it was a complete lack of faith, for they had forgotten who it was that was in the boat with them. David wrote in the Psalms, *"You shall not be afraid of the terror by night, / Nor of the arrow that flies by day"* (Psalm 91:5).

If we can nip worry in the bud early on, we may be able to avoid the devastating spiral into the depths of anxiety and terror. There has never really been any doubt about the negative effects of worry and stress, yet it is epidemic in the Western world. We have succeeded in making our lives so complicated, we have to hire life coaches to help us manage it all. University of Toronto psychology professor Jordan Peterson claims that most, if not all, mental illness is a "complexity related phenomenon." What he means is that our lives have become so complex that many of us can no longer bear it. This then manifests as mental illness in the area of "our greatest genetic susceptibility." He uses the analogy of a balloon that expands beyond its tolerance and then bursts at its weakest spot. For some, it is anxiety, for others, depression or PTSD, and in extreme situations, suicide. Not everyone agrees with him, but he does make a compelling argument.[12]

If we can nip worry in the bud early on, we may be able to avoid the devastating spiral into the depths of anxiety and terror.

Many people read the Sermon on the Mount like it is poetry, often completely missing the fact that it offers practical and helpful advice on a variety of subjects. Worry is right up at the top of the list, so let's look deeper into what Jesus teaches on the subject.

> *Which of you by worrying can add one cubit to his stature?*
> —Matthew 6:27

WORRY DOES NOT ACCOMPLISH ANYTHING

I have no idea why anyone would want to add an entire cubit to their stature. To add another eighteen inches would make most of us over seven feet tall! That likely is not His point. He really is just saying that worry has no power to accomplish anything, so just stop doing it.

Dr. Richard Carlson PhD, an American author, psychotherapist and motivational speaker, was famous for these two rules for life: Rule 1 - Don't sweat the small stuff. Rule 2 - It's all small stuff.[13] This, of course, is a bit of an overstatement, but it does remind us that too often we make mountains out of molehills. There is no way to verify the following list with complete accuracy, but it is said that most things people worry about will never happen.[14]

> 40% of all things that we worry about could never come to pass (like being hit by a meteorite).
>
> 30% of all our worries involve the past and therefore cannot be changed.
>
> 12% of our worries concern the affairs of others that aren't any of our business.
>
> 10% are health related worries (real or imagined) which only get worse as we worry about them.
>
> 8% of our worries could be described as "legitimate."

Some people will immediately counter with "Yeah, but what about the eight percent?" Perhaps Mark Twain said it best: "I have had many problems in my life… many of which never came to pass."

Life is just way too short to worry about things that may or may not happen.

While I was writing this chapter, my ninety-two-year-old mother called me and, without even saying Hello, began with, "I'm worried about your brother!"

I immediately responded with, "Well, don't be, I just spoke to him and he's fine. You need to find something else to worry about."

She came back with, "I don't want to worry about something else."

I insisted, "Well, you are going to have to because he's fine and now you have to find something else to worry about."

Confused, she said, "I don't want to worry about anything."

In agreement, I answered back, "Perfect, then that is settled."

Unpersuaded, she said, "It's not perfect. I'm worried about your brother."

Trying to end the circular argument, "Then that's the choice you are making."

Now a bit angrier, she retorts, "I'm not choosing to worry about him. I am just worried about him!"

In a last futile attempt, I said, "I know, because it is a choice."

Finally, she said, "You are such a pain—why do I even call you? Don't you ever worry?"

Using humour to end the conversation, I reminded her, "Of course not. Worry is sin. If I'm going to sin, I'm going to pick something a lot more fun than worry."

She started laughing and forgot what she was worrying about.

> *Therefore, do not worry about tomorrow, for tomorrow will worry about its own things. Sufficient for the day is its own trouble.*
>
> —Matthew 6:34 ▲

WORRYING ABOUT THE FUTURE STEALS THE JOY OF LIVING TODAY

Worry paralyzes us. When worry settles into our minds we start to imagine all sorts of negative outcomes. Once it takes root it has the potential to turn into lingering anxiety or fear.

When the twelve spies entered the Promised Land to check it out, they saw all the green hills, the fertile plains, the well-watered fields. They brought back a bunch of grapes so big it took two men to carry it on poles. But they also saw the giants and that played with their minds. Rather than focusing on the promise and the potential, they only saw the problem, "We were like grasshoppers in our own sight, *and so we were in their sight*" (Numbers 13:33). Really? Where did this "grasshopper" thing come from? Did they talk to the giants? Did they ask the giants, "What do we look like to you? Ants? Cockroaches? Grasshoppers? That's it, isn't it? Grasshoppers! We look like grasshoppers to you, don't we?" No, this whole thing took place in their own minds. *"We were like grasshoppers <u>in our own sight</u>..."* They were paralyzed by their own feelings of inadequacy and projected that back on the giants *"...and so we were in their sight."* We have no idea what the giants thought about the spies. They may not even have seen them. If they had and they were as terrifying as they said, would they not have killed the spies and eaten them for breakfast?

A friend of mine owned a Yacht on the east coast of Florida. He had dreams of retiring on it and cruising the Caribbean. He spent a decade wintering on the boat and never once ventured out of the harbour. Even though he dearly wanted to experience the adventure of sailing the open seas, the fear of the unknown prevented him from even trying. He worried about running out of fuel in the Atlantic, or having the engines break down, or hitting a reef, or losing his generator, etc. Every summer when I saw him back in Canada, I would ask him if he had made it offshore. And year after year, he had a new haunting concern that prevented him from venturing out.

One year he told me he was worried about pirates. "Pirates?" I asked, "You know that was just a movie, right? *Pirates of the Caribbean* is not a true story and Johnny Depp is not a real pirate." He went on to explain that there are modern-day pirates that prowl the Caribbean, boarding private boats, killing the people and stealing their stuff, which, I am sure, on some small scale does exist. Deciding he had better deal with the possibility before he dared set out to sea, he figured the best thing to do would be to buy a handgun. But when he went to the gun shop they wouldn't sell him one… because he was a Canadian.

I laughed and said, "Seriously? I thought they gave guns away as an incentive to open a bank account down there!" Apparently, they draw the line at selling guns to Canadians, which makes sense since most of us have never seen a handgun in person and we would likely be a menace to a society of highly responsible American gun owners. At any rate, he couldn't get a gun and that meant he would not be able to shoot to death anybody that approached his boat uninvited. That meant the risk of pirates was just too great and he had better remain in port and keep scrubbing his boat with a toothbrush.

One of the great regrets people have at the end of their lives is that they did not take a few more risks. Do we really want to put our lives on hold because we are worrying about some irrational, improbable or implausible thing that could possibly never happen?

> *Now if God so clothes the grass of the field, which today is, and tomorrow is thrown into the oven, will He not much more clothe you, O you of little faith?*
>
> —Matthew 6:30 ▲

WORRYING IS A SIGN THAT WE REALLY DON'T TRUST GOD

This is the most important reason of them all. Jesus comes right out and says that being fearful about the needs of this world is a sign that we don't trust Him.

In many ways the COVID-19 global pandemic was a test of our faith. It was a medical pandemic, but it managed to produce another pandemic of worry and anxiety. Sales of legal cannabis doubled to $17.5 billion.[15] Sales of anti-anxiety drugs spiked 34% to over $16 billion.[16] (Ironically, the manufacturers of these drugs were companies like Pfizer and Moderna - i.e. the same people who were already making billions on vaccines.) And at the end of the day none of these drugs, legal or illegal, can do a single thing to cure anxiety; all they can do is numb our tiny little brains and mask the symptoms.

It is hard to speak for the rest of the world, but in our nation of Canada people lived in an almost constant state of fear. The media, government leaders and healthcare professionals bombarded us daily with gruesome case count numbers and death rates. New warnings about impending perils were announced weekly, if not daily. The moment any faint level of optimism emerged there was more doomsaying from the ubiquitous Dr. Anthony Fauci (or the less impressive Dr. Theresa Tam in Canada), who would predict yet another surge upon a surge and more impending death. That is not to say that there was not a serious health threat, but the level of angst went through the roof. Christian people got caught up in the fear just like everybody else. They could recite the daily death count with the best of them, and millions jettisoned their faith altogether as we saw the biggest church drop-out rate in history.

In Manitoba, we were subject to some of the strictest health measures in the world. In 2020 we were shut down more than we were open, and 2021 wasn't much better. However, at Church of the Rock we had decided that either our God was bigger than COVID-19 or He wasn't, and so if our doors could be open, they were. Our staff showed up for work every day, even during the early days when people acted like the world was ending. Our team continued to work tirelessly throughout the entire pandemic, often seven days a week. We created and streamed spiritual content every night of the week in an attempt to continue to minister faith, not fear, to our congregation. During the darkest days of the pandemic, when death rates were at their highest—by the grace of God—we never had a single transmission from one staff member to another. (We did see several staff members contract COVID-19 elsewhere, but all recovered.)

King David wrote,

> *He who dwells in the secret place of the Most High*
> *Shall abide under the shadow of the Almighty.*
> *I will say of the LORD, "He is my refuge and my fortress;*
> *My God, in Him I will trust."*
> *Surely He shall deliver you from the snare of the fowler*
> *And from the perilous pestilence.*
>
> —Psalm 91:1–3

God specifically promised that He would deliver us from the perilous pestilence, which incidentally includes COVID-19.

Jesus doesn't spend a lot of time in the Sermon on the Mount teaching us how not to worry. Mostly, he just tells us to stop doing it. "Don't worry, be happy." The apostles continued to reinforce the concept, and it was the Apostle Paul who gave us a prescription so simple that, if we could just learn to exercise it, we could vanquish worry the moment it rears its ugly head.

> *Be anxious for nothing, but in everything by prayer and supplication, with thanksgiving, let your requests be made known to God; and the peace of God, which surpasses all understanding, will guard your hearts and minds through Christ Jesus.*
>
> —Philippians 4:6–7

Paul tells us that, if we would just take our concerns to God in prayer instead of ruminating on them, an inexplicable peace would guard our hearts and minds. Hearts and minds—the very places that worry resides. We have all experienced this. We start to imagine unpleasant scenarios revolving around a particular concern, and then we find we can't stop thinking about it. We try to shake it off but there it is, back on replay. Soon the thoughts have made their way down into our hearts. Our stomach is now in a knot, as worry has turned into anxiety and possibly irrational fear. Paul says you have got to bring those concerns to God.

The word *supplication* means to make a specific request. So, ask God what you would actually like Him to do to resolve the situation and then enter into *thanksgiving*, which means to give Him thanks for the answer. Paul claims that this simple exercise will bring a peace that does not even seem to make sense (*"surpasses all understanding"*). As troublesome and bothersome as worry, anxiety and fear are, they really might be that easy to defeat.

One day a businessman ran into a former client. The client knew the businessman had been plagued with high blood pressure and ulcers. Genuinely concerned, he said, "How's your health been?"

The businessman enthusiastically responded, "Great! My blood pressure is normal, the ulcers are gone and I don't have a worry in the world!" The client asked him what he had done to turn things around. "I hired a professional worrier," he explained, "Whenever I need to worry, I tell him, and he does all of my worrying for me."

Impressed, the client asked how much something like that cost. When the businessman told him it was $100,000 per year, the client asked incredulously, "How can you afford to pay him $100,000?"

Without missing a beat, the businessman replied, "I don't know, I let him worry about it."

Notwithstanding the obvious humour, maybe there is a lesson to be learned here—let HIM (God) worry about it! After all, Greater is HE who is in us than he who is in the world.

Chapter Four

The Last Shall Be First

It's going to be fun to watch and see how long the meek can keep the earth once they inherit it.

—Kin Hubbard

THE SERMON ON the Mount promises that the kingdom of heaven belongs only to the poor in spirit and those who embrace sorrow and suffering as part of the journey. Next, Jesus makes an even less believable promise when He says, *"… the meek will inherit the earth"* (Matthew 5:5 ▲).

Almost nobody believes that the meek will inherit the earth. J. Paul Getty, the founder of Standard Oil, is said to have put it this way, "The meek shall inherit the Earth, but not its mineral rights." Julius Caesar, Genghis Khan, Napoleon Bonaparte, William the Conqueror, Alexander the Great, Ivan the Terrible… none of these people were meek. Having the word "Conqueror," "Great" or "Terrible" in your name usually implies that you are anything but meek.

Maybe Jesus was trying to say something else, like, "Nice guys finish last," but was misquoted? Not likely. He was merely reiterating Psalm 37:11, *"The meek shall inherit the earth, / And shall delight themselves in the abundance of peace."* The more probable interpretation of this is that it is referring to a future reality. The word "inherit" always refers to something coming in the future; the time frame is mostly unknown, as someone has to die first. Maybe the people that need to die off for the meek to inherit the earth are the non-meek. When Christ returns at the end of the age, they will all be judged for not accepting the gospel, and the meek, those who were willing to submit themselves to His lordship, get to rule the Earth at his side for 1,000 years. (It's a very cool story and you can read about it in Revelation 20:4–6.)

So, if you are a Christian, you can be assured you are on the right side of history. But in the meantime, we need to figure out how we are going to live in this transitional age. Are we going to stoop to the level of the dog-eat-dog world, where we fight and bite one another trying to become the next alpha dog in our little corner of the backyard, or are we going to embrace the greater perspective of the Sermon on the Mount and live a life that transcends the ordinary?

It would be a mistake to think that God is looking to turn us all into underachievers so we can inherit the earth. On the contrary, He desires to take those who will become utterly dependent on Him and turn them into super-achievers. This is what He did with Noah, Moses, Joshua, Gideon, David, Daniel, and even the likes of Peter, Paul and Mary (the disciples, not the musicians). These names are part of a very long list of people who discovered that the last shall be first. Noah was ridiculed for 100 years for building a boat in the desert during the time before it had ever once rained, yet he was literally the *last* man standing after the flood—which made him the *first* in the new re-creation of the earth. Gideon was the "least in his father's house" of the "weakest clan in Manasseh"[1] (last born in the last clan) before he became the conqueror of the Midianites and the Judge of all Israel. The *last* became *first*.

Moses spent forty years on the backside of the desert tending his father-in-law's sheep before he earned his PHD (Potential Hebrew Deliverer). He was an eighty-year-old shepherd boy working for the "old man." By the way, the Bible calls Moses the world's meekest man:

"Now the man Moses was very meek, more than all men who were on the face of the earth" (Numbers 12:3). Once again, the last became first.

Each one of these champions of Scripture first learned the painful lesson of humility and submission and, therefore, meekness. There are at least three examples in the Bible of truly meek men who, in a sense, literally inherited the earth. Joseph, Daniel and Mordecai were each Jews living in pagan lands.[2] All three were humble, meek servants to the foreign kings of foreign empires. They were all rewarded for their faithfulness and eventually became oligarchs and rulers over the people of their captor nations.

> It would be a mistake to think that God is looking to turn us all into underachievers so we can inherit the earth. On the contrary, He desires to take those who will become utterly dependent on Him and turn them into super-achievers.

Mordecai's story is particularly interesting because he had a nemesis, Haman, who was the exact opposite of him. The Jewish captive Mordecai was meek and humble, while Haman, the Persian advisor to the king, was proud and ambitious. Yet, it was Mordecai who continually received promotion and recognition from the king. In a jealous rage, Haman conspired to have Mordecai and all the Jews hung on gallows, but in a fascinating reversal of fortune, Haman was hung on his own gallows while Mordecai was elevated to become the second ruler in the kingdom next to the king himself (Esther 10:3). It is one of those incredible stories where truth is stranger than fiction.

Jesus is quite serious when He says the meek shall inherit the earth.

We need to remember that meek does not mean weak.[3] In biblical times, the word meek was used to describe a wild stallion that was broken for riding. So, regardless of whatever it has come to mean today, its original meaning was "power under the control of another."[4] Even a broken stallion has the strength to crush its rider if it wanted to, but instead, it has allowed itself to come under the submission of its master. This is precisely the kind of person God is looking for. Truly meek Christians should expect that God will reward them, not only in the age to come but also in this age now.

> *For exaltation comes neither from the east*
> *Nor from the west nor from the south.*
> *But God is the Judge:*
> *He puts down one,*
> *And exalts another.*
>
> —Psalm 75:6–7

Our son likes to go by his first initial ("J"), so his friends call him Jay. He spent his childhood and adolescent years pursuing a love for sport. Whether it was soccer, volleyball or track and field, he excelled. It didn't hurt that he always had a height and weight advantage over his contemporaries. I remember times on the soccer pitch where he would be going in for a tackle and his opponent would literally jump out of the way and give up the ball rather than risk colliding with him. Sometimes boys with this kind of physical edge become the bullies in the crowd. Not Jay—he was always a team player, looking out for the next guy. And, fortunately for him, he did not inherit his father's A-type personality.

Jay doesn't need to be the loudest voice in the room or the centre of attention (although he can be). In the biblical sense of the word, I would describe him as meek. He is a quintessential example of power under control. Because of his size, Jay often ended up playing on teams with kids a year or two older than he was. We always encouraged him to make sure that he lived true to his Christian faith—be respectful, disciplined, hardworking and helpful; arrive early, stay till the end and help put away the gear. He didn't swear or tell dirty jokes or get into the stuff teenage boys are naturally attracted to. Jay was a gracious loser and a humble winner, the latter of which is the more important of the two.

On any team, there would always be a few super-outgoing, cocky types who considered themselves the team leaders. One of his teammates was so determined to be considered the captain that he wore a captain's arm band on the soccer field, even though he wasn't the captain, Jay was. In fact, Jay was chosen to be team captain time after time, even though he never once clamoured for the honour. When he made the provincial soccer team that represented Manitoba at the 2005 Canada Summer Games, he was once again chosen as captain. One day, the coach pulled us aside and paid us the ultimate compliment as parents: "There might be some that would not have seen your son as the obvious choice for captain, but to me, he exemplifies what I want to see in a team player and that's why I chose him. I wish I had twenty players on the bench like Jay."

Even the world recognizes character over charisma. Now that Jay is a grown man, he has taken these traits into the world of business. Nothing has changed, as he still continually gets promoted over his peers. Perhaps it seems counterintuitive in a society that celebrates demonstrative leadership, but Christians will always have an edge because God is in their corner.

The meek truly do inherit the earth. It is one of the little-known secrets of success from the Sermon on the Mount. It does not matter what endeavour, field of work or sport—we can try to compete for recognition and strive for acknowledgment or we can let God reward our meekness and move us to the front of the pack.

There is, however, yet another rung in the ladder on the journey from last to first. Being poor in spirit, mournful and meek involves intentionally emptying ourselves of the nature of the world, which is a deliberate pre-requisite to being filled back up with the nature of God.

> *Blessed are those who hunger and thirst for righteousness,*
> *For they shall be filled.*
>
> —Matthew 5:6 ▲

People often think sex is the most powerful human desire. It's not even close. Just think of how many times a day you need to eat, and then make your own comparison. Oddly enough, Napoleon understood this principle better than almost any other military leader in history. One of the reasons he managed to get his armies to march clear across the Alps into Italy was that he always kept their hunger satisfied. He was known to say, "An army marches on its stomach." That always produces a menacing mental image for me.

If you take all the vices in the world and roll them all together, they still cannot compare to food as our greatest desire… and weakness. Gluttony is named as one of the medieval church's seven deadly sins, yet today's church is afraid to even mention it for fear of being accused of body shaming. Comedian Jim Gaffigan, asks the question, "Why is 'still life' art always a bowl of fruit and never a box of donuts?" The answer: "Because fruit will sit for days but the donuts will be gone before anybody could possibly paint a picture of them."[5] Jesus does not shy away from this one (the topic, not the box of donuts), and in the Sermon on the Mount He challenges our extraordinarily pathetic level of human weakness and our preoccupation with basic earthly needs.

> *Therefore do not worry, saying, "What shall we eat?" or "What shall we drink?" or "What shall we wear?" For after all these things the Gentiles seek. For your heavenly Father knows that you need all these things. But seek first the*

kingdom of God and His righteousness, and all these things shall be added to you.

—Matthew 6:31–33 ▲

If we could just somehow replace our hunger for the things of this world with the things of God, Jesus promises us that He will take care of all the things we truly need. Once again, few of us really believe it. It doesn't help that we have many high-profile prosperity preachers teaching that God rewards us with earthly things. They point to their lavish homes, luxury cars and Learjets as evidence that is how it really works.

I have a pastor friend in Uganda who has planted hundreds of churches and built dozens of orphanages. He is one of the most effective spiritual leaders I know, anywhere! One day I asked him what was the biggest obstacle that the church faced in Uganda. I was expecting him to say political corruption, poverty, lack of resources, or the AIDS crisis (that was at one time worse than any nation on earth). Without hesitation, he said it was the American prosperity preachers that had filled the TV airwaves in Uganda. He said they had polluted the African Christian mindset with an American materialism that had rendered the church impotent. Pastors of struggling rural churches, where the people were poor but still happy, now insist on driving around in Mercedes Benzes while their people live in shanties with dirt floors. He made an interesting observation: "If this was the true gospel, it should work for anyone anywhere in the world. And for the Ugandan people, it doesn't work here."

When our church was in its early years, we had a young Malaysian student named Mae join our church. By the time she graduated from university, she had decided that she wanted to pursue a career in missions. Once she secured a position with a missions sending organization, off she went to Uzbekistan. (I had to look it up on a map to see where it was. It's right between Turkmenistan and Tajikistan. So, now you know too.) She raised her own support and we helped her out with a few hundred dollars a month. She moved around that part of the world and eventually ended up in Eastern China, reaching out to the highly marginalized Uyghur people. The Uyghur are a Turkic Muslim people group who are highly persecuted by the Chinese government. Many became refugees and fled to Turkey. Mae followed them.

Recently, she arrived back in Canada for a short visit, which she does every few years. She has been on the mission field for over twenty years now. I asked her how she could possibly survive with the small amount of support she receives from the West. She said, "That is a good question. I do not have nearly enough support, but somehow God always supplies, and I have never once not had enough for food or rent or clothes." I marvelled as I listened, because I realized she was living out Jesus' command not to worry about these things far better than I was. And what's more, He had never let her down.

The greater perspective of hungering and thirsting after the things of God is to be applied to every follower of Christ. Hanging out with a missionary for an hour is, however, a good way to remind us of that.

When our meeting was concluding, Mae was going to walk to the bus stop and wait in the -20°C winter night to ride the bus halfway across the city. When I offered her a ride to her accommodation, she could hardly believe that a senior pastor would go so far out of the way for her. I just said, "No problem," but deep down I was embarrassed. She had just travelled halfway across the world to see me! In that moment, I was humbled because I realized how much better she was at living out the Sermon on the Mount than I was.

It is not complicated. If we can turn our hunger towards the things of God, He will take care of everything else. But because we are immersed in an ethos much more materialistic than even what Jesus described 2,000 years ago—*"after all these things the Gentiles seek"*—it is that much harder to internalize the *greater perspective*.

I am always reluctant to tell stories of missionaries because people dismiss them as unrelatable. "Sure, that is a nice story, but I live in the real world, not on the mission field." We forget that the Sermon on the Mount was not taught in the Capernaum Missions Training Institute to twelve Bible students. It was delivered to literally thousands and thousands of people as far as the eyes could see on the hills of Galilee. The *greater perspective* of hungering and thirsting after the things of God is to be applied to every follower of Christ. Hanging out with a missionary for an hour is, however, a good way to remind us of that.

The key to hungering and thirsting is to empty oneself. For most of us, this is a foreign concept. We keep our stomachs, fridges and cupboards full, not to mention our closets, basements, garages, storage sheds and bank accounts. But hopefully every Christian has at least attempted a food fast of some sort once in awhile. Fasting is strongly recommended for spiritual growth.[6] I often laugh when people tell me their stories of the first time they tried to fast and they only lasted four hours because they had a headache or extreme hunger pangs. I remind them that they fast eight hours every night, yet they have never died in their sleep from starvation. For those of you who have managed to get to day two or day three on a fast, it is at that point that you begin to experience the powerful physiological urge of hunger. Your body subconsciously makes its way to the fridge, and you discover yourself staring longingly at a container of three-day-old Chinese food that is destined for the garburator. We will never feel true hunger if we are continually stuffing ourselves with food.

The same thing is true for spiritual things. It is impossible for us to feel spiritual hunger if we are continually stuffing ourselves with the things of this world. Again, becoming poor in spirit, mournful and meek is the emptying process that makes us utterly dependent on God. The things of this world become strangely dim, and we finally begin to long for something beyond this world. C. S. Lewis brilliantly described it this way, *"If I find in myself a desire which no experience in this world can satisfy, the most probable explanation is that I was made for another world."*[7]

Chapter Five

The Way Up Is Down

Be nice to people on your way up because you'll meet them on your way down.

—Wilson Mizner

LOUIS WAS A regular air traveller. He had racked up many frequent flyer points and was accustomed to being invited up to Business or First Class. On this particular day he was flying in Coach, and takeoff had already been delayed thirty minutes. He headed up to First Class and found the steward. He complained vehemently about his inconvenience in an entitled sort of way, even as all the other passengers were obliged to listen. The steward pulled out a pen and pad and asked, "Sir, what is your name?" Again, with all the other passengers watching on, he pronounced it carefully and spelled it out, anticipating an upgrade to First Class. Politely, the steward put away the pad and said, "Thank you, Sir. I must remember that and make sure I avoid any flight with you listed as a passenger."

If the Sermon on the Mount is the Stairway to Heaven, then why do the principles seem to move us downward? Well, because on "opposite day" the way up is always down. And down is often up. The kingdom of heaven teaches us the same.

This theme appears a few times in the Sermon on the Mount in various forms and throughout the Gospels in numerous places. Three times, Jesus declares, *"Whoever exalts himself will be humbled, and he who humbles himself will be exalted*" (Matthew 23:12, Luke 14:11, Luke 18:14). In Luke's version, the expression serves as the conclusion to the parable about being invited to a wedding feast. Jesus says it is better to take the lower seat than the higher one. For if you take the best seat, you might be asked to give up your place for a more honourable guest. But if you start at the lower seat, you might actually be invited to move up (Luke 14:7–11). In other words, the way up is down and the way down is up.

> *Let nothing be done through selfish ambition or conceit, but in lowliness of mind let each esteem others better than himself.*
> —Philippians 2:3

Jamaica's Usain Bolt was the world's fastest sprinter. He ran the 100 metres in 9.58 seconds. That is faster than the 9.79 seconds Canada's Ben Johnson ran in 1988 while he was juiced up on all kinds of steroids. (Ben was stripped of his Olympic gold medal and his world record.) It may be a long time before Bolt's record falls. He has won eight Olympic gold medals. He didn't even do silver or bronze. At the 2012 London Olympics, he defended both his 100-metre and 200-metre titles to become the first man in history to do so. Basking in his success, Bolt told the press, "I'm now a legend. I'm also the greatest athlete to live."[1]

The President of the International Olympic Committee, Jacques Rogge (a three-time Olympian himself), was immediately offended by Bolt's hubris and criticized his showboating, claiming it demonstrated a lack of respect for the other competitors. "The career of Usain Bolt has to be judged when the career stops," said Rogge, citing the success of US runner Carl Lewis. "Let Usain Bolt be free of injury. Let him keep his motivation which I think will be the case… Let him participate in three, four games, and he can be a legend."[2] It was amusing how quickly he got put in his place. I remember thinking how ridiculous it was to be so successful and yet to feel a need to be so self-aggrandizing about it at the same time.

I told people I was going to write a book about it, entitled *Legends for Dummies*. Chapter One will say, "If you are a legend and you actually tell people you are a legend, then you will be un-legended." There is no need for a Chapter Two.

In a book I actually did write, *A Greater Purpose*,[3] I spend hundreds of pages describing that the higher calling is to live for a purpose greater than oneself. When any of us reach the pinnacle of success, it is too easy to forget that it is really not all about us. This is not to say we should not strive to be the very best we can be. I dedicated an entire chapter to this in my second book, *A Greater Passion*.[4] Hard work and self-improvement are not unimportant, but we need to put it all in the right (greater) perspective. University of Toronto's Jordan Peterson says it this way, "Compare yourself to who you were yesterday, not to who someone else is today."[5] That is very good advice.

In our city of Winnipeg, Canada, the local churches managed to work together for *a greater purpose* by building a unique Christian culture that caused people to take notice. It came about because we valued one another's contributions and never relied on one or two superstars to carry the day. We hosted conferences together, citywide prayer meetings, pastors retreats and outreach initiatives. During the 1990s, we staged the largest March for Jesus in North America year after year. During our peak, we were seeing some 50,000 lovers of Jesus march through our streets singing God's praises. In the early 2000s, we shifted gears and had dozens of churches participate in a citywide outreach called Love Winnipeg. Again, it was the biggest such event in North America. We did random acts of kindness, evangelism, street carnivals, fed the poor, clothed the homeless, beautified neglected neighbourhoods, etc. Framed on my office wall is the letter we received from the then mayor, Sam Katz, thanking the church for our outstanding contribution to the good of the city.

In the next decade, we began an annual citywide church service called One Heart. We initially staged it in the MTS Centre (now the Canada Life Centre), where the Winnipeg Jets hockey team plays, and it was not unusual to get fifty churches and 10,000 people out. In 2016 we decided it was time to go big. The Investors Group football stadium (later renamed IG Field) was about to open. When we approached them about using their venue for our One Heart church service as a test run for traffic control, parking and security, they were intrigued. For them it was a low-risk chance to iron out some bugs, and for us it was an amazing opportunity to hold the biggest citywide church service in our city's history. Eighty-eight churches cancelled their Sunday services to participate and over 16,000 people showed up that beautiful sunny May morning. It was a herculean task, involving building a stage, bringing in a sound system, ushering, directing traffic and a thousand other details.

Because it was happening in the Winnipeg Blue Bombers' stadium, it seemed appropriate to have a cameo appearance by one of the Bombers. The most famous Blue Bomber at that time was retired receiver Milt Stegall, and he agreed to come. He holds eight CFL records, including Most Touchdowns. Milt was recognized as the league's Most Outstanding Player in 2002, inducted into the Hall of Fame in 2012, and if that wasn't enough, voted the Best-Looking Man in the CFL.[6] He also has a street named after him—Milt Stegall Drive. After retiring from the sport, he became a regular half-time colour commentator for all the CFL games on the TSN sports channel. He is also a devout Christian and all-round great guy.

Then it came time to nominate a keynote speaker for the event, and my peers called on yours truly to bring the sermon. It was a great honour. I had addressed the massive March for Jesus on many occasions but I had never actually preached to such a large crowd before. I was certainly running a far distant second to Milt Stegall in regard to crowd anticipation, and I was under no illusion that the moment would ever live up to Jesus' Sermon on the Mount, or Peter's Day of Pentecost sermon. I determined I would just do my best and try not to embarrass myself.

> This "first and last," "up and down" stuff is completely counterintuitive to a culture that urges us to "swing for the fences," "shoot for the stars," or "grab the brass ring."

Prior to the start of the event, Milt and I were chilling on the sidelines together. He was wearing a sports jacket like he wears on TV, and I was wearing a Blue Bomber jersey that the club had given me for the event. A young female radio reporter came up to me and said, "I have been looking all over for you. I apologize, but I didn't know who you were and had to have someone point you out."

In my most humble way I said, "Well, not everybody knows who I am." She explained that she was going to go live in a couple of minutes and wanted to do an interview.

I agreed, and when she was ready, she began, "I am here at the annual One Heart citywide church service for the very first event to be held at the Investors Group Field. I am joined today by former Blue Bomber and CFL legend… Milt Stegall!"

I gasped, "You think *I'm* Milt Stegall?"

Flummoxed she asked, "Oh… uh, well, yes, I thought you were, sorry. So which Blue Bomber are you, then?"

Now, remember, I am the one wearing a Bomber jersey. I said, "I am not a football player."

In a more confused than mean-spirited way, she asked, "Well, then, why would I want to talk to you?"

Attempting to salvage some shred of self-respect I said, "Look, you came looking for me!"

Then, pointing out Milt, I explained, "This is Milt Stegall… I'm Mark Hughes." By this time Milt was killing himself laughing and I was looking for a rock to crawl under.

Realizing her mistake, the reporter asked quietly, "I am so embarrassed, do you think this could just be our little secret?"

Regaining my composure, I said, "Not a chance, I am going to tell this story every chance I get."

A few minutes later, Milt did a great job with his address from the stage, and I followed up with the sermon. Fortunately, I was able to not let my "life's most embarrassing moment" throw me completely off my game, and I think I did a passable job.

I have thought about that moment many times and it always reminds me of the story of Jesus' triumphal entry. It was Palm Sunday and he came riding into Jerusalem on a donkey. The crowds were laying down palm branches and greeting Him like a king, shouting, *"Hosanna! Blessed is He who comes in the name of the LORD!"* (John 12:13). Imagine for a moment if the donkey thought all that was for him… now you know the feeling I had that day.

This "first and last," "up and down" stuff is completely counterintuitive to a culture that urges us to "swing for the fences," "shoot for the stars," or "grab the brass ring." Personal ambition in modern culture is generally (not always) valued as a virtue. Our world is a highly competitive place. If we are going to make the best sports team, get into the best schools or be rewarded with the management position, we had better put ourselves out there. The Scriptures teach something altogether different, that it is better to let someone else promote us than to be self-promoting by putting ourselves ahead of others. This kind of nuanced maturity only emerges when we discover the *greater perspective* found in the Sermon on the Mount.

Charles Colson served in the United States Marine Corps in the early 1950s, rising to the rank of captain. In 1955 he was promoted to Assistant to the Assistant Secretary of the Navy. In 1959 he graduated from law school and founded the law firm of Colson & Morin, which grew in prestige in Boston and then in Washington, DC. Chuck was thirty-eight years old when he was invited to become Special Counsel to President Richard Nixon. He became the dirty tricks man. He was immoral, dishonest and conniving. There was nothing he was unwilling to do to advance his career and the Presidency that he served. He was once called the "evil genius" of an evil administration."[7] Chuck was largely considered the brains behind the Watergate scandal.[8] On June 17, 1972, five men were caught breaking into the Democratic National Committee's offices in the Watergate building in Washington. The intention was to bug the offices so that Nixon's campaign team could listen in to their conversations. The scandal eventually led right to the top, and President Nixon resigned in disgrace. Criminal charges eventually led to the conviction of forty-nine people.[9] Colson was sentenced to one to three years and was disbarred from practising law. He had gone from being one of the most powerful people in the world to becoming a common criminal.

While Colson was awaiting sentencing, his close friend Thomas L. Phillips, chair of the board of Raytheon Company, gave him a copy of *Mere Christianity* by C. S. Lewis. It was a life-changing moment for Colson and he gave his life to Christ. Having read about the forgiving message of the gospel, he figured he would be exculpated with a slap on the wrist, avoiding actual jail time. Instead, he ended up serving seven months in prison. While he was there, God began to deal with him in a profound way.

Seeing the brokenness of these incarcerated men, Colson developed a vision to help them. In a way, he never left prison. In 1976 he founded Prison Fellowship and started going back in to minister to these men. In a few short years he went from the highest corridors of power to the lowest cell blocks of prison. By the time he died in 2012, he had established 1,000 chapters of Prison Fellowship, with programming that reached more than 365,000 incarcerated men and women each year. He received far more honours and awards after his time in prison than during his years in the White House. In 1993 Colson was awarded the Templeton Prize for Progress in Religion, which is given each year to the one person in the world who has done the most to advance the cause of religion. He donated the one-million-dollar cash prize to further the work of Prison Fellowship.

He would never again sit in the Oval Office and have the ear of the President; he would never even be able to practice law again; he found a new and *greater purpose,* but only after he discovered a *greater perspective*. I am not suggesting that any of us should have to go to prison to discover our divine calling, but I am suggesting that if we would humble ourselves under the mighty hand of God, He will exalt us into whatever unique role He has for our life. The way up is down.

Chapter Six

From the Inside Out

The world would take people out of the slums. Christ would take the slums out of people, and then they would take themselves out of the slums.

—Ezra Taft Benson

IN 2015, DISNEY/PIXAR FILMS came out with a clever animated feature movie called *Inside Out*.[1] It was the story of a young girl named Riley, who discovered that her emotions had lives of their own and could personify themselves in a cartoon form and help her navigate the stresses of growing up. The five emotions were Joy, Sadness, Fear, Anger and Disgust. Each one had a particular colour, so it was always clear which one was at play in Riley's life at any given moment. Even better, each emotion was appropriately voiced by a popular comedic actor, like Amy Poehler (Joy), Phyllis Smith (Sadness), Bill Hader (Fear), Mindy Kaling (Disgust) and Lewis Black (Anger). The emotions vied for Riley's attention and ultimately shaped how she conducted herself outwardly. The movie took the idea of having a devil and an angel on each shoulder to a whole new level. Critics and audiences loved it, and parents found some very teachable moments to help their children deal with the wide range of emotions that rule all of us.

Although it is not a perfect analogy for how spiritual life works, we would do well to realize that people live their lives from the inside out, not the outside in. It is for this reason that the Beatitudes invite us to discover who we are ahead of telling us what to do. For instance, *"Blessed are the pure in <u>heart</u> for they shall see God"* (Matthew 5:8 ▲, emphasis added). The Sermon on the Mount clearly aims for the heart first because we all live from the inside out whether we recognize it or not.

> *You will know them by their fruits. Do men gather grapes from thornbushes or figs from thistles? Even so, every good tree bears good fruit, but a bad tree bears bad fruit. A good tree cannot bear bad fruit, nor can a bad tree bear good fruit. Every tree that does not bear good fruit is cut down and thrown into the fire. Therefore by their fruits you will know them.*
>
> —Matthew 7:16–20 ▲

We all appreciate the importance of good fruit, a metaphor the Bible uses to, at least in part, refer to good behaviour. And we can see here that Jesus is saying that a tree will be judged according to its fruit. So far, so good (or bad). But that is not at all the point of this verse! The essence of the matter is what kind of tree are we? Who we "are" determines what we "do." Any attempts to change outward behaviour without changing the inward self is doomed to fail. Jesus is pointing out that if the tree is bad, the fruit will be bad. We need to stop trying to improve the fruit and start growing a better tree.

In the midst of all the moral and political problems of first century Palestine, it is interesting to notice that Jesus reserved His harshest criticism for the religious leaders of His day. There were plenty of people more unscrupulous than the Pharisees. Herod was guilty of killing off thousands of people, including innocent children; the Romans treated their subjects with violence and abuse; and the Greeks had turned sordid sexual practices into a religion.[2] In contrast, one could say it looked like the Pharisees were trying. So why did Jesus pick on the poor Pharisees? Not only was He clearly unimpressed with who they were on the outside, He really despised who they were on the inside. At least the pagans didn't pretend to be righteous.

> *Woe to you, scribes and Pharisees, hypocrites! For you are like whitewashed tombs which indeed appear beautiful outwardly, but inside are full of dead men's bones and all uncleanness. Even so you also outwardly appear righteous to men, but inside you are full of hypocrisy and lawlessness.*
>
> —Matthew 23:27–28

For a Pharisee, godliness was merely a pretense. As long as it all looked good on the outside and you appeared to be keeping all the rules, it didn't much matter what was on the inside. Jesus had little patience for this type of religiosity. What was so offensive about the Pharisees' implied message was that it was essentially self-centred instead of God-centred. If we can be good enough to get to heaven on our own actions or righteousness, then why do we need a Saviour anyway? Don't forget, that is exactly why the Jews, for the most part, rejected the Messiah, and the influence of the Pharisees and Sadducees played no small part in that. They, in effect, prevented many people from coming to Christ because they had the Law of Moses. "If it was good enough for Grandpa, then it's good enough for me."

Externally motivated religion doesn't work, and it never did. The Apostle Paul said it best when he wrote, *"For what the law could not do in that it was weak through the flesh, God did by sending his own Son in the likeness of sinful flesh, on account of sin: He condemned sin in the flesh"* (Romans 8:3). He was not criticizing the Law of Moses, for we know that it was righteous; rather, he was saying the problem is the weakness of our own humanity. No matter how hard we try, we will never get it right if we attempt to keep the Law from the outside in. As Doctor Phil would say, "How's that working for ya?" It isn't! Only the work of the cross has the power to change us from the inside out. It is one of the great mysteries of the faith that, when we accept Christ, He sends His Holy Spirit to dwell within us and begin the transformative process of changing us into the likeness of Christ.[3]

Jeffrey grew up in a fairly typical Canadian home. His parents were non-religious and tilted toward the lenient side, allowing him to bump along in life and find his own way. Jeffrey was going to go to college, but he was making such good money as a bartender that it was hard to move on. He loved the lifestyle of closing up the bar late and then heading to an after-hours party with some of the regulars. The drugs always flowed liberally at these events. Jeffrey got to know all the players in the supply chain. When people came into the bar and were looking for some drugs, asking the bartender was always the logical first stop. Jeffrey saw the opportunity and started up a little sideline business. He was making really good money now, but it wasn't getting him ahead because he was snorting the profits.

If everybody knew the bartender was the dealer, it was pretty certain the narcs knew as well. Eventually, Jeffrey was picked up and convicted in court. When it came time for sentencing, the judge recognized there wasn't much hope for this young man in prison, as it would likely just take him further down the path he was already on. So, the judge offered a choice—eighteen months in jail or eighteen months in a Teen Challenge program. Jeffrey jumped at the chance, not really knowing what he was getting himself into. For one thing, if at any point he dropped out of the program, then he had to serve his entire sentence in jail. Long story short, he completed the program and today is a new man. He is drug free, alcohol free, able to hold down a proper job, and most importantly, he is radically in love with Jesus.

Teen Challenge was started in the 1960s in New York City by Pentecostal preacher David Wilkerson. The story is chronicled in his best-selling book, *The Cross and the Switchblade*.[4] Even decades later, it is still a remarkable read about how God used him to transform the violent gangs on the streets of New York. Today, the program that grew out of Wilkerson's experiences is in 110 nations around the world and is often considered the most effective addiction rehabilitation program in history. Most secular programs have about a 10% success rate. However, studies have shown that 74% of those who finish the Teen Challenge program are drug free six months later and 67% are sober seven years later.[5] These kinds of results are virtually unheard of in the addictions recovery world.

Jeffery's slide into the world of addiction was typical. Like most people who experiment with addictive substances, he suffered very little in the way of consequences at first. But then the addiction starts to control the person instead of them being able to control it. Once the behaviour is engaged in for a time, they lose all power to stop it on their own. As it progresses, it gets beyond the addict's willpower or "wanting to stop." They become hopelessly obsessed with an inexorable addiction that cannot be subjugated until an outside force intervenes. The real problem is no longer even the substance itself but the obsession which takes hold in the mind.

What is really at the core of the issue is that we all have a God-shaped void in our life that the addiction tends to fill—but only temporarily. Teen Challenge (and Celebrate Recovery,® which we use in our church) removes the individual from the destructive environment they were in and immerses them in an intense spiritual environment where, gradually, they learn to fill that void with Christ. The transformation happens almost organically, a change from the inside out. The reason so few other programs are effective and why so many suffering from addictions never get free is that they have not replaced the addiction with something greater, more meaningful, more powerful and more personal. *"Therefore if the Son makes you free, you shall be free indeed"* (John 8:36).

Without Christ, every one of us develops a somewhat addictive personality. We busily try to fill the God-shaped void with the things of this world—sports, success, recognition, business, money, things or what have you. Without Christ, we will never be all that we can be nor will we live out our *greater purpose*. Without Christ, we will all have some rotten fruit hanging from our branches. And so, Jesus, in His most famous discourse, aims directly for the heart.

> *You have heard that it was said to those of old, "You shall not commit adultery." But I say to you that whoever looks at a woman to lust for her has already committed adultery with her in his <u>heart</u>.*
>
> —Matthew 5:27–28 ▲▲, emphasis added

> *You have heard that it was said to those of old, "You shall not murder, and whoever murders will be in danger of the judgment." But I say to you that whoever is <u>angry</u> with his brother without a cause shall be in danger of the judgment. And whoever says to his brother, "Raca!" shall be in danger of the council. But whoever says, "You fool!" shall be in danger of hell fire.*
>
> —Matthew 5:21–22 ▲▲, emphasis added

Adultery and murder seem like a big deal, and they are, but they are not the core of the matter. The root causes, respectively, are lust or anger in the heart. The Sermon on the Mount is all about learning the inside out principle. The most obvious manifestation is in the area of moral behaviour, but it is not limited to religious piety.

Whether we want to acknowledge it or not, we live our entire lives from the inside out. Every success or failure in every area of life is related to the inside out paradigm.

At the risk of appearing formulaic, here is one way to delineate it:

Your beliefs become your thoughts,
Your thoughts become your words,
Your words become your actions,
Your actions become your destiny.[6]

Those of us who are married have seen this play out in real time. First, we came to *believe* we might be in love. Then our beliefs became our *thoughts* and we began to lose all sensibility and could not stop thinking about the other person. Then our thoughts became our *words* and we started saying dangerous things like, "I love you," "I can't live without you," and, "Will you marry me?" Then, in a state of all loss of good judgment, our words became our *actions* and we got married. If, in fact, it wasn't just temporary insanity, our actions became our *destiny* and we are still married today.

That is why there are the three rings of marriage: The engagement ring, the wedding ring and the suffe*ring*. Of course, I am joking. I discovered the secret to a happy marriage very early on—I don't try to run Kathy's life… and I don't try to run mine.

YOUR BELIEFS BECOME YOUR THOUGHTS

King Solomon once mused, *"For as he* [a person] *thinks in his heart, so is he"* (Proverbs 23:7). We tend to think on the things that we believe in our heart. And consequently, we often end up living those things out. If you think about what you think about, you rarely think about things that you don't believe. For example, if you don't believe you could ever run a marathon, you are not going to sit around and daydream about it. But if you actually did believe it, and it was something you had an ambition to do, thinking about it would be exactly where you would start.

> Whether we want to acknowledge it or not, we live our entire lives from the inside out. Every success or failure in every area of life is related to the inside out paradigm.

When tennis legend Andre Agassi was only four years old, he had already started believing that one day he would win Wimbledon. It was a strange thing, considering that most four-year-olds would not have any idea what Wimbledon is. Agassi never let go of the dream and thought about it every day. By age twelve, he and his doubles partner won the 1982 National Indoor Boys under 14 Doubles Championship in Chicago. By thirteen, Agassi's father had scraped enough money together to send him to Nick Bollettieri's Tennis Academy in Florida for three months. After thirty minutes of watching Agassi play, Bollettieri called his father and said: "Take your check back. He's here for free."[7] Now Andre could think about his dream day and night. He remained there until he was fifteen and then dropped out of school completely to compete full-time. He never lost sight of his goal and in 1992 he won Wimbledon, tennis's historic coveted prize. In fact, he went on to far exceed his goal, winning the Olympic gold medal in 1996, and in 1999 he became one of only five men at the time to have won a Career Grand Slam.[8] Further, Agassi holds the distinction of being the only male in history to have won the Career Super Slam.[9] Not a bad run for a high school dropout with a big dream.

Igor Sikorsky grew up in the Soviet-occupied Ukraine at the turn of the twentieth century. After reading the works of futurist Jules Verne, at the age of twelve he became obsessed with human flight. His father told him to get those ideas out of his head and insisted that man would never fly. Igor defied his father and continued to think and believe that it was possible. Patterned after sketches by Leonardo Davinci, he began to build working models of helicopters powered by rubber bands. He never stopped thinking about human flight and, moving to America, he pursued a career in the fledgling field of aviation. Sikorsky designed dozens of fixed wing aircrafts in his career, but in 1939 he designed the world's first successful helicopter, the VS-300. When he built his helicopter factory in Stratford, Connecticut, he had these words printed over the front entrance: "According to the laws of aerodynamics, the bumblebee can't fly, but the bumblebee doesn't know the laws of aerodynamics, so it goes ahead and flies."[10]

Jesus said, *"If you can believe, all things are possible to him who believes"* (Mark 9:23). Success or failure in life essentially begins with what we believe in our heart. Of course, many people believe unhelpful and unbiblical things. Depending on who is doing the counting, there are somewhere between 6,000–8,000 promises in the Bible and *"all the promises of God in Him are Yes, and in Him Amen, to the glory of God through us"* (2 Corinthians 1:20). So why would we want to think about anything else?

YOUR THOUGHTS BECOME YOUR WORDS

Once again, while trash-talking the Pharisees, Jesus said, *"Brood of vipers! How can you, being evil, speak good things? For out of the abundance of the heart the mouth speaks"* (Matthew 12:34). People with foul mouths are foul people. You know the ones—the profanities just roll off their tongues with the greatest of ease. I have publicly lamented that our world has become a vulgar place. You cannot turn on the TV today without being violated by increasingly disgusting language. Words that, a generation ago, were illegal on broadcast television are now commonplace.

The words themselves, however, are not the real problem; the root of the matter is the darkness in people's hearts and minds. We even see Christian people being drawn into this kind of communication. It is doubtful that they recognize they have acquiesced to worldly values. While I was growing up, my father, the lawyer, always said, "The use of vulgarity merely reveals your lack of vocabulary." That challenge motivated me to avoid vulgar language, even before I met Christ.

I am fond of the story of the pastor who rides his bike down the street and sees twelve-year-old Billy with a for sale sign on a lawnmower. The pastor asks why a boy his age is selling a lawn mower. Billy responds that he is raising money to buy a bike. The pastor tells him that he needs a new mower for the church and that he would be willing to trade his bike for it. Billy agrees, but the pastor wants to make sure the mower starts.

After pulling on the rope multiple times, he says to Billy. "It won't start!"

Billy explains, "You have to cuss at it to get it to start."

The pastor says, "Oh, it has been so long since I uttered a cuss word, I don't think I would remember how."

Billy replied, "Oh, you just keep pulling on that rope, preacher... it'll come back to you."

In Mark chapter nine, Jesus' disciples encountered a man whose mute son suffered seizures. When the disciples failed to heal the boy, the father brought him to Jesus.

> *Jesus said to him, "If you can believe, all things are possible to him who believes." Immediately the father of the child cried out and said with tears, "Lord, I believe; help my unbelief!"*
>
> —Mark 9:23–24

At first the man said he believed. Did he? Maybe not. Probably not. Everybody is capable of saying something, in a cursory fashion, that they do not believe. We have all done it. We get asked a question and we say Yes, but after a moment's thought we realized the answer is more likely No. If you listen to anyone long enough, their words will eventually reveal what they really believe. It is the toothpaste test. When the pressure is on, what's on the inside comes out.

In the movie *A Few Good Men*, Tom Cruise is playing Lt. Daniel Kaffee, a military prosecutor trying to get to the bottom of a hazing death on a base at Guantanamo Bay. Col. Jessep, brilliantly played by Jack Nicholson, repeatedly lies about the incident on the stand. Kaffee understands Jessep's pride and bravado, and he continually pushes his buttons.

> Col. Jessep: "You want answers?"
>
> Kaffee: "I think I'm entitled."
>
> Col. Jessep: "You want answers?"
>
> Kaffee: "I want the truth!"
>
> Col. Jessep: "YOU CAN'T HANDLE THE TRUTH!"[11]

And at that, Jessep snapped and admitted he ordered the code red. The exchange has become not only an iconic moment in cinematic theatre but an even better example of Jesus' powerful principle that out of the abundance of the heart the mouth speaks (Luke 6:45). What we believe in our heart will ultimately come out of our mouth. So, we had better put the right thing into our heart.

Jesus said, "Above all else, guard your heart, for everything you do flows *from it*" (Proverbs 4:23 NIV). If you spend thirty minutes listening to a sermon once a week but thirty hours watching trashy TV shows, what is going to come out of your mouth? Garbage in, garbage out.

Conversely, if we fill our heart with God's Word, what is going to come out? If our faith is based on what we believe in our heart, it will ultimately be reflected in what we say. Therefore, the words we speak are fundamental to our faith. If you do a biblical study on the subject of faith, you will find that Scripture essentially makes little distinction between what we believe and what we say, the reason being that they are basically one and the same. When we came to Christ, we did so by aligning what we said with our mouths with what we believed in our hearts. *"If you <u>confess with your mouth</u> the Lord Jesus and <u>believe in your heart</u> that God has raised Him from the dead, you will be saved"* (Romans 10:9, emphasis added).

YOUR WORDS BECOME YOUR ACTIONS

It happened in the spring of the year, at the time when kings go out to battle, that David... remained at Jerusalem (2 Samuel 11:1).

It's funny how we get in the most trouble when we are not where we are supposed to be, doing what we are not supposed to be doing. Bored and antsy, King David looked out the penthouse window of the palace, and what did he see but a beautiful woman bathing on her rooftop. We are not sure what she was wearing at the time, but it is a good guess that people bathed the same way then that they do now… naked. He could have looked away; he could have gone and written another one of his famous psalms or even taken a cold dip in the royal pool. But he just kept looking, and leering. There was no doubt that the thoughts of lust filled his heart. Still, he did not look away. After a few more minutes, he forgot that he was a married man, and this bathing neighbour was a married woman. In fact, her husband, Uriah, was one of David's captains, a man of honour and duty. It didn't matter. His thoughts became his words and he said to his servants, "Go get her for me!" What choice did they have? He was the king. When they arrived with the object of his desire, he wasted no time bedding her. His words had now become his actions.

What choice did she have? He was the king. It was, without question, David's most woeful and pathetic moment. The "man after God's own heart" allowed his own heart to wander, and there he was.

Maybe it was to be a one-night stand. Maybe David would get his act together and repent of his misgivings and try to make it right somehow. But soon she was discovered to be pregnant… with his child. So David sent a message to his commander Joab in the field, "Send Uriah the Hittite back to town ASAP!" Perhaps he was going to confess all to Uriah and fall at his feet and beg for forgiveness. But it wasn't to be so. David sent Uriah down to his house to be with his wife, and he threw in some gifts of food (champagne and caviar?). A romantic night, a perfectly reasonable plan—make him think the baby is his—no harm no foul.

But Uriah slept on the king's doorstep. The next morning, when questioned why he did not go to his house he said,

> *The ark and Israel and Judah are dwelling in tents, and my lord Joab and the servants of my lord are encamped in the open fields. Shall I then go to my house to eat and drink, and to lie with my wife? As you live, and as your soul lives, I will not do this thing.*
>
> —2 Samuel 11:11

Uriah was a much better man than his king! When his disingenuous and devious efforts to cover up the affair failed, David sent Uriah to the front lines so that he would be killed, and then he took his widow Bathsheba as his own wife. This treacherous course of action sent his virtue to a new low. There were so many moments in the narrative where his actions could have been reversed but he continued to dig the hole as he sank to lower and lower depths as his thoughts became his actions.

This is probably a good moment to remind ourselves that none of our actions in life are done in isolation. Our activities always affect other people and start in motion a series of events that can potentially impact generations to come. It is particularly distressing when we see leaders fail. The unavoidable consequences are that people will conclude, "If King David, or Bill Hybels, or Ravi Zacharias… (it is a very long list) can't resist temptation, what hope is there for me?" Being world famous leaders does not make them better people than us. We are vulnerable to temptation and failure. But more importantly, we can never forget that our God is bigger than anything the enemy can throw at us. He has given us everything necessary to live above the temptations of this world, and it all starts with guarding our hearts and minds. We can see why Jesus, in the Sermon on the Mount, concerns Himself so much with the thoughts and intents of our hearts. He knows that rarely is any outward act initiated in a vacuum. There are beliefs, thoughts and words behind every deed.

Although the Bible contains a few of these very sordid examples of the "inside out" principle creating negative outcomes, there are far more examples on the positive side of the ledger. Every act of faith follows the same pattern: beliefs—thoughts—words—actions—destiny. Jesus put it this way,

> *For assuredly, I say to you, whoever says to this mountain, 'Be removed and be cast into the sea,' and does not doubt in his*

heart, but believes that those things he says will be done, he will have whatever he says.

—Mark 11:23

In fact, we all begin our journey with Christ from the inside out.

Some years ago, I was looking for a truck to purchase. I was very specific as to what I was searching for—a 1967 to 1972 Chevrolet C-10, with jacked up suspension and oversized tires. Yes, I know, I was a bit of a hoser. I also wore cowboy boots and a plaid flannel shirt. Having no internet in those days, I checked the classified ads every day with no luck. Kathy suggested I might have better success if I actually prayed about it, so I did.

That very night, we went to visit friends on the other side of town. We parked our car and were walking toward their house. And there, parked on the street, was a 1970 Chevrolet, jacked up with big boots. I remember placing my hands right on the cab and saying to Kathy, "This is it. I want this truck right here!"

She rolled her eyes and said, "That's nice."

The next Saturday, I spotted an ad for a 1970 C-10. I made the call and got the address to go have a look. It did not dawn on me until I was driving down the street that it was the same one we had seen the week before where our friends lived. I came around the bend and there it was, with a For Sale sign on it. The exact same truck! It felt surreal. What were the chances the very truck I laid hands on would be for sale the next week?

It goes without saying that I bought the truck. Every single morning as I walked out the front door and saw the truck, I was reminded of the faithfulness of God. I sometimes think that He was trying to teach me the difference between relying on myself as opposed to relying on Him. Needless to say, something that extraordinary doesn't happen to me every day… but maybe it should.

"If you can believe, all things are possible to him who believes" (Mark 9:23).

A Wisconsin dairy farmer was visiting a Texas rancher one day. The boastful Texan said, "If I get in my truck and start driving at dawn, I won't reach the other end of my property until sundown."

The dairy farmer humbly responded, "Yeah, I had a truck like that once too."

YOUR ACTIONS BECOME YOUR DESTINY

Living by faith in Christ always requires a corresponding action to that which we believe, think and speak. We can hold a truth more dearly than life itself, but if we never act upon it nothing will ever become of it. As you survey the Bible, you will discover that every demonstration of faith required a human act of obedience to bring forth the desired result. Lazarus was only raised from the dead after the disciples took action and rolled away the stone. The multitudes were only fed after the disciples, in a decidedly unlikely fashion, distributed a mere five loaves and two fish to over 5,000 people. Namaan the leper was only cleansed after he reluctantly agreed to wash in the Jordan River seven times.

Interestingly, and probably not coincidentally, many destiny moments involved the Jordan River. At one point, Israel's entire future—the Promised Land—was on the other side of that river. But before they ever reached the banks of the Jordan, God gave Joshua some very unambiguous instructions as to how their destiny was to be acquired.

> *This Book of the Law shall not depart from your mouth, but you shall meditate in it day and night, that you may observe to do according to all that is written in it. For then you will*

make your way prosperous, and then you will have good success.

—Joshua 1:8

In other words, "Don't stop thinking about it, don't stop talking about it!" But God also told Joshua to act. Every one of us will face significant challenges in life wherein acting on our faith will be the only path to success.

Kevin was in a serious accident at ten years old and lost his left arm. It was tragic for the family; no parent wants to see their children debilitated. He spent the next year going through the necessary rehabilitation and got on reasonably well. Kids are remarkably resilient. When rehab had run its course, the doctor pulled his parents aside and said, "The best thing you can do is get Kevin back into regular ten-year-old activities and especially sports." In discussing with their son what sport interested him, he said, "Judo." Judo? They were thinking more like soccer, where you didn't need your arms. Kevin said, "I don't want to play soccer; I want to do judo."

His parents relented and took him down to the local judo studio. They said, "Would you take our kid? He has no arm."

The instructor thought for a moment and said, "Why not?"

For the next three months the instructor worked with Kevin and taught him one move and one move only. They went over it and over it again. Then Kevin entered his first competition. To his complete surprise, there he was, the kid with no left arm, and he had won every fight with one single move. He had landed himself in the finals. His opponent was an undefeated twelve-year-old that looked like Goliath's kid brother. Once in the ring, Kevin was getting beaten badly and was just barely able to stay in the fight. The referee was ready to call the match when the instructor caught Kevin's attention and mouthed the words, "Do the move, do the move!"

Kevin mustered every ounce of strength he had and did the move. To his surprise, in a matter of seconds, he pinned the twelve-year-old and won the match. As Kevin received the first-place trophy, he said to his instructor, "How did I win?"

The instructor enlightened him, "First, you only had one move, but it is one of the most difficult moves there is and you do it very well. And second, there is only one defense against it, and that is for your opponent to grab your left arm." It is fascinating what can happen when we just do what we are told.

The inside out paradigm is one of those things that appears logical when you think about it out loud. Of course, our beliefs become our thoughts, our thoughts become our words, our words become our actions, and our actions become our destiny! Still, many of us don't think about things so linearly. We would rather circumvent the process and find a shortcut to success. But shortcuts don't exist in real life—Jesus gave us the Sermon on the Mount to teach us a *greater perspective* on how life really works.

> The outward work can never be small if the inward one is great, and the outward work can never be great if the inward one is small.
>
> —Meister Eckhart, 14th Century Christian Mystic

For the Christian, living from the inside out means *putting into practice* that which we first *put into perspective.* It also means experiencing life and life more abundantly.

Chapter Seven

Messing with Moses

> *Man has made 32 million laws since the Commandments were handed down to Moses on Mount Sinai… but he has never improved on God's law.*
>
> —Cecil B. DeMille

IN MEL BROOKS' 1981 film *A History of the World: Part 1*,[1] Brooks casts himself in the role of Moses. He comes down from Mount Sinai carrying three stone tablets containing five commandments each. Just as he is announcing the fifteen commandments to the children of Israel, he drops one of the tablets mid-sentence, shattering it on the ground. It plays out in real time like this, "*OH HEAR ME! The Lord Jehovah has given unto you these fifteen… CRASH … Oy. Ten! Ten commandments for all to obey!*" It is a laugh-out-loud funny moment, just as long as you don't get too bent out of shape over Mel Brooks messing with Moses.

After all, Moses is one of the top three characters in all of Scripture, alongside Elijah and Jesus. It was Moses and Elijah who appeared with Jesus before the disciples on the Mount of Transfiguration, and the two Old Testament figures have almost mythical historical significance. So, imagine when Jesus starts "messing with Moses" in the Sermon on the Mount. It's not that He mentions Moses by name but that, to the uninitiated, it seems like Jesus is criticizing the Ten Commandments. He takes the nearly

1,500 years (to that point) of historical understanding of the law of Moses and offers a *greater perspective*. He re-interprets them in the light of the Great Commandment (to love God and love others), which is the essence of the *spirit* of the Law not the *letter* of the Law.

Five times, Jesus introduces a thought with the phrase, "*You have heard it said.*" Each one of these was a reference to something that Moses had said. Some of them, like the directions regarding murder and adultery, were central to the Ten Commandants. How was it that Jesus could take the liberty to re-interpret them? Because He's Jesus, that's why! He was, by definition, the Word of God made flesh.[2] He was the only human who ever truly knew the perfect and accurate meaning of every scripture. So, if Jesus wants to correct our understanding of things, we should listen up.

> *You have heard that it was said to those of old, "You shall not murder, and whoever murders will be in danger of the judgment." But I say to you that whoever is angry with his brother without a cause shall be in danger of the judgment. And whoever says to his brother, "Raca!" shall be in danger of the council. But whoever says, "You fool!" shall be in danger of hell fire.*
>
> —Matthew 5:21–22

Jesus starts with the granddaddy of all commandments—you know, the "don't murder" one—and then implies that being angry at your brother without cause has just as serious of consequences. It is doubtful that He is saying that calling someone a "fool"[3] is on the same level as killing another human being. For one thing, Jesus Himself called the Pharisees fools.[4] Awkward! No, what Christ is doing in each of these examples is sticking a knife into the narrow self-righteous religious interpretation of the Law and the false notion that just doing the bare minimum to fulfill the letter of the Law means we are good to go, i.e., as long as I haven't killed anybody, then I have done my part and God must be pleased with me.

Nothing could be further from the truth. Just because you don't kill people doesn't mean you are a good person. Maybe you are not killing people but you hate them and are angry with them. If you are bitter and contemptuous toward others, you are actually a "pretty bad person" and that puts you in danger of judgment and even hell fire.

Jesus' modus operandi here is to reference the commandments and then kick them up a notch. His intention is not to make them even more inaccessible but to drive home the point that what matters the most to God is what is going on in the heart.[5]

> *You have heard that it was said to those of old, "You shall not commit adultery." But I say to you that whoever looks at a woman to lust for her has already committed adultery with her in his heart.*
>
> —Matthew 5:27–28

We see the same line of reasoning with adultery. It could be paraphrased this way: "Don't think that just because you haven't committed adultery you are morally pure! If you are lusting after other women, you are committing adultery in your heart." Jesus is not only raising the bar on how we should be looking at the Ten Commandments but also addressing how what is going on inside our hearts is just as important (or maybe more important) as what we are doing on the outside. The Apostle Paul helps clarify this as he reminds the Corinthians that the new covenant is *"not of the letter but of the Spirit; for the letter kills, but the Spirit gives life"* (2 Corinthians 3:6). The Pharisees expended much of their energy trying to adhere to the letter of the Law but never understood the spirit of it. As a result, they were not good people. They were self-righteous, judgmental, unloving, uncaring, petty little weasels for whom Jesus reserved most of His disapproval. The sad thing, more often than not, is that we look more like the Pharisees than we look like Jesus.

> *Furthermore it has been said, "Whoever divorces his wife, let him give her a certificate of divorce." But I say to you that whoever divorces his wife for any reason except sexual immorality causes her to commit adultery; and whoever marries a woman who is divorced commits adultery."*
>
> —Matthew 5:31–32 ▲

Jesus takes a similar track on the issue of divorce. Under Mosaic Law, an unfaithful wife could be put away by serving her with a certificate of divorce (Deuteronomy 24:1). The Jews abused this and used it as a "get out of jail free" card. If a man was not pleased in his marriage, he just wrote up a certificate of divorce for his wife and sent the old ball and chain packing. It was bad enough that wives were regarded as men's property in ancient times, but a divorced woman was very lowly esteemed, virtually a societal outcast. She had no rights, no financial means and no claim to the family property. She was cast out with nothing and had a very slim chance of finding another husband, as she was now labelled with the shame of divorce. The man, on the other hand, just traded her in on a newer model and carried on his merry way.

On the topic of newer models, Henry Ford, the founder of Ford Motor Company, was asked at his fiftieth wedding anniversary about his secret to a good marriage. He replied, "The formula is the same as in car manufacturing. Stick to one model."[6] (From 1908 to 1927 Ford only built the Model T. He also used to joke, "Any customer can have a car painted any color that he wants so long as it's black."[7])

Jesus was history's greatest champion for women and was offended by the practice of the certificate of divorce. He rebuked it and made it clear that, unless she was truly unfaithful, the man's remarriage was nothing more than adultery.

In 1631 King Charles commissioned the printing of 1,000 King James Bibles. The typesetter made an egregious error, and the word "not" was left out of the seventh commandment. Instead of reading, "Thou shalt *not* commit adultery" it read, "Thou *shalt* commit adultery." Nobody was laughing—especially King Charles, who fined the printer Barker and Lewis £300 (equivalent to more than $70,000 today) and stripped them of their printing licences. They were bankrupted by the ordeal. The king ordered those Bibles recalled and burned. Ten of them went unaccounted for and are today considered collectors' items known as the Wicked Bible. Most recently one sold at auction for $56,250.[8] In human terms, adultery is much more costly than that.

Understand, this emotional, painful and obviously more complicated subject deserves a more thorough discussion than we can offer here. But even Jesus just cuts to the chase and tells them they had gotten it all wrong. The bottom line for us is that, even though it is not the unpardonable sin, God hates divorce (Malachi 2:16). The tragedy we see in the church today is that we still have Christians coming to their pastors looking for a loophole. The God we serve is in the marriage restoration business, not the divorce business. He claims that *love never fails* (1 Corinthians 13:8). That means that there must be a way to save even the most broken and unhappy marriages! And not to just patch them up and let them live in relative misery but to restore them to better than ever. We have seen it countless times and I marvel at how powerful God's grace can be in the midst of even the most hopeless relationships.

One of my favourite reconciliation stories happened years ago at a Billy Graham crusade. A divorced couple had both ended up single and lonely. They were living in the same city but had not seen each other for several years. A Christian friend of the woman told her that Billy Graham was in town and invited her to come and see him preach that night. She agreed. At the same time her estranged husband was sitting in his apartment reading the newspaper. He saw the notice for the crusade that night and something inside him told him he needed to go. That night they were both in the stands of the stadium on completely opposite sides—one in the east stands, the other in the west.

> The God we serve is in the marriage restoration business, not the divorce business.

Billy Graham preached one of his inimitable sermons on hope. He repeated again and again that it did not matter what misfortune life had served up, with God there was always hope. I can almost hear him preaching this as I type. It was his masterclass message. At the conclusion he called people forward to accept Christ as he had done countless times in his ministry before. Both the man and the woman immediately responded and came down onto the field as George Beverly Shea sang "Just As I Am."[9] As Billy Graham led them in prayer, they followed along with their eyes closed and gave their lives over to Jesus for the first time. Upon opening their eyes, imagine their surprise when they found themselves standing right next to one another. Being that they were both in a contrite and forgiving mood, they decided to meet for coffee and catch up. One thing led to another, and over time they found their hurts were healed and their relationship was restored. They remarried and gave marriage another shot, only this time they had Christ at the centre. There is no relationship so damaged that God cannot invade both lives and bring divine transformation.

Messing with Moses

> *Again you have heard that it was said to those of old, "You shall not swear falsely, but shall perform your oaths to the Lord." But I say to you, do not swear at all: neither by heaven, for it is God's throne; nor by the earth, for it is His footstool; nor by Jerusalem, for it is the city of the great King. Nor shall you swear by your head, because you cannot make one hair white or black. But let your "Yes" be "Yes," and your "No," "No." For whatever is more than these is from the evil one.*
>
> —Matthew 5:33–37 ▲

In the Old Testament it was common for people to make a vow or pledge to God or another person.[10] There was nothing wrong with that as long as they did what they said they were going to do.[11] By Jesus' day it was a common practice to swear to God, or to heaven, or Jerusalem, not unlike when people today say, "I swear to God," or, "I'll swear on a stack of Bibles," or, "I swear on my mother's grave." Jesus' point was to just do what you said you were going to do. Never mind the swearing of an oath. *Let your "Yes" be "Yes," and your "No," "No."* Just tell the truth and do what you said you would do. Capiche?

> *You have heard that it was said, "An eye for an eye and a tooth for a tooth." But I tell you not to resist an evil person. But whoever slaps you on your right cheek, turn the other to him also.*
>
> —Matthew 5:38–39 ▲

Most of us will flippantly use the expression "turn the other cheek" metaphorically (which is still an appropriate usage), without giving a second thought to Jesus' intended meaning. He was saying that if someone deliberately smacks you in the face, the Christian response is to let him have a swing at the other cheek as well. It is hard to imagine any of us actually doing this! Yet, incredibly, it is fully consistent with the counterintuitive nature of the Sermon on the Mount.

There is a great story about a retired Irish boxing champion who later became a fiery street preacher. One day he was standing on a street corner preaching when a very belligerent man sucker-punched him in the face. After overcoming the initial surprise, he said to the pugilistic opponent, "You get one more free shot at the other side." The man struck him again on the other cheek. Then, to the surprise of everyone gathered, the preacher/boxer beat the tar out of the man. As the man fell to the ground, conscious but hurting, the crowd stood in stunned silence. The preacher answered, "Jesus said to turn the other cheek. After that He gave no further instructions!" Once again, the key is to look at the heart issue and not the outward action. I am not sure the Irish preacher understood the spirit of this one.

It should be a bit concerning to us that, after 2,000 years of Christianity, many have never fully comprehended this essential aspect of the New Testament. By over-focusing on external things, we have created a church culture where the barometer of spirituality is what we look like on the outside. It was Jesus' single biggest contention with the Pharisees.[12] The church has sometimes gained the same reputation of being puritanical people who "don't smoke and drink and chew or go with girls that do" but love to judge those that do. Many in the church today don't look a whole lot different from the Pharisees of yesterday. We have even created a hierarchy of sins and put sexual sins at the top. C. S. Lewis challenged this notion years ago:

> The sins of the flesh are bad, but they are the least bad of all sins. All of the worst pleasures are purely spiritual: the pleasure of putting other people in the wrong, of bossing and patronizing and spoiling sport, and back-biting, the pleasures of power, of hatred.[13]

In 1862 Danish missionary Ludwig Nommensen arrived on the island of Sumatra in Indonesia. He had read about the Batak people, whom Marco Polo had reported as being cannibals. Nobody tried to eat him, but the mission did not go well at first. Nommensen began by learning the Batak language with the intention of translating the New Testament. Eventually he became friends with the local tribal chief, Pontas Lumbantobing. After a year of observing him, Pontas said to the missionary, "Your religion is the same as ours. We believe that you should not steal, lie or murder as well."

Ludwig responded, "Yes, but our God gives you the power to keep his law." The chief challenged him to prove it and gave him access to his people for a half a year to try to influence them to become better people. Pontas became one of his first converts and initially 2,000 people came to Christ. When Nommensen died, the Batak church had 34 pastors, 788 teacher-preachers, and 180,000 members in more than 500 local churches.[14]

God is still interested in His standard of righteousness. That has not changed in the slightest. The big difference in the New Testament is how we approach the problem of sin. Man is not actually capable of obeying God strictly on his own volition and will power.[15]

If Christians today could truly grasp that God gives them the power to change from the inside out, we would not have room enough in our churches to contain the people that would want to come to Christ.

Chapter Eight

The Inverted Law

Do I not destroy my enemies when I make them my friends?
—Abraham Lincoln

THE AMERICAN CIVIL War was a dark chapter in US history. In the four-year conflict from 1861–1865, a staggering 620,000 Americans lost their lives fighting their neighbours to the North or the South. At the heart of the war was the issue of slavery. The Confederates in the southern states saw it as their God-given right to keep black slaves as their unpaid hired help. The more enlightened North knew that the time had come to end this barbaric colonial practice. Most historians agree that President Abraham Lincoln had no desire to see his nation go to war.[1] He did everything within his power not to provoke military combat, but when the fighting broke out, he had little choice but to defend the principles of the Union.

At the height of the Civil War, Lincoln was giving a speech where he stated that the southerners of the Confederate states should be thought of as erring human beings, not as enemies to be exterminated. An elderly woman in the room chastised the President, shouting, "You should be thinking of how to destroy them!"

Lincoln responded, "Why, Madam, do I not destroy my enemies when I make them my friends?"[2]

Abe Lincoln was, just like the rest of us, far from being a perfect human being, but he was a lover of God's Word[3] and understood what I call the Inverted Law. This concept is at the heart of the Sermon on the Mount, the inverse of what conventional wisdom or human nature would dictate. Once again, we will look at the pivotal and admittedly emotionally vexing *love your enemy* segment, only this time we will discover why we should do something so counterintuitive.

> *You have heard that it was said, "You shall love your neighbor and hate your enemy." But I say to you, love your enemies, bless those who curse you, do good to those who hate you, and pray for those who spitefully use you and persecute you, that you may be sons of your Father in heaven; for He makes His sun rise on the evil and on the good, and sends rain on the just and on the unjust. For if you love those who love you, what reward have you? Do not even the tax collectors do the same?*
>
> —Matthew 5:43–46

In reading David Neff's interview with Amy Jill Levine, a Jewish scholar of the New Testament (which seemed ironic at first until I realized we have Christian scholars of the Old Testament), I was fascinated by a comment she made. When asked what made Jesus unique among historical religious figures, she answered, "You have to look at the entire person to see his distinctiveness. Other people told parables. Other people referred to God as Father. Other people debated how to follow Torah. Other people lost their lives on Roman crosses… But He's the only person I can find in antiquity who says you have to love your enemy."[4]

The love Jesus expects us to have for our enemies is not some ethereal, non-committal, patronizing sentiment with no practical application—He actually tells us what it looks like. It means doing good things for people who absolutely hate our guts. It means blessing people who gossip about us, criticize us and malign our character. It means praying for people who abuse us, slander us, scheme against us and try to ruin our lives. These are the hardest people in the world to love. They are far more difficult to love than a casual acquaintance that made a joke at your expense, or a political opponent that criticized us from across the aisle or even some unknown terrorist on the other side of the world. These are generally people involved with our lives in some way.

The things our enemies say and do toward us are not emotionally detached in nature; they are personal and intended to hurt us. Let's be honest, if it is dependent on our own strength we are not going to love these people. We are far more likely to want revenge, or at the very least, wish misfortune upon them.

When George Costanza started doing the opposite of his first instinct, in a very imperfect way he had discovered the Inverted Law. He unwittingly had tapped into a higher law than the law of human nature. Here are three reasons why the Inverted Law has the power to change everything.

THE INVERTED LAW IS THE HIGHER CALLING

The life of the Christian must always stand apart as unique from the cultural zeitgeist. The message of the gospel is intended to raise us up to *a greater perspective* than the base instincts of fallen man. The Sermon on the Mount is the seminal teaching on how the gospel intersects with a secular (or even religious) culture and it helps us understand what it means to have a biblical worldview. A worldview is simply the lens through which we view the world, and we all have one, even if we do not realize it.

The biblical worldview cuts across the grain of every other. It influences how we look at sexuality, marriage, gender, interpersonal relationships, economics and, above all, the value of human life. As previously mentioned, no teacher from any other world religion ever taught their adherents to love their enemies. Even Judaism taught the Jews that it was acceptable to kill their enemies. However, Jesus said it wasn't okay—we should love them instead. This was, and still is, a revolutionary idea.

When Peter cut off the ear of the servant of the high priest, Jesus rebuked him: *"People who live by the sword die by the sword"* (Matthew 26:52 *Voice*). I am guessing Peter thought at the time, "Note to self, cutting off an ear—not cool! Perhaps not a true expression of love."

Shortly thereafter, Jesus was under trial by Pontius Pilate. When Pilate asked Him if He is the King of the Jews, Jesus answered,

> *My kingdom is not of this world. If My kingdom were of this world, My servants would fight, so that I should not be delivered to the Jews; but now My kingdom is not from here.*
>
> —John 18:36

He clearly was fighting for a higher kingdom; Jesus was not prepared to raise a worldly weapon, even in His own defense. The Anabaptist Christians have correctly interpreted that Jesus exemplified a radical form of pacifism. This ethic carried forward and was a central characteristic of the early church, who were not willing to ever resist their enemies with mortal force. They chose to be killed rather than to kill.[5] Their biblical worldview precluded the taking of another life even in self-defence. Few Christians today hold this level of conviction. If we truly believed that our citizenship is in heaven, we would not fear our own deaths and would value others' lives above our own.

Catholics have done a much better job articulating this than Evangelicals. The late Archbishop of Chicago, Cardinal Joseph Bernardin, dubbed it the "consistent ethic of life."[6] Quite simply, it meant committing oneself to consistently living in ways that uphold the irrevocable worth of every human being. In practical terms it would mean opposing abortion, infanticide, capital punishment, assisted suicide, euthanasia, unjust war, poverty and racism. This moves the needle from being pro-life on the abortion issue to being completely pro-life on every issue. Very few people fully embrace the *consistent life ethic*. Only four percent would even be considered anti-abortion, anti-assisted suicide and anti-capital punishment.[7]

This is where the evangelical pro-life messaging has fallen short. We have been commendably immovable in our opposition to abortion. But in the very next breath we support capital punishment and assault rifle ownership, and we are often the first ones to get behind a military invasion of our geo-political enemies. The challenge for us is that our pro-life position appears hypocritically inconsistent. To the casual observer it looks like we are okay with killing adults, we just don't like killing unborn babies. The *consistent life ethic* is far more congruent with the New Testament teachings of Jesus. If we tilted further that way, our messaging on the abortion issue would be less likely to fall on deaf ears, as our arguments would carry far more gravitas and credibility.

> Our pro-life message might be much stronger if we sounded more like the Sermon on the Mount and less like the Book of Leviticus.

At this point you could roll out some reasonable objections. You can make a pretty strong biblical case in favour of capital punishment from Romans 13. But then we read the gospels and have a very difficult time imagining Jesus volunteering to pull the lever or swing the executioner's axe. We can imagine Him rescuing a woman from death by stoning, though.[8] You could cite the popular American gun slogan idiom, "guns don't kill, people do,"[9] and you would only be partially right. You cannot put 450 million guns in a complex society with lots of mental illness, social unrest and angst, and not expect a lot of people to die violent deaths. You could also invoke St. Augustine's brilliantly constructed theory of Just War.[10] It is well worth taking a look if you have never read it. However, keep in mind that this, of course, was Augustine's position, not Jesus' position. The few violent sounding statements that Jesus did make were never intended to be taken militaristically. For instance, when He said, *"And from the days of John the Baptist until now the kingdom of heaven suffers violence, and the violent take it by force"* Matthew 11:12). it was a reference to spiritual aggression, as both He and John the Baptist were nonviolent men.

On a personal note, in the early years of my ministry I would preach on capital punishment and Just War. But the more time I spent in the Gospels, and particularly the Sermon on the Mount, I found my position on these things gradually shifting. I eventually found it impossible to make a biblical case that Jesus was anything but a pacifist. It is simple logic—if you love your enemies, you don't kill them. Full disclosure: I am a gun owner, but I do not own any weapons that were designed to kill people. Nor do I ever kill people with the guns I do have. I am being funny here but not flippant; I have many friends that tell me they would not hesitate to use their guns to kill in self-defence. Please don't assume I am advocating taking away hunters' and sportsmen's guns, for I am not. At the end of the day, I am just making a point that our pro-life message might be much stronger if we sounded more like the Sermon on the Mount and less like the Book of Leviticus.

Even Jesus' disciples took an inordinate amount of time to figure this one out. James and his brother John, (you know the one, the Apostle of Love?) wanted to call fire down from heaven and consume the Samaritans when they refused to receive Jesus' message (Luke

9:54). It was on the very last day of Jesus' ministry that Peter used his sword to cut off the ear of the servant of the high priest (Matthew 26:51). After over three years with Jesus, he still didn't get it.

Yet, years later these men were champions of the Inverted Law. Peter expresses how it is the very nature of the *greater perspective*:

> *Do not repay evil for evil or insult with insult. On the contrary, replay evil with blessing, because to this <u>you were called</u> so that you may inherit a blessing."*
>
> —1 Peter 3:9 NIV, emphasis added

Even if there was no personal benefit to the Inverted Law (although we will see shortly that there absolutely is), we would do it anyway because it is how we are called to live as disciples of Christ.

Consider this story of another man named Peter. Peter Miller was a pastor in Ephrata, Pennsylvania, during and after the American War of Independence. He was highly educated and was asked by Thomas Jefferson to translate the Declaration of Independence into seven different languages. Prior to the war he had been with the German Reformed Church, but he left to join the Seventh Day Baptists. This enraged Michael Witman, one of the deacons at the Reformed Church. He made it his personal mission in life to make Miller's life miserable. He slandered and criticized him at every opportunity and physically abused Pastor Peter by slapping or spitting on his face. Miller never retaliated or spoke a cross word toward Witman but endured it as his cross to bear.

Witman had considerable influence in their town, as he was the owner of one of the hotels. One night two guests were staying at his inn, and they got to talking over dinner. Witman was careless with his words and spoke in favour of the British. He even mentioned that he had gone to General Howard of the British army and offered his services as a spy. Unbeknownst to Witman, the two guests were spies themselves—for the Americans. They were about to arrest him for treason when he escaped out an open window and fled into the night. Ironically, he went to the village of the Seven Day Baptists to hide from capture. Eventually, he realized there was little hope for himself and he surrendered to the Americans. He was taken to General George Washington at Valley Forge, where he was tried for treason and sentenced to hang.

Upon hearing this news, Peter Miller took his cane and walked through the snow for sixty miles to Valley Forge. He was acquainted with George Washington and was granted an audience with him. He pleaded for the life of Michael Witman but Washington responded that he could not grant Miller's request to pardon his friend.

Miller exclaimed, "My friend! I have not a worse enemy living than that man."

Incredulously, Washington responded, "What! You have walked sixty miles to plead for the life of your enemy? That, in my judgment, puts the matter in a different light. I will grant you his pardon."

Washington signed the pardon and handed it to Miller. Now he had to walk the fifteen miles to West Chester, where Witman was to be hanged that afternoon, and stop the execution. Miller arrived just as they were escorting him to the scaffold. Seeing him walking up through the crowd Witman remarked, "There is old Peter Miller. He has walked all the way from Ephrata to have his revenge gratified today to see me hung." At that, Miller waved the pardon in the air, halting the execution and saving his enemy's life. The two embraced for the first time since their falling out and made the journey home to Ephrata together. They remained friends for the rest of their lives.[11] It is an extraordinary story of unrequited love and reconciliation from someone who had truly discovered the *greater perspective* of the Sermon on the Mount.

THE INVERTED LAW HAS THE POWER TO CHANGE US

In 2001 Mother Teresa of Calcutta, who died in 1997, was undergoing the process of what the Catholic Church calls *beatification*. In their tradition, this is the first step of the process to designate someone a saint. She was beatified in 2003 and canonized as a saint in 2016. What is somewhat interesting is the process, as the Vatican lines up people to testify in favour of and against the person's acts and character. The opponents were at one time called Devil's Advocates, and this is where this oft-used expression originated. They have since dropped that term, as it has now been commandeered by our culture to denote anyone that wants to defend an unpopular position.

One of Mother Teresa's opponents was celebrated British atheist Christopher Hitchens. He had been a long-term critic of Mother Teresa and published a book on her in 1995, called *The Missionary Position: Mother Teresa in Theory and Practice*.[12] It did not treat her kindly. So, it should have come as no surprise when Hitchens made an appearance at the Washing Archdiocese to weigh in on her character when they were considering her sainthood. Among other nasty things he said about her, he called her a "fanatic, a fundamentalist, and a fraud."[13] There is no doubt that this seemed like a vindictive thing to say of someone who had lived their life serving others and was now deceased. Nor am I making a case here for or against the sacrament of canonization. But one thing should not escape our notice; if people lined up to criticize Mother Teresa of Calcutta, what chance do we have of getting through life without criticism or judgment?

As mentioned in Chapter One, Jesus began the Sermon on the Mount with what we call the Beatitudes, or in a more common vernacular, the "Blessings." There is nothing appealing about any of them on the surface. At first blush they look like curses rather than blessings. They start off with the confusing blessing of being poor in spirit and end with the utterly ridiculous blessing of being persecuted and reviled.

> *Blessed are those who are persecuted for righteousness sake, For theirs is the kingdom of heaven. Blessed are you when they revile and persecute you, and say all kinds of evil against you falsely for My sake. Rejoice and be exceedingly glad, for great is your reward in heaven, for so they persecuted the prophets who were before you.*
>
> —Matthew 5:10–12 ⛰

"Yippee, people hate me! I am so happy I could just die!" Can you name even one person you know who rejoices and is exceedingly glad when they are reviled, persecuted and falsely accused? You don't! I don't! I can only find one example in all of the Bible where people actually rejoiced in the midst of persecution and suffering, and perhaps not surprisingly, it was Jesus' disciples… the very men who stood with Him on that mountain in Galilee when He delivered this historical and revolutionary sermon. What I am referring to is in Acts 5, when the council of the high priest in Jerusalem imprisoned them, beat them and commanded them not to preach in Jesus' name again.

> *… and when they had called for the apostles and beaten them, they commanded that they should not speak in the name of Jesus, and let them go. So they departed from the presence of the council, rejoicing that they were counted worthy to suffer shame for His name.*
>
> —Acts 5:40–41

Kaduna, Nigeria, lies right on the tenth parallel. It has been the historic dividing line between the Muslims in the north of the country and the Christians to the south. The city has been long characterized by the violence between the two faiths. James Movel Wuye is a local pastor in the city. He lost his arm when it was cut by a sword in a fight with a local Muslim man. His bitterness ran deep toward the Muslim community around him. In 1995 he went to a pastors' conference and while listening to a message on the Sermon on the Mount, God dealt with him about his hatred for Muslims. He realized he would never reach them for Christ if he didn't learn first to love them.

Shortly thereafter a journalist introduced him to Muhammad Ashafa, a local Muslim Imam, and said, "Pastor, Imam… talk!"[14] They talked and decided that they would together try to help the two groups to live together in harmony in the same city. It was difficult at first, as the bitterness between them ran deep. Pastor James admitted that one night they had to share a room together as they were travelling. During the night he had thoughts of taking his pillow and suffocating his Muslim counterpart with it. He overcame the impulse, and eventually their love and respect for one another broke though. They have been working side by side as great friends ever since. Kaduna is a much more peaceful place today than it was two decades ago, but it could never have happened if the Inverted Law had not changed a man's heart.

THE INVERTED LAW HAS THE POWER TO CHANGE OTHERS

The Inverted Law has the remarkable power to change people in a way that no amount of wrangling, correcting or contention can.

Someone once said, "Love your enemies, it will drive them crazy," but the Bible tells us what really happens.

> *If your enemy is hungry, give him bread to eat;*
> *And if he is thirsty, give him water to drink;*
> *For so you will heap coals of fire on his head,*
> *And the LORD will reward you.*
>
> —Proverbs 25:21–22

In this proverb, Solomon tells us that the Lord will reward us when we do good to our enemies. It does not say specifically how, but that doesn't matter since being in God's good graces is never a bad thing. Hundreds of years later, the Apostle Paul quotes this exact proverb in the epistle to the Romans when telling them not to look for revenge over their enemies.

> *Therefore "If your enemy is hungry, feed him; If he is thirsty, give him a drink; For in so doing you will heap coals of fire on his head." Do not be overcome by evil, but overcome evil with good.*
>
> —Romans 12:20–21

"Heaping burning coals of fire on his head" is likely a reference to an Egyptian ritual in which a person who wanted to make amends for a wrongdoing would walk around with a basin of glowing coals on his head as evidence of genuine repentance. Solomon is using the idiom metaphorically here (so please do not try this trick at home). It means that the conviction of the Holy Spirit will come upon that person and they will recognize their folly.

Few people change when we judge them or correct them. Usually, they just get mad at us. Yet this truth seems to elude most people as they continue futilely trying to change the behaviour of others. It just doesn't work. We really cannot change others; we can only change ourselves. Only God can change others! Martin Luther King Jr. put it this way:

> Now, for the final reason why Jesus says, "Love your enemies." It is this: that love has within it a redemptive power. And there is a power there that eventually transforms individuals. That's why Jesus says, "Love your enemies." Because if you hate your enemies, you have no way to redeem and to transform your enemies. But if you love your enemies, you will discover that at the very root of love is the power of redemption. You just keep loving people and keep loving them, even though they're mistreating you. Here's the person who is a neighbor, and this person is doing something wrong to you and all of that. Just keep being friendly to that person. Keep loving them. Don't do anything to embarrass them. Just keep loving them, and they can't stand it too long. Oh, they react in many ways in the beginning. They react with bitterness because they're mad because you love them like that. They react with guilt feelings, and sometimes they'll hate you a little more at that transition period, but just keep loving them. And by the power of your love they will break down under the load. That's love, you see. It is redemptive, and this is why Jesus says love. There's something about love that builds up and is creative. There is something about hate that tears down and is destructive. "love your enemies."[15]

When our kids were little, the neighbourhood was teeming with young people. They would be out on the street playing ball hockey or in the school yard behind our house playing soccer. In every community there is always a bad apple or two, and ours was named Jason. There were actually two Jasons. My kids called one "Jason" and the other one "the bad Jason." If a bike went missing, it was

Jason, the bad Jason. If the garbage cans got rolled down the street, it was Jason, the bad Jason. I used to joke that, with Jason living on our street, every day was "Friday the thirteenth." (You would need to be a movie buff to get that reference.)[16] It wasn't that he was a horrible kid; he just had no adult guidance in his life. He didn't appear to have a father anywhere and his mother was at work most of the time, leaving him to his own devices. It was a bad combination.

One day I looked out our back window toward the school yard and saw Jason, the bad Jason, shooting hoops with a shiny new basketball. Normally I would not take notice of such a thing, but I had just bought my kids a new ball and I couldn't help but wonder. I went into the garage, and sure enough, it was gone.

I walked across the field to the basketball court and confronted him. "Hey, Jason, why did you take my basketball?"

He shot back in an indignant voice, "Well, I don't have my own ball, so what was I supposed to do?"

Ok, fair question, I thought. His mother isn't going to buy him a ball and he has no father in the picture. So, in a fatherly way I made a deal with him. I told him he could use mine anytime he wanted as long as he knocked on the door and asked for it. Then I told him, "But not today, because you stole it." I snatched the ball from his hands and headed home, where I put it in the garage. I remember how brilliantly and compassionately I felt I had handled the situation. In my mind it was tough love. I was willing to share the ball but I was still teaching him a lesson in respect and responsibility at the same time.

The VERY next day I looked out the front window and saw Jason, the bad Jason, going down the street, bouncing my basketball. He had not knocked on my door. He had not asked to borrow it. He had just walked into my garage and taken it. I ran out the front door and called after him, "JASON!"

This time, with ball still in hand, he took off running down the street. With his head start I knew I would not catch him on foot, so I grabbed one of my kid's bikes and mounted it for the chase. It was a little pink girl's Barbie bike. Imagine, if you will, the noted TV preacher, whom everyone on the block knows, chasing a boy down the street on a little pink bike shouting, "JASON! JASON! COME BACK HERE WITH MY BALL!" I managed to overtake him, reclaim my ball and threaten him that next time he broke into my garage I was going to call the cops. Then I began the "ride of shame" home. The whole neighbourhood was now out on their front steps watching me ride back to my house on a little pink Barbie bike with the ball in my hand that I had stripped away from the fatherless kid that lives in the apartment down the street. I was thinking to myself, "What is wrong with me? Have I lost my mind over a stupid basketball?"

It didn't take me long to decide what to do. The next day I saw Jason walking down the street. This time he didn't have my ball… I had it in the house, not in my garage. I grabbed the ball and headed out the door. I calmly called after him, "Jason!" Once again, he broke into a sprint. Fortunately, I convinced him to stop and did not have to chase him on a little pink Barbie bike a second time. I walked over and handed him the ball and said, "Jason, I want you to have this ball. I know you need one and have no way to get one. I will just buy my kids another." He was a bit stunned at his reversal of fortune and didn't say anything. He silently took the ball, turned and carried on down the street. I wanted to be careful not to congratulate myself again, but I was pretty sure I had gotten it right this time. Even if nothing ever came of it, I had done the right thing.

To this we are called, to *"overcome evil with good."* What happened in the aftermath was remarkable. Jason never once broke into my garage again, nor did he terrorize my house or my garbage cans. When he would walk by our place he would shout, "Hello, Mister Hughes!"

I would call back, "Hey, Jason, how's it going?"

He was a man of few words, "Fine."

It was the Inverted Law at work. It not only changed him, but maybe more importantly, it changed me. I have missed many opportunities to do good since then, simply because I forgot how powerful this principle is. But on that day, I felt like George Costanza in a rare, brilliant moment on "opposite day."

Chapter Nine

The Titanium Rule

There is no difficulty that enough love will not conquer: no disease that love will not heal: no door that enough love will not open.... If only you could love enough you would be the happiest and most powerful being in the world.

—Emmet Fox

IF YOU ASK the average non-Christian what Jesus taught us about treating our fellow human being, they will likely quote the Golden Rule: "Do unto others as you would have them do onto you." Jesus did say a version of this in the Sermon on the Mount—*"Therefore, whatever you want men to do to you, do also to them, for this is the Law and the Prophets"* (Matthew 7:12 ▲)—but what they may not know is that the Golden Rule did not originate with Jesus. There is a version of it in almost every major religion in history, from Confucianism to Buddhism. The first reference in other cultures may go back to ancient Egypt.[1] More significantly, the Golden Rule is nowhere near the highest altruistic virtue because it is still a relatively self-centred virtue, i.e., we only treat others the way WE want to be treated by them.

Business guru Tony Alessandra came up with what he called the Platinum Rule: "Treat others the way THEY want to be treated."[2] He cleverly pointed out that it was based on what your customer wanted, not what you would want. The "metallic" rules don't end there, either. There are at least four of them:

Platinum Rule – Do unto others as they would have you do unto them.
Golden Rule – Do unto others as you would have them do unto you.
Silver Rule – Do unto others as they did unto you.
Iron Rule – Do unto others before they do it to you!

Again, none of these even come close to how Jesus really taught us to treat one another. Canadian author Leonard Sweet got it right with what he coined the Titanium Rule: "Do unto others as Christ has done to you."[3] You can find it almost word for word in John 13:34, *"A new commandment I give unto you, that you love one another; as I have loved you."*

> If we don't understand that the nature of God is love, we will never understand the New Testament and we will never comprehend why Jesus commands us to love even our enemies.

The Apostle Paul extrapolated on precisely what it would look like to love someone the way Christ loved us. His thoughts are found in 1 Corinthians 13, and we almost only ever recite it at weddings because we secretly believe that only newlyweds—and only on their wedding day—could possibly ever be that *patient, kind, good, humble, selfless, enduring, forgiving, truthful* and *hopeful* (1 Corinthians 13:4-8). Paul called this kind of loving interaction with another human being *"a more excellent way"* (1 Corinthians 12:31b).

We may have read the Sermon on the Mount a thousand times and yet, somehow, missed just how extraordinarily radical it was then, now, or in any age. All of Jesus' teachings, including this sermon, are intrinsically rooted in one single overarching, all-powerful concept—LOVE.

The Apostle John exclusively refers to himself as *"the disciple that Jesus loved"* (John 21:7). Nobody is sure why he thought he was Jesus' favourite over his brother James or even Peter, but who are we to argue? We weren't there. John earned the nickname "Apostle of Love" because nobody wrote more about the love of God than he did. He repeatedly states that *"God is love"* (1 John 4:7–12). If we don't understand that the nature of God is love, we will never understand the New Testament and we will never comprehend why Jesus commands us to love even our enemies. Here is the Sermon on the Mount version of the Titanium Rule.

> *You have heard that it was said, "You shall love your neighbor and hate your enemy." But I say to you, love your enemies, bless those who curse you, do good to those who hate you, and pray for those who spitefully use you and persecute you, that you may be sons of your Father in heaven; for He makes His sun rise on the evil and on the good, and sends rain on the just and on the unjust. For if you love those who love you, what reward have you? Do not even the tax collectors do the same?*
>
> —Matthew 5:43–46 ⛰

One of the more obvious reasons why Jesus tells us to love our enemies is that this is exactly how God treated us when we were His enemies (Romans 5:8). The reference to bringing rain and sunshine on the just and unjust alike is indicative of the fact that God still loves all people, saints and sinners alike, as we are all created in His image. Christ is not asking us to do anything He Himself has not already done for us. He is merely asking us to return the favour. The problem is, nobody loves their enemies. Well, Frank Sinatra said he did, *"Alcohol may be man's worst enemy, but the Bible says love your enemy."*[4]

For the rest of us, loving our enemy, instead of hating them, is the hardest thing we will ever do. It is another one of those "opposites" we talked about in the introduction.

We have been trained from a very young age to hate our enemies. Almost 100% of all action movies that come out of Hollywood have the same basic plot. It invariably looks something like this:

> In the first five minutes of the movie, a violent villain violates a victim. A very vexed victor arises and vows to vacate the villain. Our visceral response to the vulgar villain vaults to a vector of vengeance. Invariably, the victor vanquishes the villain by eviscerating him. The victim is vindicated, and the victor is venerated. Our vitriol is validated, and we grow only in our value for vengeance. (This is my best attempt at impersonating Dr. Suess.)

Speaking of which, even children's cartoons follow a similar yet only slightly less violent presentation of the classic struggle between good and evil. We never see any examples of the affable Mickey Mouse or Sonic the Hedgehog loving their enemies. To love an enemy is incongruent with human and animal nature because, quite frankly, it is exclusive to the one true God's divine nature.

I met Pastor Frantisek in 1987. His home country of Czechoslovakia had been in the grip of oppressive communism since 1945. He still managed to build the largest evangelical church in Prague despite the opposition he faced in doing so. His government had agreed to allow Frantisek to travel to North America to tell the West how open they were to freedom of religion. After all, here was a flourishing evangelical congregation of 500 people that the government was so graciously allowing to exist. He spoke in several churches in Canada and carefully avoided any mention of the politics back home, choosing to instead speak of the amazing things God was doing in Prague. On a Sunday evening while he was in Winnipeg, a group of a dozen pastors and their spouses were gathering for dinner. One of them had brought Frantisek as a guest. After the meal, we asked him to tell us more about his ministry back home. He seemed a bit nervous at first, but slowly decided he was in a safe place and could talk openly.

He began to tell us the real story. The Communist Party of Czechoslovakia had plainclothes secret police called the StB, which was an acronym for *Státní bezpečnost* or State Security in English. The Party used them as an instrument of political repression. They spied on suspected opponents of the government using telephone taps, intercepting private mail and conducting house-to-house searches. They had an army of 200,000 volunteer collaborators, whose missions were to spy on their friends, families and neighbours and report any suspicious activity that might be considered "subversion of the republic." The StB would then forge false criminal evidence against them and blackmail them or kidnap and torture them and administer drugs in order to force confessions out of them. For Frantisek, a Sunday never went by without several official StB members (not to mention an unknown number of collaborators) sitting in his congregation. They would make notes on every word Frantisek spoke and report back to their superiors. On numerous occasions, agents broke into his home in the middle of the night and beat him senseless with metal rods right in front of his family. They never showed badges, read him his rights or even identified themselves for that matter. Many times, he ended up in the hospital. Sometimes they would kidnap him and torture him at an undisclosed location.

Frantisek soldiered on faithfully. His message of following Christ was perceived as disloyal to a government that demanded unquestioned loyalty. Finally, the StB decided that they had had enough of Frantisek and sent in a higher-ranking officer who was authorized to kill. As serious as the story was, I had to laugh when he told us that, translated into English, they referred to him as "the Terminator." The movie by the same name, starring Arnold Schwarzenegger as a cyborg assassin, had come out a couple of years earlier and everyone in the room chuckled. He had no idea what was so funny. The Terminator sat through a couple of Sunday services himself and had decided that Frantisek needed to be terminated. The only reason Frantisek knew this was that he had spies of his own. He was no dummy.

Then, in an ironic twist of fate, the Terminator had a heart attack and ended up in the hospital, dying. When Frantisek discovered this, he went to visit the man in intensive care. He shared with him about the gospel and the love of God. The hitman said nothing. The next day, Frantisek returned to visit him and shared the gospel for a second time. On the third visit, the Terminator became clearly aggravated, asking, "Don't you know who I am?"

Frantisek assured him. "Of course, I do."

Then he asked, "Don't you know why I have come?" Again, the pastor acknowledged that he did. Finally, the StB agent started to become emotional and said, "Then, why are you treating me with such kindness? What is your interest in me?"

Pastor Frantisek explained to this man that he himself had experienced the love of God when he did not deserve it. Christ had come into his broken life and given him a fresh start, a new life and a meaningful career in ministry. He then told him that the one thing that God asks in return is that he would love others the same way God loved him, even if that person was his enemy. At that, the Terminator broke down into deep sobs. Once again Frantisek shared the message of the gospel, but this time the career assassin accepted Christ into his life. That evening the Terminator passed away.

One day the two of them will meet again in heaven—the pastor and the assassin reunited in Christ—all because one man took the command seriously to *"love one another as I have loved you"* (John 15:12). Some people find it offensive that a person can live their entire life as a rank murderous sinner and then make a death bed conversion and be admitted to heaven. "That's not fair!" Of course, it is not fair. There is nothing fair about grace. None of us, not a single one of us, deserve to go to heaven. That is what is so amazing about grace, and so incredible about God's love.

In North American culture, most of us will never have enemies who are determined to take our lives, rape our wives or kidnap our children (although, sadly, these things can still happen anywhere in the world). For many of us, faced with only first world problems, we think our "enemies" are people who park in our assigned spot at work, let their dandelions blow seed fluff into our well-manicured lawns or make fun of us behind our backs. That doesn't make them any easier to love, and they still get categorized in the enemy box. G. K. Chesterton humorously put it this way: "The Bible tells us to love our neighbours, and also to love our enemies; probably because they are generally the same people."[5] I have managed to make my fair share of enemies in life because I am not always as tuned in to people's deeply held sentiments as maybe I should be.

A few years back, we had next-door neighbours who could be accurately described as borderline pantheists. They loved nature in a way that I didn't really appreciate. A handmade wooden strip canoe hung in their garage and was ferried to wilderness lakes on the rooftop of their hybrid SUV. They picked every weed by hand, fertilized the garden with fish guts and mowed the grass with a rotary push mower. In the end, their grass was scraggly, thin and light green. On my side of the environmental divide, the grass was thick, dark green and fueled by poisonous chemicals. (I am not bragging, and I have since improved my game significantly.) Most egregious was the fact that I operated gas powered mowers, weed whackers, chainsaws and leaf blowers. Then, as if to add insult to injury, every spring I would fire up my 250 HP outboard in the driveway. Billows of grey smoke drifted across their yard and down the street like the mosquito fogging machines of the past. By the next day, however, the boat would be gone, as I towed it out to the lake behind a Hemi-powered Dodge Ram truck.

For some reason, I was oblivious to how annoying these things were to my neighbours. After all, I am the nicest guy you will ever meet. Who wouldn't like me? Well, my neighbours, for starters. I would always say to Kathy, "I don't know why Louise next door doesn't like me. She won't even make eye contact some days."

Kathy would usually reply with, "Well you're not the easiest person to live with, so it must be almost as hard living beside you." I had no idea what she was talking about.

Then, one year, the husband, Gerald, got cancer and died. They knew we had been praying for him and it was very sad to see how it ended. That first winter without him was a harsh one. We had huge snowstorms that filled everybody's driveways weekly. I would wait until Louise was out of the house and then run over with my obnoxiously loud gas powered 12 HP Binford 3800 Snow Thrower and clear her driveway. It was my way of loving my neighbour/enemy and I was hoping I didn't get caught. After about three or four snowstorms, I saw Louise heading up our driveway to the front door. I said to Kathy, "Here comes Louise. If she is looking for me, tell her I'm not home. And tell her you have no idea how her driveway got cleared."

After a moment of pleasantries, she came right out and asked, "Has Mark been the one snow blowing my drive?" I was busted. There was no way Kathy was going to lie for me.

Without hesitation, Kathy gave me up and said that I had been doing it because I was concerned that she would not be able to get out of the driveway. Tearing up, Louise said, "Please tell him thank-you and let him know how much I appreciate it."

Huh? I did not see that coming. I was expecting a lecture about destroying the planet. From that day forward Louise has gone out of her way to smile, say Hello and ask me how I am. How did such a small thing make such a big difference in a relationship? Maybe, just maybe, Jesus was on to something with all that loving your brother/neighbour/enemy stuff!

Chapter Ten

For the Love of Pete

It is easier to love humanity than to love your neighbor.
—Eric Hoffer

JESUS HAD AN encounter one day with a very astute lawyer. Of course, in that day lawyers were not people that you had to pay thousands of dollars to keep you out of jail for cheating on your taxes. In this context, lawyers were experts in the Mosaic Law. They studied it, translated it and scribed it onto papyrus. They may not have always understood the intent of what they were working on but they were highly knowledgeable about the content of the Word of God. This particular lawyer asked Jesus what he must do to obtain eternal life. Christ turned it back on him and instead asked him what he thought the Law said about it.

> *So he answered and said, "You shall love the LORD your God with all your heart, with all your soul, with all your strength, and with all your mind," and "your neighbor as yourself."*
>
> *And He said to him, "You have answered rightly; do this and you will live."*
>
> *But he, wanting to justify himself, said to Jesus, "And who is my neighbor?"*
>
> —Luke 10:27–29

It is fascinating that, even when we know what the right thing to do is, our first human response is to look for a loophole. So, instead of just answering the lawyer's question directly, Jesus tells him a story. Christ loved to make people think for themselves and answer their own questions. If you can help people figure out their own questions for themselves, they will be more likely to accept the answer. It is much more effective than just telling people what to do or what to believe.

The story He tells is one we know today as the parable of the good Samaritan. In it a Jewish man falls among thieves and is robbed, beaten and left for dead. What's more, both a Levite and a Priest, potential rescuers, cross on the other side of the road to avoid dealing with it. If you get the impression that Jesus may be giving the religious leaders a proverbial poke in the eye, you would be right. And let's not forget that when it comes to the New Testament, it is us Christians who are the "Levites" and the "priestly" generation.[1] Then, in a move reminiscent of Moe Howard of the Three Stooges, Jesus hits them with the "double zinger" and pokes them in both eyes at once—He presents the dreaded Samaritan as the hero of the story! The lawyer, like all Jews, would have hated the Samaritans, considering them to be half-brother religious dogs that had bastardized Judaism.

It is the Samaritan who stops to care for the man, bandages the poor fellow up, puts him on his own animal, and takes him to an inn. He pays the bill and promises to cover any unexpected future expenses. It was an extraordinary act of kindness from a stranger. Then Jesus asks the clearly obvious question: *"So which of these three do you think was neighbor to him who fell among the thieves?"* (Luke 10:36). Duh, I don't know! Well, it was the Samaritan of course, and Jesus tells the lawyer to go and do likewise to others.

This parable is particularly personal to me, and not in a good way. Some years ago, a friend and I were in Ottawa for an evangelism course. During the lunch break we were heading down the sidewalk to find a restaurant. I was doing what I always do—talking—and my friend was doing what my friends always do—listening. A homeless man who walked with crutches had fallen on the sidewalk and was splayed on the ground in front of us. I honestly did not consciously see him as I stepped clear over him and kept walking and talking. Then a strange feeling came over me and I stopped. Oh, not because I now noticed the man but because I was still talking and sensed I had lost my audience. I looked back to see that my friend was helping the poor man to his feet. In that moment I had an epiphany—I was the Levite in the parable of the good Samaritan.

That moment still haunts me to this day. Ignoring the plight of another human being was so natural that I did not even notice that I was doing it. I have not done something quite that egregious since, but the point of the parable is that the Samaritan's response of uncommon kindness should be common for the follower of Christ. *"Therefore, to him who knows to do good and does not do it, to him it is sin"* (James 4:17).

There are two questions from this story that we don't want to miss.

1. WHO IS MY NEIGHBOUR?

The answer to this question is ridiculously simple. Using this parable as a guide, our neighbour is not every person in the world but anyone that is in need that crosses our path. Yes, that makes for a big neighbourhood!

2. HOW DO I LOVE MY NEIGHBOUR AS MYSELF?

This may be the more difficult question of the two. If you were sick, how much would you be willing to pay for a cure? Likely everything you have. If your child was sick, how much would you be willing to pay for a cure? Again, everything you have. If your next-door neighbour was sick, how much would you be willing to pay for a cure? Maybe $50 on the GoFundMe app? I know because that is exactly what I did the last time I participated in a GoFundMe campaign. If it is someone on the next floor down at the office, it is more like $5—the price of a Get Well Soon card. I am not saying this to be condemning, only to remind us that in practical terms we do not love others the same as we love our own. Loving others as yourself is extraordinarily difficult and arguably impossible without special grace that comes from God.

This brings us to the hub—the crux, the heart, the critical moment, the very essence—of the Sermon on the Mount and the entire New Covenant ushered in by Jesus. In Matthew 5:17 Jesus says, *"Do not think that I came to destroy the Law or the Prophets. I did not come to destroy but to fulfill."* ▲ This is perhaps Jesus' most profound statement, for the complete outworking of it is so multi-faceted that it is far beyond the scope of this book. He came as the literal fulfillment of the Jewish Passover, the sacrificial lamb, the Day of Atonement and a whole host of other Old Testament types and shadows, things so incredible that the disciple John put it this way,

> *And there are also many other things which Jesus did, which, if they were written one by one, I suppose that even the world itself could not contain the books that would be written.*
>
> —John 21:25

In the simplest of terms, Jesus offers us a way to approach the entire Mosaic Law, fulfilled in the two-part directive that we call the Great Commandment.

> *You shall love the LORD your God with all your heart, with all your soul, and with all your mind."… You shall love your neighbor as yourself. On these two commandments hang all the Law and the Prophets."*
>
> —Matthew 22:37–40

When we break down the Great Commandment into the two parts of "loving God" and "loving others,' it is not an accident that loving God is first. It is impossible to love others, outside of your friends and family, if you do not first have a love for God. We sometimes refer to that as loving "vertically." The more love we give God upwardly, the more we realize how much more He loves us back down. It is that vertical column of love that creates a desire to love others "horizontally." It is the picture of the cross. You must erect the vertical post first before you can hang the horizontal beam. Love for others flows out of the love we receive from God. John, the Apostle of Love, was pretty clear on this in his epistles.

> *But whoever has this world's goods, and sees his brother in need, and shuts up his heart from him, how does the love of God abide in him?*
>
> —1 John 3:17

> *If someone says, "I love God," and hates his brother, he is a liar; for he who does not love his brother whom he has seen, how can he love God whom he has not seen? And this commandment we have from Him: that he who loves God must love his brother also.*
>
> —1 John 4:20–21

One of the great debates of the last 2,000 years has been, "Are the Ten Commandments still valid, or have they been abolished?" The answer is Yes and Yes. When people say that we no longer are bound by the Ten Commandments, I like to ask them which one of them we are no longer required to keep. The murder one? The stealing one? The adultery one? (I get a lot of blank looks.) The Great Commandment is, no doubt, a replacement for the Mosaic Law, but it doesn't dismiss the Law so much as it fulfills it. The simple explanation is that the Law of Love is the only one you have to keep, because if you love God and love others you won't kill them, steal from them, covet their spouse, etc.

> Loving others as yourself is extraordinarily difficult and arguably impossible without special grace that comes from God.

The Great Commandment produces exactly what we see in the Sermon on the Mount. It is not about trying to obey God from the outside in, but from the inside out. When we develop a heart that loves God and loves people, the Ten Commandments seem like the bare minimum as to how we treat God and man. "Not killing" becomes a piece of cake. (Fortunately, most people are already pretty good at this.) But "not stealing" also becomes second nature. "Not committing adultery" is no longer even a question! Blessing people instead of cursing them seems like the only way to go. Loving our enemies? Hmmm... we might need some further help with that one!

Maximilan Kolbe was ordained as a Franciscan priest with the Roman Catholic Church in 1918. Of Polish/German descent, he was educated in Rome in philosophy, theology, mathematics and physics. After earning a doctorate in philosophy, he returned to Poland and founded a seminary, a monastery and a radio station. In the 1930s he headed a mission to Japan, where he built a monastery at the outskirts of Nagasaki.[2]

He moved back to Poland just prior to the Nazis invading his country in 1939. He was a vocal opponent of Hitler and the Nazi regime, taking to the radio waves to report on their activities. During this time, he was instrumental in hiding 2,000 Jews from Nazi persecution.

In February 1941 he was arrested by the German Gestapo and eventually incarcerated at the notorious Auschwitz death camp. In July 1941 a man from Kolbe's barracks vanished, presumed to have escaped. In order to discourage further escape attempts, the camp commander ordered ten men from his barracks to be starved to death in Block 13.

When one of the selected men utterly broke down, lamenting the fact that he was a father and had a family (most all of them did), Max Kolbe volunteered to take the man's place. The man who had disappeared from the barracks had not escaped and was later found drowned in the camp latrine, but the punishment ensued anyway. During the time in the cell, Kolbe led the men in songs and taught them to pray. After three weeks of total dehydration and starvation, they should all have been dead. Yet Kolbe and three others still remained alive. Wanting to end the ordeal, the commander ordered death by injection of carbolic acid, and the four men were murdered.

The Catholic Church later recognized his extraordinary sacrifice and Father Kolbe was beatified as a confessor by Pope Paul VI in 1971 and then canonized by Pope John Paul II on October 10, 1982.[3] In Catholic circles he is venerated as the patron saint of amateur-radio operators, drug addicts, political prisoners, families, journalists, prisoners and the pro-life movement.[4] He lived out Jesus's words in John 15:13, *"Greater love has no man than this that a man lay down his life for his friends."*

Laying down your life for your friend, brother, neighbour, etc. doesn't necessarily mean dying in their place. If that was the case, then you could only really do that once! On a more practical level, it means caring enough about them that you would be willing to inconvenience our own lives for their benefit. It is something we can and should do every day.

> *For if you love those who love you, what reward have you? Do not even the tax collectors do the same? And if you greet your brethren only, what do you do more than others? Do not even the tax collectors do so? Therefore you shall be perfect, just as your Father in heaven is perfect.*
>
> —Matthew 5:46–48 ▲

Some years ago, when we were living in our first house, we had a next-door neighbour that we really loved. Vlad was a salt-of-the-earth type who worked in a factory making tractors. For a young homeowner like me, he was a great resource. He knew how to fix everything and was always willing to offer a hand. People like Vlad are the type of people that make neighbourhoods a community. One day he informed us that he had received a generous buyout to take early retirement and he was moving out to the country. And just like that he was gone.

It's always a little disquieting to get a new next-door neighbour, especially when their bathroom window is six feet from yours. There are really no secrets in tightly packed communities. When the new neighbour, Pete, rolled in with the moving van, my heart sank. His buddies showed up to help him move in… on their Harley

Davidsons. Most of his furniture went right into the garage—the couch, the fridge the TV and the stereo. By afternoon the music was blaring, the beer was flowing and the smell of marijuana was wafting out the garage door and down the street.

My kids asked, "Dad, what is that smell?"

I accurately answered, "That is the neighbourhood going to pot."

They also had pet ferrets that often escaped from their cages and terrified our kids. I realized it had only been one day and I already pretty much hated my neighbour. I knew it was going to be a good test for my faith, but I still wasn't happy about it. I never made any effort to get to know Pothead Pete and his biker babe wife, Runaround Sue.

That first spring after moving in, they rototilled their entire back yard and planted a huge garden. I naturally assumed they were probably growing illegal weed. They then turned on the sprinkler and went away for the weekend. By Sunday morning the entire back yard looked like a lake. The water was inching closer to their window wells and was soon going to be flooding into their basement. I had a decision to make—would I get a beverage and watch the destruction ensue, or in an extraordinary act of Christian charity would I walk over and turn off the stupid sprinkler? I am being sarcastic here, and of course I turned off the water. The command to love your neighbour is not contingent on them somehow deserving or earning it.

That summer the backyard garden turned into six-foot-high rag weeds. The front yard was two-foot-tall quack grass filled with dandelions.

Pete didn't own a lawnmower. He had lots of small motors but they were all on motorcycles. It was probably a selfish motive, but I started mowing his grass. He would come out and say, "Whoa, dude, you don't need to do that! I was going to get a mower and do it myself."

I was thinking, "No, I really did need to do this because you never are going to buy a mower!" As an agriculture grad I gave Pothead Pete and Runaround Sue some pointers as to how to tend a garden. I helped him mend his fence that was falling down. It was the strangest thing, over time I came to both know him and, on some bizarre level, actually like him.

Pete never really changed, but as I got to know him I came to realize he was just a hoser doing the best he knew how. It was my attitude toward him that needed to change, and when it did, it made all the difference in the world.

Chapter Eleven

The F-Bomb

He that cannot forgive others breaks the bridge over which he must pass himself; for every man has need to be forgiven.
—Thomas Fuller

In 1998, Rev. Dale Lang, pastor of St. Theodore's Anglican Church in Taber, Alberta, felt God tell him that he would gain a national audience to speak to young people. At the time he had no way of knowing what that meant or what price his family would have to pay to see it come to pass.

On April 20, 1999, two Grade Twelve students walked into Columbine High School in Littleton, Colorado, with automatic weapons and opened fire. Thirteen students and teachers were murdered and twenty-one people were injured. The assailants then turned the weapons on themselves and committed suicide. In a cruel twist of fate, the event inspired multiple copycat murders in schools around the world that left dozens more dead. The first of these was only eight days later, on April 28, 1999. Todd Cameron Smith walked into the W. R. Myers High School in Taber and opened fire with a .22 calibre rifle. Before he could be wrestled to the ground, he wounded two students and killed a third. The student who died was Jason Lang, Rev. Lang's seventeen-year-old son.

In what can only be described as an act of uncommon forgiveness, Dale Lang went on national television the very next day and forgave the killer. Even when Smith received a sentence of only three years, Lang repeated his position of absolute forgiveness. "It didn't make me angry at him, it made me feel sad for him," said Lang.[1] The generally cynical media took notice and marvelled as to what kind of man this was, who would forgive the murderer of his only son. For the next ten years Rev. Lang's schedule was jam-packed as he crisscrossed the nation sharing the incredible message of compassion and forgiveness to tens of thousands of students. Rev. Lang tirelessly fulfilled his calling and shared the story over 1,500 times in a single decade. Though his schedule has normalized somewhat, he still gets called on to bring the message of forgiveness and hope to young people.

What would have happened if the Lang family had not been able to forgive Todd Smith? What would have resulted if their hearts were filled with bitterness and they did not have a message of hope for the young people that were trying to make sense of the tragedy? People would have understood, even expected it, but the doors to hundreds of schools would not have opened to him. Rev. Dale would not have had anything but pain to share with others. Jason would have died for no reason, since no good would have come from it. But by the power of forgiveness, a redemptive purpose that impacted a nation rose out of a great tragedy.

Few of us will ever have to deal with anything quite on the level the Lang family faced. It is disquieting, however, to realize how many of us are unable to forgive the much smaller transgressions we endure.

> *For if you forgive men their trespasses, your heavenly Father will also forgive you. But if you do not forgive men their trespasses, neither will your Father forgive your trespasses.*
> —Matthew 6:14–15 ▲

The stakes could not possibly be higher. Jesus specifically states that our Father in heaven will not forgive our sins if we do not forgive those of others. Without trying to unnecessarily frighten anybody… we should be absolutely terrified by this truth! How many of us go through life with people we cannot or will not forgive? Are we really doomed if we do not release them from their transgressions against us? Yes! Look, these are Jesus' words—not Paul's, not Peter's, not John's, not mine. There is no wiggle room here for other possible interpretations.

So many of us feel we are justified in carrying a little bit of offence, as long as it doesn't unduly affect our lives. I remember one day mentioning to a friend that I had heard that his brother had sold the family cottage where they all spent their summers. My friend was completely unaware that it had happened. I asked him how it was possible that I knew something like that and he didn't. He calmly said, "Oh, I don't talk to my brother. What's the point of holding a grudge if you don't hold it forever?" He smiled when he said it, but I sensed the pain behind the comment. I guess you need to admire his honesty, but what could these brothers possibly have between them that would warrant a lifelong grudge? And what price are they paying, even on an emotional level, never mind the spiritual one?

Most of us grew up learning that the A-bomb (or atomic bomb) was the most powerful manmade force. That may be so, but forgiveness might be the most powerful divine force. If the A-bomb blows things up, the "F-bomb" (forgiveness) has the power to put them back together again. With forgiveness we can heal hurts, end arguments, restore trust, turn enemies into friends and resolve virtually any interpersonal conflict. As it has been said, "He who forgives ends the quarrel."[2]

In Matthew 18, Peter asks Jesus a question that was undoubtedly rooted in a personal conflict. Perhaps it came out of a disagreement with one of the other dopey disciples. He inquires, *"Lord, how often shall my brother sin against me, and I forgive him? Up to seven times?"*

(Matthew 18:21). We can imagine that, by suggesting seven times, Peter was now sitting at offence number eight with the always confrontational Sons of Thunder, John and James, and was looking for reprieve from the endless forgiving. Peter, always willing to go the extra mile, was content with forgiveness number seven, but eight? Surely that was a bridge too far.

Jesus' response must have left Peter absolutely incredulous: *"I do not say to you, up to seven times, but up to seventy times seven"* (Matthew 18:22). Quick, do the math! That would be 490 times. However, if you are counting, you have missed the point. Jesus is, in effect, saying, "You need to forgive everybody all the time."

People who have been hanging around Church of the Rock any length of time will have heard me say that on multiple occasions. It is a motto I live by. I have made the decision that I will forgive everybody all the time and there will be no exceptions to the rule. I do not care what people do to me, say about me or think about me. I have decided in advance that I will forgive every one of them every single time.

I have never had this conviction tested to the level that Rev. Dale Lang and his family have (and I pray I never will), but I have had many, many opportunities to put it into practice. Today we live in a culture of offence. People feel free to be offended with anything and anyone. Social media has become something of a repository of bitter offence. It seems many are willing to trade their self-respect for attention. Trolls hide behind their keyboards and launch flaming missiles at others, often anonymously and cowardly.

When you are in the public eye, you are an easy target. I get insulted almost every single day. Sometimes it is from people I know, but mostly from people I don't. One day, I got an email from a stranger who went to all the trouble to write to me to ask, "Why are you even on TV? You look like a wrinkled-up crackhead or drug addict. I don't know how your wife can stand you!" I try not to take things too personally, but it was hard to see this as anything but personal.

I would be lying if I said I was so thick-skinned that nothing bothered me. We are all human. Even televangelists have feelings—hard to imagine, really. It is helpful to remind ourselves that Jesus also had His detractors, and He was perfect. His words are strangely encouraging, *"Woe to you when all men speak well of you, for so did their fathers to the false prophets"* (Luke 6:26).

Of course, forgiving a stranger may actually be easier than forgiving, let's say, the person we wake up beside every morning. The reason being, we don't really care what strangers think of us. It is the people closest to us who matter the most, and as we are all aware, it is the people closest to us that we hurt the most.

One evening we were at the dinner table and my daughter made a very funny smart-aleck remark. I can no longer recall exactly what she said, but at any rate, I cracked up because I love good-natured banter. Kathy turned to her and said, "Whatever you do, don't turn out like your father."

I looked at Kathy and said, "You know I am sitting right here, don't you?"

To which she replied, "Do you have to take everything so personally?"

I said, "Kathy, how can I not take it personally? You're telling our daughter not to turn out like me!"

To which she rebuked me again saying, "Everything has to be about you, doesn't it?"

I sat there, silent and somewhat bewildered. Then I smiled, realizing this story was going to make a great sermon illustration someday. Which it did!

The point is, we cannot go through life being offended by every little thing. We all need to stop taking ourselves so seriously, learn to forgive everybody all the time and maybe start enjoying the humorously distorted moments in life.

But hang on! Jesus has not even finished His answer to Peter—not only do we have to always forgive, there are also no limits to what is forgivable. He then tells a parable about a king whose servant owes him 10,000 talents (Matthew 18:23–35). The king commands that the man, along with his wife and children, be sold as slaves until the debt is paid. The servant begs for patience, claiming that, given time, he will repay the entire amount. The king is moved with compassion and forgives the man the entire debt. So far, so good. But then the servant went out and found a fellow servant that owed him 100 denarii. This time it was his peer begging for patience. One would expect the servant to have had compassion, just as his master had, but instead he grabbed him by the throat and threw him into debtor's prison until all the debt was paid. The other servants who had witnessed the whole affair were upset and snitched on him to their master. The king was understandably and deeply disappointed that this man did not have pity on his colleague. This time, he delivered his servant to the torturers until the debt could be paid.

Seriously? Who has torturers on standby?

To truly appreciate the significance of this parable we need to do a little math. A talent, by weight, measures 59 kilograms. 10,000 talents are therefore 590,000 kgs. If it was talents of gold, which at this writing are $73,000/kg, then we are talking about a debt of $43 billion (CAD)—or roughly the entire personal net worth of Bill Gates. Because the number is nothing short of outlandish, Jesus must have been referring to 10,000 talents of silver, which is a mere $925/kg, making the total value of the deal a much more affordable $546 million. Regardless of whether it was gold or silver, it is a debt so great that the disciples would have been dumbfounded when they heard the number. The servant had no possibility of ever being able to repay it; that is the intention of this story. By contrast, a denarius was the average daily wage for an agricultural worker in Jesus' day. The value of the 100 denarii the fellow servant owed the first servant is a bit hard to put a modern-day number on, but for argument's sake, let's be generous and compare it to an unskilled farm labourer's wage of $15 an hour, 10 hours a day, for 100 days. If we do that, we are still looking at no more than $15,000 that his fellow servant owes him.

Clearly, Jesus is using hyperbolical language here. The king forgives a $546 million debt, one that no mere servant would ever be able to repay in a thousand lifetimes, compared to a real-life debt of $15,000 or probably less, a debt that could realistically be repaid.

The whole point of this illustration is to remind us that the debt we owe to God for our own sin and despicable behaviour is so immense that it could never ever be repaid, no matter how hard we try. And yet, He is willing to have compassion upon us and forgive us the entire amount, no matter how great. In return, however, He expects us to forgive our fellow human beings the infinitesimally small transgressions that they have committed against us.

Jesus concludes the parable by saying, *"His master was angry, and delivered him to the torturers until he should pay all that was due to him"* (Matthew 18:34), which again, if you were following the details of the story, would be "never." Then He summarizes the lesson with this imperative, *"So My heavenly Father also will do to you if each of you, from his heart, does not forgive his brother his trespasses"* (Matthew 18:35).

Strictly speaking, we are required to forgive everybody all the time. Otherwise, our own transgressions will be recompensed back upon us, and that, my friends, is a price too high for anyone to pay.

Here is something of a marvel. When I speak on the subject of forgiveness not being optional but mandatory, almost without exception, I will hear from someone who feels that forgiving their perpetrator is an insurmountable request. Their memory is still raw, the wound is too deep, and the individual is impenitent and does not deserve to be forgiven. No doubt all of that is true. If the offending party deserved to be forgiven, we wouldn't have to give it to them. It is the reason for the idiom "to err is human; to forgive, divine." The very nature of forgiveness is to release the guilty, undeserving, even wretched party from their transgression. The indebted servant in the parable did not earn the expunging of his debt; it was an act of compassion on the part of his master. Todd Smith did not deserve Rev. Dale Lang's forgiveness. He deserved hatred and anger, but that is not what he received. If the Langs could find a way to forgive their son's murderer, shouldn't it be possible for any of us to do the same for undoubtedly much smaller infractions?

Still, people object. The response usually goes something like this: "You cannot possibly understand what I have gone through. I have to see this person at family events. They have shown no remorse whatsoever." Again, that is probably all true. One of the greatest challenges of forgiveness is when the unkindness, betrayal, violation or injustice is continually in your face. It is much easier to forgive someone from a distance, or as comedian George Burns used to say, "Happiness is having a large, loving, caring, close-knit family in another city." The degree of difficulty, however, does not change the fact that we still must forgive others if we want to be forgiven ourselves. To hold on to the offence is too high a price to pay.

At the same time, we need to remind people that they do not have to continue to entertain a relationship with someone that continually hurts them. Forgiveness does not mean putting yourself in continual danger. Nobody should subject themselves to abuse or violence, and sometimes removing oneself from the situation is part of the process. If, however, the relationship is tolerable, forgiveness in the lingering close contact will build the most character and maturity in us.

Judas was stealing money from Jesus on a continual basis.[3] Jesus also knew that Judas would betray Him.[4] Even so, He walked in love and forgiveness toward Judas every single day. How would we treat someone if we knew they were going to betray us?

> If the Langs could find a way to forgive their son's murderer, shouldn't it be possible for any of us to do the same for undoubtedly much smaller infractions?

My father and mother were divorced when I was a young adult, and my father remarried. It made for an awkward family dynamic that is all too familiar to many of us today. Only a few short years later, my father died after a short battle with liver cancer. Near the end, while I was visiting him as he lay dying on his hospital bed, he was a bit anxious about something. He said to me, "I think I have made a big mistake on my will." He was lawyer and dealt with wills every single day, so I dismissed it and calmed him with, "I am sure that whatever you did was the right thing." He elaborated that he wanted his estate split nine ways—to go to his six children and his new wife's three children after she passed away. That surprised me a little, as he was not close with her children. But if that is what he wanted, who was I to object?

A week after that conversation, he passed away. Sure enough, his will was as he said, and initially his entire estate was bequeathed to his second wife. It was not until later that I understood what "mistake" my father had referred to on his death bed. Unbeknownst to any of us, immediately after his death she changed her will and left my father's estate exclusively to her three grown children. Shortly after that, she herself became ill and was hospitalized. At that point her children moved into my father's home, and to add insult to injury, that house was just a block away from mine and I drove by it every day. And I have continued to drive by it for over twenty years.

To this day, people who are not even related to my father dwell in his home and live off his estate. I face the injustice every single day and get the privilege of practicing "forgiving everybody all the time," every single day. I honestly see it as a gift because I feel it makes me a better person. I could be resentful, bitter or even angry, but I have decided to love my neighbours… and in my case, my neighbours are spending my inheritance! You do have to appreciate the irony of it all.

One of the secrets to understanding the F-bomb principle is to recognize that bitterness enslaves you, not the one with whom you are offended. The word "offence" appears fifty-two times in the Bible. In the Greek New Testament, the word used is *skandalizo,* from which we get our English word "scandalize." The term was used to describe a trap that would be used to snare an animal. What many people do not realize is that when we get offended with someone, we are the one who steps into the trap, not them. Why people think they are somehow punishing the other person is an inscrutable mystery. The offender often has no idea they have hurt anyone, and they go on their merry way, which, of course, enrages us even more. Proverbs describes it as a self-imposed prison: *"A brother offended is more unyielding than a strong city, and quarreling is like the bars of a castle"* (Proverbs 18:19 ESV).

One Monday morning, I was doing my daily commute to the office. I was mostly awake, holding a cup of joe in one hand while the other was on the wheel. In the next lane in front of me was a 1976 Pontiac Parisienne, a gem of a car and possibly the largest automobile ever produced. I could not see a driver. Only a tuft of white hair and a set of knuckles were visible over the steering wheel. (It is an inverse proportion: the older and smaller the man, the bigger the car.) I was keeping my eye on him, as I knew there was no possible way he was able to shoulder check and he was already meandering back and forth across the centre line.

Just then, he pulled a hard left into my lane without looking or signaling his intent. I reacted quickly, evading a collision, but dumped my coffee unto my lap. I began cussing him out—in the way pastors do—"Hey, you… crazy… old guy." (I am terrible at cussing.) He never even saw me and carried on in his mission to terrorize as many people as possible before he dies. It is like the old adage, "I want to die peacefully in my sleep like my grandfather, not screaming in terror like the other passengers in his car at the time."

When I arrived at the office, I had to explain why my crotch was soaking wet. By the time I was halfway down the hall, I had told the story five times and was becoming more animated and agitated with each telling. "This wet crotch is not what it looks like! I did not pee my pants!" Then it dawned on me. I was allowing someone who did not even know that I existed to ruin my day. I thought, "By this time of the morning, he has probably cut off ten more people in traffic. It is what he does, the reason he gets up in the morning; everybody needs a purpose in life."

My response to my frustration was violating my own conviction to forgive everybody all the time. It is so easy to forget that we are the primary victim of our own offence. Lewis B. Smedes brilliantly put it this way, "To forgive is to set a prisoner free and discover that the prisoner was you."[5]

Approaching the final days of the Vietnam war in 1972, soldiers on both sides had lost all sense of humanity. North Vietnamese troops had attacked and occupied the little village of Trang Bang and a group of civilian and South Vietnamese soldiers were fleeing the village. A Republic of Vietnam Air Force pilot mistook the group as enemy Viet Con and bombed them with napalm. Four civilians were killed and many more horribly burned by the flames. One of them was nine-year-old Phan Thi Kim Phúc, who tore her clothes and ran down the street, shouting, "Nóng quá, nóng quá!" ("too hot, too hot!"). *Associated Press* photographer Nick Ut snapped a picture of the distressed and naked Kim and the *New York Times* printed the photograph on the front page the next day. It later earned Nick Ut a Pulitzer Prize[6] and was chosen as the World Press Photo of the Year for 1973.[7] It is a disturbing image but needs to be seen to appreciate the horrors of war and the poignancy of this story.

After he snapped the picture, Nick Ut took Kim Phúc and the other injured children to Barsky Hospital in Saigon. The attending physician was a Winnipegger by the name of Dr. Norm Merkeley (who just happened to also be my cousin's father). He was an adventuresome individual and would often volunteer to serve in dangerous and war-torn places. Dr. Merkeley determined that the third-degree burns were so severe that Kim probably would not survive. Fortunately, her situation drew the attention of several world-renowned skin specialists, who eventually performed no less than seventeen surgeries. Two of Kim's cousins were not so lucky and died in the attacks. She was able to return to life more or less as usual. In 1982, she found a New Testament in the library and, after reading it, converted to Christianity. Given permission to study abroad in Cuba, she met and married her husband, Bui Huy Toan, another student. In 1992, on a flight from Cuba, their plane landed in Gander Newfoundland for refuelling. The couple defected and was granted asylum by the Canadian government.[8] They settled in Ajax, Ontario. Kim lived a quiet life in Canada and, due to her faith, was able to deal with the physical and emotional pain that haunted her every day.

In 1996, Kim agreed to speak at the Veterans Day ceremonies at the Memorial Wall in Washington, DC, something she had not done before. As she stood before the soldiers, many of whom had fought in Vietnam, she offered forgiveness even to those who had caused her such great harm. She talked at length about the power of forgiveness. "I just let them know it's about the love of God and the love of people. That is more powerful than any weapon of war."[9]

After her address a note was handed to her from someone in the crowd: "Kim, I am THAT man." His name was Rev. John Plummer, a former soldier, and upon meeting Kim, he publicly collapsed into her arms as she repeated gentle words of forgiveness. The story took on a life of its own and was the subject of a powerful book, *The Lost Art of Forgiving: Stories of Healing from the Cancer of Bitterness.*[10] Bizarrely, Plummer later admitted that he was a low-level staff officer who was neither the pilot nor the one who ordered the attack. He was just caught up in the emotion at the Wall that day. In Kim's typically classy manner, she said, "Whether or not he played a major or a minor role, the point is I forgive him."[11]

And that is the point! It never really matters who is at fault. The onus is always on us to forgive everybody all the time. The F-bomb has many benefits of its own to improve ourselves emotionally, relationally and spiritually, but at the end of the day, in terms of non-negotiables, it is as close to number one as you can get.

Chapter Twelve

A Woke Nightmare

"Do not think that you have to be woke to be kind. And do not think that because you aren't woke you don't have to be kind."

—Conor Barnes

WE HAVE ALL heard the term "woke" repeatedly in the last few years. It may seem like some urban hip-hop dictionary term that has only recently become part of the English lexicon, but it has actually been around for decades. Originally, it was part of a Black activism call to equality, and a few purists still use it that way.

The origin is interesting and storied. It is from a line in a 1938 song by Lead Belly called "The Scottsboro Boys" based on a tragic incident from 1931, when nine black youths were falsely accused of raping a white girl and then sentenced to death. Fortunately, upon appeal, the youths were acquitted when famous legal defender Clarence Darrow took on their case. The lyrics of the Lead Belly song were a reminder, "I made this little song about down there, So I advise everybody, be a little careful when they go along through there —best stay woke, keep their eyes open."[1] It was a warning to people of colour that they needed to take heed, as justice was not always on their side.

Merriam Webster defines "woke" as "aware of and actively attentive to important facts and issues (especially issues of racial and social justice),"[2] which again, in and of itself, is not ignoble. The problem is that the term has been co-opted by the mainstream media and politicos and has become yet another means of cultural polarization to describe current political or social agendas. For example, a pro-choice or pro-carbon tax position would be defined as "woke" even though they have nothing to do with racial justice. The woke mantra today is "Stay woke, stay angry."[3] And that is exactly what we see: activists, influencers, journalists, talk show hosts and social media keyboard cowboys, all angry, disaffected, critical, judgmental and divisive. Wokeness has staked out the territory of a social agenda that includes very narrow views on the environment, feminism, LGBTQ+ issues, race, gender and similar culture issues. Typically, it takes the form of "virtue signalling," which is the practice of publicly expressing opinions or sentiments intended to demonstrate one's moral superiority on a particular issue, most often unaccompanied by any real demonstration of action.

Former President Barack Obama, in an interview he did at the Obama Foundation Summit in Chicago in 2019, did us all a favour when he gave wokeness a poke in the eye and challenged every one of us to do better:

> This idea of purity and that you're never compromised and you're always politically woke—you should get over that quickly. The world is messy. There are ambiguities. People who do really good stuff have flaws… I do get a sense sometimes now among certain young people, and this is accelerated by social media—there is this sense sometimes of the way of me making change is to be as judgmental as possible about other people, and that's enough. If I tweet or hashtag about how you didn't do something right or used the wrong verb, then I can sit back and feel pretty good about myself. Did you see how woke

I was, I called you out. Then I'm going to get on my TV and watch my show… That's not activism. That's not bringing about change. If all you're doing is casting stones, you're probably not going to get that far."[4]

By now we are all sick of the term "woke." However, it still symbolizes what is wrong with our world today. Specifically, it provides the picture of a culture that is deeply divided, hypersensitive, easily offended, judgmental, angry and sometimes downright apoplectic. Most of us living today have never seen as divisive a time as we are facing now. The fracture lines run deep—politically, racially, religiously and especially morally. You can now turn on the TV any night of the week and see an angry mob upset about something, somewhere, burning cars and looting stores. Jesus warned us that this kind of cold-hearted, easily offended culture was going to be a sign of the end times.

> *And then many will be offended, will betray one another, and will hate one another. Then many false prophets will rise up and deceive many. And because lawlessness will abound, the love of many will grow cold. But he who endures to the end shall be saved.*
>
> —Matthew 24:10–12

Wokeness and cancel culture have taken public ridicule and shaming to a whole new level. An eighty-five-year-old Don Cherry was cancelled after thirty-nine years on *Hockey Night in Canada* for referring to immigrants as "you people."[5] Former news anchor Megan Kelly was cancelled from NBC when she impotently defended "black face" as a Halloween costume.[6] Chris Harrison was cancelled as the host of the TV show *The Bachelor* when he suggested people should show some grace to a young contestant who, some years back, had attended an Old South party.[7]

The intention here is not to defend any of these people (and get cancelled myself) but to ask this question: Who are all these perfect people out there who have never made a mistake? Don Cherry had been saying boneheaded, politically incorrect things publicly for thirty-nine years, but when he crossed the woke police his career came to a crashing unceremonious end. How is it that we have so heartlessly judged others, even to the point of costing them their careers and destroying their reputations, for what appear to be minor and forgivable errors in judgment? None of the three aforementioned are sexual predators, none of them killed anyone, none of them were even charged with a crime. Their misdemeanours do not compare to those of sexual predators like Bill Cosby, Harvey Weinstein or Jeffery Epstein. Yet, in the last few years, dozens and dozens of celebrities—from Al Franken to Wynona Rider—have been cancelled for not measuring up to the woke culture.[8] They have become victims of a hypersensitive, super-judgmental society that throws stones at others without ever examining their own human weaknesses.

J. K. Rowling is a household name, arguably one of the most successful novelists of our time. Her Harry Potter series has sold half a billion copies, making it the highest selling novel of all time. The movie series by the same name is the highest grossing film series ever.[9] But her star fell from grace when she had the temerity to question whether trans-women were the same as biological women.[10] She has gone to great lengths to try to explain that she is not transphobic and is supportive of trans-people and their rights.[11] Rowling's position is hardly radical. Polls show that 75% of Americans agree "with her" that there are only two genders. (Ironically, she didn't even say that.)[12] Nevertheless, Rowling has been viciously attacked on social media, accused of hate speech and physically threatened, having become a victim of widespread cancel culture. She was suspiciously absent from the *Harry Potter 20th Anniversary: Return to Hogwarts* special on HBO.[13] The cast of the Harry Potter series—Daniel Radcliffe, Emma Watson and Rupert Grint—have been outspoken in their criticism of her.[14] It seems to have escaped their notice that their fame wouldn't even exist without Rowling. She, of course, never needs to work again, but that is not her objection. Rowling feels that she has been maligned as a person, denied her right to freedom of speech and labelled as something she is not. She particularly dislikes being called a TERF: Trans-Exclusionary Radical Feminist,[15] a term that doesn't even come close to describing her, but labelling people is one of the cheap and dirty lowbrow tricks of people who are not capable of defending their positions intellectually. There is likely no person in history that has been more criticized for saying so little.

> Who are all these perfect people out there who have never made a mistake?

I used to lament that our culture valued "tolerance" as the highest human virtue, which never held a candle to the virtue of "love" that the New Testament teaches. Now I have come to miss it. Somewhere along the way, the call for tolerance was mysteriously supplanted with an abject sense of intolerance. There is zero tolerance for the opinions of a J. K. Rowling, Megyn Kelly, Don Cherry or any viewpoint that does not fall perfectly into line with the extreme politically correct narrative of today.

Then there has been the COVID-19 effect, which turned families, friends, communities and even churches against each other. People fought over lockdowns, masks, vaccines and vaccine mandates. Some of us got suckered into the fight and forgot that we live for a higher cause—we were supposed to be part of the answer, not part of the problem. It was distressing to see how many church people were being discipled by cultural values rather than biblical values. Perhaps it should not have been surprising, since most of us consumed countless hours of secular news, social media and political commentary during the coronavirus pandemic.

By this point, some may have already concluded that this chapter should not be part of a book on the Sermon on the Mount. Traditional Christian convention is that political commentary should be left out of a work on spiritual matters. But what is more spiritual than the attitudes people hold and the words they speak to one another? Isn't that precisely what the Sermon on the Mount was meant to correct? In many ways, Jesus' audience was no different from today, as they, too, had become steeped in the cultural mores of their day. They believed all kinds of things about marriage, divorce, sexuality and interpersonal relationships that were both unhelpful and unbiblical. The message of the gospel was meant to confront and correct the bankrupt values of a fallen world. The Sermon on the Mount, in particular, was intended to give the sincere listener *a greater perspective* as to how life should be lived and especially how we should be treating our fellow human beings. No subject was off limits in this discourse.

Again, the Sermon on the Mount is the basis of our biblical worldview. Socialists have their worldview influenced by the writings of Karl Marx. Libertarians, from English philosophers John Locke and John Stuart Mill. The Muslim worldview is rooted in the teachings of the Qur'an. Buddhists take cues from their historic teachings, and so forth. Wokeism is just another worldview that has risen out of the values of pop culture, Hollywood and social media. The Sermon on the Mount is a biblical worldview that cuts across the grain of every other worldview. Many of the values of Wokeism and cancel culture run completely contrary to the values of Christianity. Though we want to love our adversaries, we need to remember we are still in a cultural war, and the winner gets to decide what our children learn in school.

In the late 1990s, the now deceased political policy analyst Joseph P. Overton (1960–2003) proposed a theorem on political acceptableness. Posthumously, it has become known as the Overton Window.[16] He stated that an idea's political viability depends mainly on whether it falls within a particular range of public acceptability. According to Overton, the window frames the range of policies that a politician can recommend without appearing too extreme to gain or keep public office given the climate of public opinion at that time. Visually it looked like this:

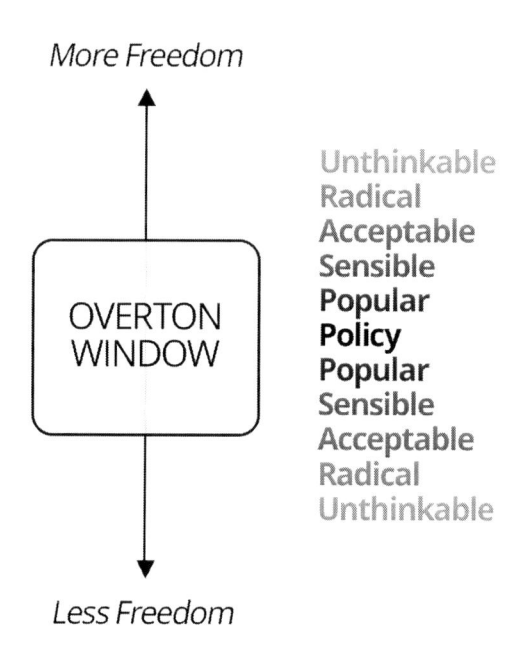

More Freedom

OVERTON WINDOW

Unthinkable
Radical
Acceptable
Sensible
Popular
Policy
Popular
Sensible
Acceptable
Radical
Unthinkable

Less Freedom

Overton oriented his diagram on a vertical axis to avoid a comparison to political left/right.[17] Unfortunately, if you search this idea online you will see most diagrams drawn on a horizontal axis complete with each extreme coloured in red or blue.[18] That was not his intent. It was his way of illustrating how various cultures move toward either more or less freedom, irrespective of their actual political construct. For example, communism and fascism are on the opposite ends of the left/right political spectrum but both of them are highly restrictive of personal freedoms.

Most political parties and their leaders in Canada are now left of centre. I used to joke with my American friends that their sometimes-maligned *socialist* Bernie Sanders would be a *conservative* in Canada. There was very little in his political platform that would not have been popular in our nation (universal health care, fair minimum wages, pro-choice, etc.). Be that as it may, the real concern is that our freedoms are being lost as the Overton Window shifts. This became even more apparent during the COVID-19 pandemic when it was open season on the unvaccinated. Not only were they basically under house arrest in nations like Canada, they were fired from their jobs and ineligible to go into a restaurant or movie theatre or ride on a train, bus, or plane.[19] In some provinces (and nations), people were fined for refusing the vaccine.[20] I am not defending their position— I am defending their right to be treated with respect and dignity. Politicians lined up clear across Canada to support such measures, and they received very little public pushback. And yes, we were in a pandemic, we all understand that. The point is that the Overton Window shifted dramatically. Politicians could now support draconian positions that, only a few months earlier, were on the *unthinkable* extreme but were now considered *sensible* and *acceptable*.

Some of us watched in disbelief as the fundamental human rights of the unvaccinated got dismissed without proper due process, legislative debate, or any form of open public dialogue. It was the most draconian and totalitarian thing I have ever witnessed personally, and yet most of us nodded in silent agreement.[21] Could any of us have imagined just a few years earlier the idea of a medical certificate (vaccine passport) being required to travel on a plane or train, or to go to a restaurant or a ball game? Dubbed "anti-vaxxers," they were routinely vilified by elected politicians and censored on social media. Big Tech volunteered to become Big Brother and made sure independent thinkers, irrespective of their credentials, were not able to post anything contrary to the official party line.[22]

I do a monthly news magazine format webcast on current affairs called *The eXchange*. YouTube censorship bots flagged and banned an episode for merely mentioning the word Ivermectin. I was not promoting it or suggesting its use. I was merely asking why respected physicians, who were trying to present clinical findings on the drug as a possible treatment for COVID-19, were unceremoniously shut down.[23] And for my sin of association, I also got shut down.

In January of 2022, Canadian truckers staged a major protest as they came from across Canada and converged on our nation's capital city, Ottawa.[24] They clogged the city, holding it hostage and demanding that the vaccine mandate for truckers be rescinded. At that point all Canadian and American truckers required a vaccine passport to go back and forth across the US/Canada border. Whether the protest was legal or not is not my point. Because the Overton Window had shifted, the truckers' perspective, which would have been *popular* a couple of years earlier, had now become *unthinkable* and contemptible. For some, their livelihoods were being stripped away and they were willing to resort to radical measures to convince politicians, media and average Canadians to think the same. Though some saw the protest as a victory, since many restrictions were eased shortly thereafter, it was a full seven months later before vaccine passports were lifted for crossing over the Canadian border. Many workplaces and universities across Canada still required vaccines, boosters and mask-wearing even though COVID-19 vaccines had been proven to no longer provide protection against the new variants of the virus.[25] Infection rates among vaccinated and unvaccinated were virtually the same. Again, restrictions that would have been completely *unthinkable* pre-pandemic were now clearly in the *sensible policy* range. And yes, we understand we were in an unprecedented situation, but it was shocking to see the degree of cultural change that was precipitated in such a short period of time.

My real concern has less to do with political liberties (which, though important, is not the subject of this book) and more to do with our religious freedom. The message of the gospel used to be within the *popular* range of the Overton Window a generation ago. During my forty-year career in ministry, it has shifted from *popular* to *sensible* to *radical*. It is hard to imagine how, in one generation, the notion of monogamous heterosexual marriage had become a *radical* idea. As an exclusive ideal, it is now unquestionably categorized as *unacceptable*.

I keep asking myself the question, what kind of train have we boarded and where is it taking us? Who will be the next on the list to be cancelled? We know who will be. We will! As Christians, we are already in the crosshairs; we are as politically incorrect as they come. We believe that life begins at conception, that marriage is sacred, that gender is by divine assignment, that all people were created equally and that the colour of our skin should not be a factor one way or another. We maintain that we are all sinners, incapable of living righteously on our own accord, and therefore we are all in need of a personal Saviour to redeem our lives and guide us day by day through the work of His Holy Spirit. That is not a particularly popular message for a secular world that no longer believes there is an absolute right and wrong but instead embraces a moral relativism that changes as the winds blow. And those winds are already blowing against us.

In 2013, Trinity Western University (TWU) in British Columbia began working toward establishing a law school on their campus.[26] They had already gained provincial approval only to have legal challenges launched against them because of their "community covenant." As a Christian university, they required certain moral behaviour from their students. The covenant that all students were asked to sign, among other things, restricted them to heterosexual sex within marriage. It disallowed premarital, extramarital and homosexual relationships within its student body. The Law Societies (governing bodies of the legal profession) in British Columbia, Ontario and Nova Scotia ruled that they would not license any TWU grads to practice law in their provinces. They stipulated that they were not saying Christian law schools cannot exist, only that graduates from TWU could not work as lawyers.[27] If the right to work in one's chosen profession is not a constitutionally protected right, then we are in big trouble.

The fundamental argument against the "community covenant" was that it excluded LGBTQ+ students from enrolling in the TWU law school. Nobody seemed to care that it also precluded common-law couples, premarital sex and adulterous relationships. Various court challenges ensued, escalating it all the way to the Supreme Court of Canada. The nine justices ruled seven to two against TWU.[28] There were no LGBTQ+ students trying to get into their law school, but the Supreme Court decided that the individual rights of a hypothetical student overrode the religious freedom of an entire university. One wonders what they would have ruled had it been a Jewish or Muslim university?

Eventually, TWU dropped their mandatory "covenant" in favour of a voluntary one, which of course defeats the purpose.[29] And, as of this writing, TWU still does not have a law school. Without trying to be overly dramatic, it felt like a distressing moment in Canadian history.

One can feel the constrictions narrowing around what one can or cannot safely say. Many preachers have already voluntarily acquiesced in the pulpit, fearing the cultural pressure, and hopelessly trying not to offend the modern enlightened soul that might be sitting in the pew. The bigger question is, where is this all going? Is there any end in sight for this woke nightmare?

Maybe we can't change the media, pop culture, Hollywood or Big Tech. But we can change the immediate world around us—our families and friends, the communities in which we live, the places we work and the schools we attend. Want to know how? Keep reading!

Chapter Thirteen

Mercy over Justice

I have always found that mercy bears richer fruits than strict justice.

—Abraham Lincoln

THE INJUSTICE THAT prevails in our world today has not escaped anyone's notice. The vast majority of people, who just want to live normal decent lives, have become understandably frustrated with discrimination/violence/eroding freedom/government waste/inane or incompetent political leadership—take your pick.

The Sermon on the Mount provides us with the antidote for a fallen world, so we want to be careful that we don't fall into the trap of casting aspersions on others and, in effect, become guilty of the same intolerance with which we find ourselves treated. Jesus sternly instructs His followers not to fall into the entaglement of offence (*skandalizo*).[1]

Woe to the world because of offenses! For offenses must come, but woe to that man by whom the offense comes!

—Matthew 18:7

I have always believed that you can measure a person's spiritual maturity by the ease with which they are offended. People who are quick to react and take offence demonstrate that they have not yet learned Christ's way and are still worldly in their emotions. You would be hard pressed to find a single example of where Jesus was offended with another human being.[2] The more mature a follower of Christ, the more likely they will be able to take matters in stride without becoming bitter. We make a deliberate point of looking for people with this kind of maturity when trying to fill positions of leadership in our organization. It is not uncommon for otherwise talented people to be overlooked because they cannot pass the Offence Test. Our unregenerated human natures have a proclivity to look for someone to single out, blame and punish when things aren't going well.

In the Bible, whenever something went wrong God's people looked around for someone to stone. When under David's watch the base camp at Ziklag was burned with fire and the women and children taken captive, *"the people spoke of stoning David"* (1 Samuel 30:6). For obvious reasons, I try to avoid hiring staff who are inclined to this kind of problem-solving protocol. More seriously, the inadequacy of retributive justice is that it doesn't have any transformative power. It might be cathartic, but it is not redemptive.

Jesus underscores a simple yet entirely profound understanding of the judgmental spirit that plagued his day as much as it does ours today. In keeping with the counterintuitive nature of Christ, His advice (command) flies in the face of modern convention.

> *Judge not, that you be not judged. For with what judgment you judge, you will be judged; and with the measure you use, it will be measured back to you. And why do you look at the speck in your brother's eye, but do not consider the plank in your own eye? Or how can you say to your brother, "Let me remove the speck from your eye"; and look, a plank is in your own eye? Hypocrite! First remove the plank from your own eye, and then you will see clearly to remove the speck from your brother's eye.*
>
> —Matthew 7:1–5

For Christ these were not mere platitudes but life-altering proverbs. One of the greatest of examples of this is Jesus' interaction with the woman caught in adultery (John 8:3–11). The Pharisees brought the woman to Him, claiming they had caught her in the very act of adultery. If that was the case, then the man was also caught. Where was he in the story? This justice is already looking a bit one-sided. If that was not enough, the story seems to indicate that she was dragged into the street naked, adding insult to the injury.

In a pious and self-righteous manner, the Pharisees turned to Jesus and said, *"Now Moses, in the law, commanded us that such should be stoned. But what do You say?"* (v. 5). They had to ask the question twice because Jesus had stooped to the ground and was writing something in the dirt. We don't know what it was. Perhaps it was some of their sins, or maybe He was just averting His eyes from the already shamed woman. Finally, He uttered the now famous words, *"He who is without sin among you, let him throw a stone at her first"* (v. 7). At that, from the eldest to least, they dropped their stones and walked away. Jesus turned and spoke to the woman, reminding her to *"go and sin no more"* (v. 11).

Were the Pharisees correct? Did the Law command that she should be stoned? Yes, it did, and it would have been justice. But what would that have accomplished? Nothing! There would have been a dead naked woman lying in the dirt and blood running down the street. She may have been an abandoned wife, a mother to children, or at the very least, somebody's daughter. The smug self-righteous men who would have killed her would have stood around congratulating themselves like dandies at the end of a fox hunt.

Mercy, on the other hand, changed everything. The men were now reminded of their own imperfection. The woman was given a second chance, and as I like to ask, do we think she ever committed adultery again? I doubt it. She had narrowly escaped death and had become the recipient of one of the great attributes of God—mercy. James reminds us that *"mercy triumphs over judgment"* (James 2:13).

Fiorello LaGuardia[3] was the mayor of New York City during the Great Depression and throughout the entire Second World War. He was adored by New Yorkers and given the nomenclature "the Little Flower" (English for *fiorello*). He stood at 5' 2" and always wore a carnation in his lapel. He was a colourful character, with a heart as big as his famous oversized hat. He was known to take all the children in an entire orphanage to baseball games, and on Sundays he would read the newspaper funnies out loud to kids over the radio.

In January of 1935, the mayor turned up at a night court that served the poorest ward of the city. LaGuardia dismissed the judge for the evening and took over the bench himself. One case that night involved a trembling old man who was charged with stealing a loaf of bread. After hearing the evidence, LaGuardia turned to the man and said, "Well, I've got to punish you. The law makes no exception, and I can do nothing but sentence you to a fine of ten dollars." In a surprising move he reached for his big hat and tossed in ten dollars from his own wallet. Then he continued, "Furthermore, I'm going to fine everybody in this courtroom fifty cents for living in a city that requires a man to steal bread to feed his family."

The bailiff passed around the hat and then walked over to the bewildered accused and dumped out $47.50 into his hands. LaGuardia looked out and said, "Next case, please." It was a beautiful example of how mercy can triumph over judgment.

The story is both touching and instructive. Everything we learn from the Sermon on the Mount is that our responses to our fellow human beings are to be meek, merciful, kind and never judgmental. Here is how we might look at the differences between justice, mercy and grace.

Justice is getting what we deserve.
Mercy is not getting what we deserve.
Grace is getting what we don't deserve.

Here's a practical example of how this might look. If a policeman pulls you over for speeding, justice would be that he gives you a speeding ticket; mercy would be that he lets you off with a warning; and grace would be that he gives you one of his jelly donuts!

Years ago, I had a neighbour who had a critical word to say about every person in the community. Whenever a name came up in conversation, he did not hesitate to share the dirt. At first, I found myself getting pulled in and feeling special, as if I was some sort of confidant. Then I realized I was his patsy. I was letting him dump his garbage on me and he could just as easily be saying things about me behind my back. After all, why wouldn't he? It was his schtick. It also didn't take long to observe that, behind his back, everybody, and I mean everybody, criticized him.

> *Do not judge, so that YOU will not be judged. For in the way you judge, you will be judged; and by your standard of measure, it will be measured to you.*
>
> —Matthew 7:1–2 NASB ▲▲ (emphasis added)

This neighbour had the reputation of being the town gossip. He dished it out by the bucketful, and it came back upon him in multiple buckets. Just as it says in the fifth Beatitude, *"Blessed are the merciful, for they shall obtain mercy"* (Matthew 5:7 ▲▲). We reap what we sow. Sow judgment, reap judgment. Sow mercy, reap mercy.

As I was just a young Christian at the time and trying to figure all this stuff out, I wondered how I got suckered in so easily. Gossip had never been my thing before. Why did I entertain it so readily? Proverbs has a lot to say about why: *"Listening to gossip is like eating cheap candy; do you want junk like that in your belly?"* (Proverbs 26:22 MSG). There is something initially satisfying about hearing dirt on other people but it is not satisfying for very long. We think better of ourselves only because others are being put down, which poisons our minds toward them and damages our relationship with them. In the end, entertaining criticism makes us just as guilty of judging as the person doing the yapping.

One of the big lies we tell ourselves is that we will escape incrimination if we preface our gossip with, "I am telling you this in the strictest confidence." Do we know what that really means? Nothing! The next person will just pass it on with the same empty caveat. Again, it is clear in Proverbs: *"A gadabout gossip can't be trusted with a secret, but someone of integrity won't violate a confidence"* (Proverbs 11:13 MSG). Like the guy who said to his friend, "Look, I don't like to repeat gossip… so I am only going to say this once." Or another who put it this way, "I shouldn't say anything more, I've already told you more than I heard myself."

Over the years I like to think I have done better on this, but occasionally I catch myself stepping headlong into it. One day a good friend of mine dropped by my office. He came in and we shut the door, as a group of people were meeting in the adjacent space. He started going on about his father-in-law (also a member of our church), who we both agreed was a bit of a goof. He was telling stories about him and I was laughing and agreeing. This went on for probably ten minutes. At the end of our visit, I opened my door and saw that his father-in-law had been sitting in a chair immediately outside my office. We both gasped in horror, and I was racking my brain trying to think if I had said anything untoward or if my friend was the only guilty one. It didn't matter, I was party to the conversation and could have and should have shut it down. I want to follow the example from Psalm 101:5, *"I put a gag on the gossip who bad-mouths his neighbor; I can't stand arrogance"* (MSG). The Bible teaches that bad-mouthing another person will always come around to bite you back.

> *Do not curse the king, even in your thought;*
> *Do not curse the rich, even in your bedroom;*
> *For a bird of the air may carry your voice,*
> *And a bird in flight may tell the matter.*
>
> —Ecclesiastes 10:20

Apparently, one day a man came to Muhammad, the founder of the Islamic religion, and confessed that he had made some pejorative comments about a friend. He asked if there was any way he could take them back. Muhammad told him to take the feathers from a pillow and place them on the windowsill overnight, and sleep with the window open. The man dutifully obeyed, and returned the next day, inquiring what to do next. Muhammad said, "Now put the feathers back in the pillow." The man objected, saying that the wind had come up overnight and blown the feathers all over town. Muhammad said, "Exactly, and so has been done to the words that you spoke. You can never take them back." His words may have been true, but one of the major differences between Islam and Christianity is that Christ teaches the redemptive power of repentance and forgiveness, which can atone for the mistakes we all inevitably make.

Another of the little-known traps of offence we can step into is what we call a second-hand offence. This refers to picking up an offence held by another person, an issue that may not be any of our business. For instance, someone has a grudge about something, they share it with us and, without knowing the other side of the story, we buy into it, hook, line and sinker. The Bible provides insight here too: *"He who passes by and meddles in a quarrel not his own is like one who takes a dog by the ears"* (Proverbs 26:17). Most of us are smart enough to never grab a dog by its ears. Why, then, would we pick up the offence of another person?

One day, I made a crack from the pulpit about the hairline of a staff member. I said that he has had only three hairstyles in his entire life—parted, unparted and departed. He laughed, the congregation laughed, and I forgot all about it. It was about as benign a joke as I can tell, and he was not in the least bit offended. The next week, I got a scathing email from a viewer who saw it on television. She demanded that I make a public apology to the staff member on TV, since that was where the offending joke took place. I wrote a gentle response back, suggesting that maybe if the object of the joke was not offended maybe she didn't need to be offended either. She wasn't buying it and continued to send angry emails. Even if the staff member had been offended, it was not anyone else's place to meddle in it. Surely, for the love of God, we have something better to do with our time? Or maybe not.

One day I heard a terrible rumour about the daughter of one of our staff members. It was something that should never have been repeated, even if it had been true. The person shared it in an oh-so-spiritual manner. "Pastor, I really feel you needed to be aware of this and figured you might want to deal with it." I only thought about it for a few seconds and thought to myself, "I don't believe it." I made a deliberate choice that day to believe the best about that young woman. I felt that no good could come from me letting that thought sit in the back of my mind. No one deserves that kind of rumour swirling around about them. I told this person that I did not want them to ever share that story with another human being and advised them to just leave it with me. I, of course, was planning on deep-sixing it.

A few months later I was speaking at a leadership event, explaining how we need to believe the best about people. Without sharing any names or details or in any way revealing the person's identity, I used the story as an example to make a point. At the end of the night, the young lady in question came up to me in tears and said, "Pastor Mark, that story was about me, wasn't it?" She only knew because that individual had not kept it a secret and it had come back to her. She had been struggling to live down the rumour. I admitted that indeed it was about her. She thanked me for defending her reputation and believing the best in her. She knew that a story like that could have ruined both her and her parents. I still don't believe the rumour was true, but even if it was, what good would it have done to shame a young lady as she was struggling to navigate young adulthood?

Blessed are the merciful, for they shall receive mercy—mercy triumphs over justice every time.

Chapter Fourteen

Off Broadway

*Two roads diverged in a wood, and I—
I took the one less traveled by,
And that has made all the difference.*

– Robert Frost, "The Road Not Taken"

NEW YORK CITY should be on everyone's bucket list as a place to visit at least once. It is home to the world's largest stock markets, the United Nations building, the Empire State building and, of course, the site of the tragic and ill-fated World Trade Center towers that collapsed in the terrorist attack of 9/11. There is lots to do and even more to see.

Unlike many places in the New World, Manhattan was not founded by people seeking religious freedom, but rather, as a Dutch colony, by people looking for a place to make money. And make money they did! As you walk down the streets you are confronted by the neon lights, store fronts, street vendors and hotdog stands. In Times Square, a city by-law requires that at least twenty percent of every building must be covered with illuminated signs. When I was there, a Coke sign was adorning 1475 Broadway, also known as One Times Square. At that time, they were renting the signage space for $170,000 per month. You can feel the historic worship of mammon even today.

The area is also the home to the world's largest and most important theatre district—Broadway—named after the main street running out of Times Square. The biggest shows and musicals, many of which have the most famous actors, are performed in the biggest theatres on and in the immediate vicinity of Broadway. The lesser shows are relegated to the smaller surrounding theatres and are referred to as Off-Broadway. When the musical *Hamilton* debuted on Broadway, tickets sold for $1,200 USD each and the show was sold out every night for years. When it finally moved Off-Broadway, tickets sold for the bargain basement price of $150 each.[1]

Earlier in the book, I told the story of the preacher David Wilkerson going to New York to reach the gangs in 1958. In those days, Times Square was a run-down part of Manhattan, with peep shows and strip clubs all along Broadway. The gangs ran wild in the streets and the crime rate was through the roof. Even as things started to improve and David Wilkerson became a household name (Pat Boone portrayed him in the 1970 Hollywood movie *The Cross and the Switchblade*), he never lost his vision to reach that part of the city. In 1991 he purchased the Mark Hellinger Theatre for $17 million on West 51st Street, which is located… wait for it, wait for it… just OFF BROADWAY. In 2011 we visited the church, which goes by the name Times Square Church. We were part of the 1,600 people crowded into the theatre, with another 1,600 next door in the overflow. They repeated their service three times that day and I assumed they packed all of them out. It was hard not to be encouraged by the thought that some 8,000 or 9,000 people were coming to church in a city that, while it is known for many things, serving God isn't one of them.

Interestingly, Broadway was not the original name that the Dutch West India Company gave to Manhattan's main street. It was *de Heere Straat*, or "Gentlemen's Street." It only became known as

Broadway during the nineteenth century as a metonym, or a descriptive of what it was—a broad way.[2] It was Jesus who introduced the "broad way" concept in the Sermon on the Mount.

> *Enter by the narrow gate; for wide is the gate and broad is the way that leads to destruction, and there are many who go in by it. Because narrow is the gate and difficult is the way which leads to life, and there are few who find it.*
>
> —Matthew 7:13–14 ▲

The use of the terms "narrow gate" and "wide gate" are interesting. They are almost certainly meant to be metaphorical, as Jesus' listeners would not have had any trouble imagining a narrow or a wide gate. Archaeological evidence does not seem to indicate that these would have been specific gates somewhere in Jerusalem to which Jesus was referring. If that had been the case, invariably some people would have taken it literally and promoted making annual pilgrimages to the "narrow gate."

There is, however, a bit of a parallel when we consider Herod's temple. The original Jewish temple was built in the days of King Solomon. It was destroyed by the Babylonian King Nebuchadnezzar in 586 BC. Nehemiah began rebuilding it some seventy years later. Over the next 400 years the temple and the city of Jerusalem took a lot of abuse from various marauding gentiles. In 39 BC, King Herod took over the temple and promised the Jews he would rebuild it bigger and better, which he did. It was destroyed by the Romans in AD 70 and the ruins you can view today in Jerusalem are of Herod's Temple. There is not much remaining of any earlier iterations.

The historian Flavius Josephus, who lived during the time of Jesus, did a thorough job of describing Herod's Temple in his works.[3] There appear to have been eight gates: two on the south, four on the west, one on the east and one on the north (which has not yet been unearthed).

If you travel to Israel today, you can walk the stone stairs up to the southern entrances. It can be an emotionally and spiritually meaningful experience to you realize you are literally walking on the very spot that the Lord Jesus would have stepped when He was on earth. These were massive staircases leading to—yes, you guessed it—wide gates. Herod wanted huge crowds to visit and admire his masterpiece, and so he built inviting arched gates to accommodate exactly that. These wide gates were the entrance into the outer court, a place where both Jews and gentiles were allowed to congregate. Most of the western gates are large as well, with architectural bridges leading into the inner court, which only Jews were permitted to enter.

However, one of the eastern gates, known as the Warren Gate (thus named after being discovered by archaeologist Charles Warren), is a narrower gate with a difficult traverse of stairs and corridors. It empties into the Holy of Holies and was likely used by the priests when they entered to conduct temple worship. (Imagine, if you will, the secret entrance at Church of the Rock that leads to my corner office. You will need a good imagination because there isn't one!)

Mary and Joseph had been taking Jesus to Herod's Temple from His infancy. He would have had first-hand knowledge of the facility. We certainly don't want to make too much of this, but were these wide and narrow gates the inspiration for this parable? Or had He merely just walked by a farmyard and observed both a narrow and a wide gate to the pasture?

Almost every city and town in North America has a street named Broadway. In Winnipeg, Broadway Avenue is one of the oldest and most historically significant streets in our city. It runs through the heart of downtown and makes up a section of the Trans-Canada Highway. It is lined with mature elm trees and is the home of our historic and grand Fort Garry Hotel. Most importantly, it is a "broad way," boasting a beautiful grassy median with flora and benches. In the summer it is teeming with people looking for some respite over the lunch hour, a place to escape the concrete tower they might spend the rest of day in, toiling away.

In the Sermon on the Mount, Jesus points out that people are attracted to the broad way. We tend to follow along and do what everybody else is doing. In contrast, He urges us to go through the "narrow gate" that leads to a "difficult way."

> There is a simple explanation as to why Christianity must be exclusive—Jesus, and only Jesus, died on the cross for our sins.

The "narrow gate" is very easy to interpret because Jesus is referring to Himself. *"I am the door. If anyone enters by Me, he will be saved, and will go in and out and find pasture"* (John 10:9). Likewise, He is also the "difficult way." *"I am the way, the truth, and the life. No one comes to the Father except through Me"* (John 14:6). No one gets to heaven any other way! This kind of exclusivity is not very popular today. Critics of the Christian faith don't like the fact that we make it seem like there is only one true religion in the world. The reason they get that impression is because it is TRUE! Hey, don't lynch the messenger. Jesus said it, not us! Come to think of it, they did lynch Him.

There is a simple explanation as to why Christianity must be exclusive—Jesus, and only Jesus, died on the cross for our sins. Therefore, there is no other "way" to get to heaven and no other "gate." In the Gospels we see that He repeatedly warned us that other people were not going to like it.[4] It has become a very popular notion today that, essentially, all paths to God are equal and it is just a matter of upbringing or personal choice.

Unlike some of us, Jesus didn't offend people unnecessarily. We can see this in how He was careful not to come right out and say, "Look, the whole bunch of you are going straight to hell!" Instead, He used more cryptic language to illustrate that the other paths—the broad ways—all lead to destruction.

> *I am the door. If anyone enters by Me, he will be saved, and will go in and out and find pasture. The thief does not come except to steal, and to kill, and to destroy. I have come that they may have life, and that they may have it more abundantly.*
>
> —John 10:9–10

Years ago, I was in a desert region south of Hyderabad, India, and a medical doctor approached me to ask if I would come and pray for his wife. I agreed, and we walked together for several blocks. As we entered his modest little home, I could see his poor wife lying helpless on her bed, suffering from advanced rheumatoid arthritis. I also could not miss the fact that the walls were entirely papered with posters of Hindu gods, Krishna, Ganesha and others. I said I would willingly pray but he needed to understand that I was not a healer (like Hindu gurus sometimes claim to be). I told him that Jesus was the real healer and asked if they wanted to invite Him into their home. Being that he was a medical doctor, I tried to explain my point by asking, "If you were to visit a patient, would it make sense to just send in the medical bag without the doctor?"

He thought that was sound reasoning and said he would invite Jesus into their home as ONE of their gods. I explained the exclusivity of the plan of redemption, that Jesus is the only way to eternal life. He bobbled his head in the way Hindi people politely do and said, "Don't all roads lead to Rome?"

I laughed and said, "You, of all people, would know that isn't true. From here there is only one road that could possibly lead you to Rome, and that is the one that goes north out of town. The rest of them lead you out into the middle of the desert." It was a clever argument, if I do say so myself, but sadly, he was not buying what I was selling that day. At any rate, I prayed fervently for their health, physically and spiritually, and I can only hope it was a good seed sown into good soil.

The gate metaphors are key to understanding the greater perspective. To enter the narrow gate and difficult way is to intentionally choose the more challenging path in life. The wide gate and broad way will be the default choice for most people as it will look much easier… at first. "Hey, I get to do whatever I want in life. I am not interested in restrictive rules cramping my style." Honestly, it is not really an easy street, it just looks that way. Proverbs reminds us, *"Good understanding gives favor, / But the way of the unfaithful is hard"* (Proverbs 13:15). The broad way is fraught with its own difficulties: hardships, calamity, grief and pain.

The difficult way is dubbed as such because it requires discipline, dedication, integrity, morality and sacrifice, all of which are delineated in the Sermon on the Mount. It is not a choice to be made lightly. Preachers, myself included, are probably guilty of sugar-coating the Christian walk. "Choose Jesus and all your troubles will be over" is just not true. We are, in fact, promised the opposite: *"These things I have spoken to you, that in Me you may have peace. In the world you will have tribulation; but be of good cheer, I have overcome the world"* (John 16:33).

"Off broad way" living is by far the more difficult way. Given the choice, why would we ever pick the narrow and difficult over the wide and broad? If we have gained a *greater perspective*, we will realize that one leads to destruction and the other leads to abundant life.

GREATER PERSPECTIVE LIVING MEANS ALWAYS DOING THE RIGHT THING BECAUSE IT IS THE "RIGHT" THING

The Sermon on the Mount in its entirety, for all intents and purposes, is the practical guide to living out the narrow way. It is by no means a tightrope, but it is no cakewalk either. Jesus calls us to do the right thing, no matter what the circumstances are. This disabuses the bankrupt ethic of the moral relativism that we see all around us today, which perpetuates the belief that right and wrong are not absolutes but are relative to the situation.

In an old episode of *The Simpsons*, Bart got a job tending a bar run by a gangster named Fat Tony. His new boss was giving him a lesson on morality.

> Fat Tony: Bart, is it wrong to steal a loaf of bread to feed your starving family?
>
> Bart: No.
>
> Fat Tony: Well, suppose you got a large starving family. Is it wrong to steal a truckload of bread to feed them?
>
> Bart: Uh uh.
>
> Fat Tony: And, what if your family don't like bread? They like… cigarettes?
>
> Bart: I guess that's okay.
>
> Fat Tony: Now, what if instead of giving them away, you sold them at a price that was practically giving them away. Would that be a crime, Bart?
>
> Bart: Hell, no.[5]

Stealing bread to feed one's family is the classic example moral relativism has debated at length for centuries. It was reignited during the early stages of the COVID-19 pandemic when crime surged in New York City. Congresswoman Alexandria Ocasio-Cortez explained,

> Maybe this has to do with the fact that people aren't paying their rent and are scared to pay their rent and so they go out and they need to feed their child and they don't have money…. They feel like they either need to shoplift some bread or go hungry."[6]

She didn't quite excuse it outright, but she did assume most listeners would agree that stealing bread to feed your family was not an immoral act but an act of desperation. Never mind that the problem in question was not a rash of local bakery burglaries but violent crime in the streets.

Within every day is the choice to do the right thing, or not. Baseball legend Yogi Berra used to say, "If you come to a fork in the road… take it."[7] He was quite aware of the humor in the comment. If we are going to live according to the Sermon on the Mount, the right choice will always be to do the right thing, regardless of what the circumstances or consequences might be.

> *But let your "Yes" be "Yes," and your "No," "No." For whatever is more than these is from the evil one.*
>
> —Matthew 5:37 ⛰

We have a word for it in the English language—integrity. A dictionary definition of the term is "The quality of being honest and having strong moral principles."[8] For example, "He is known to be a man of integrity." The word derives from the Latin word *integritas,* which means "wholeness, completeness, and entirety."

During the time of the Caesars, the Roman armies had regular morning inspections. Soldiers would start the day by assembling their battle armour. When the commander would walk by, the soldier would strike his right fist to his breastplate and shout, "Integritas!" The breastplate protected the heart, the most vulnerable region in the throes of battle. By the end of the fourth century (not coincidentally the time of the fall of the Roman empire), negligence and laziness had set in. The soldiers began skipping the morning inspection, as it was cumbersome and uncomfortable. Many began to go into battle with no armour at all. They became vulnerable to the arrows of the marauding Goths. In what everyone thought was impossible, the undefeatable Romans were vanquished by the invading barbarians from the North. Even when the Romans began losing some of the earlier smaller battles, no one thought to restore the armour to the infantry. To lose their armour was to lose their integrity.

Once you lose your integrity, you risk losing everything. Integrity is who you are when no one is looking. If who you are when someone is NOT looking is in conflict with who you are when someone IS looking, then your integrity is in question. Most of the time, people know the right thing to do—they are just not sure they want to do it.

Mark Twain was famous for telling a story about when he was a lad of fourteen and he stole a melon from a street vendor's cart. As he ducked into an alley and took bite, a strange feeling came over him. He knew exactly what he needed to do. He returned the melon to the cart… and got a ripe one.[9]

My motto has always been to decide in the morning, when I get out of bed, that no matter what I am faced with that day, I am going to choose to do the right thing. It is a simple exercise that, in effect, allows me to make a thousand decisions in advance.

Contrast this with the guy who woke up one morning and prayed, "Lord, so far, I have had a pretty good day. I have not lied, cheated or lost my temper. I have not been overcome with bitterness or anger, nor have I been offended with a single person. But in a few moments time, I am going to get out of bed… and from then on, I am going to need a lot more help."

One of the things we all experience in today's morally compromised world is the underground economy. People do business for cash, with no invoices recorded and no taxes collected. Even if we ourselves don't do business like this, we become party to it when we agree to let someone else do it. For example, you ask for a quote for something, and the individual says, "If you give me cash, I can do it for X dollars." We think to ourselves that we are not the scofflaw here, the other guy is. But in fact, we are. If we agree to it, we become accomplices to this individual cheating the tax system. Sometimes, these people still also ask for the GST or PST (taxes) and then pocket it in addition to cheating on their income taxes. No matter how innocent it may seem from our end, it is theft, plain and simple.

I have made it a point to tell these vendors that I am uncomfortable with the arrangement and that I would like an invoice, "preferring" (using the word loosely) to pay the taxes. Hey, I don't want to pay taxes any more than the next guy, but what is the price of my integrity? $100 at the bare minimum for sure! More seriously, most of the time they are surprised to hear this, which makes me assume most other people say "OK."

We forget that we don't live in a vacuum and that all of our choices affect someone and something else. I remember hearing the story of a man driving with his eight-year-old daughter. When he was pulled over for speeding, she witnessed her father get off by slipping the officer a $100 bill. The next week the little girl was caught cheating on a test at school. The father scolded the child, saying, "We did not raise you to be a cheater. Where did you learn this kind of behaviour?"

Imagine the father's shame when his daughter replied, "From you, Daddy, from you!"

Most of us are pretty comfortable with our level of moral relativism because we feel we can justify it. "I can't possibly be expected to be perfect, you know?" Our tendency is to use a moral-o-meter (I made that word up) as a determinant of our moral calculus. We often hear this one. "Well, I'm not perfect, but the good I do outweighs the bad." That's nice! Exactly how much bad is an acceptable amount? It seems to me that if you are 51% good and 49% bad, you're still pretty bad!

Ruthless Columbian drug lord, Pablo Escobar, had thousands of people executed for his own selfish gain, yet he was beloved by many for his extravagant generosity to his community.[10] He was a genocidal maniac that desperately wanted to be loved and respected by others. It didn't really matter how much good he did, he was still abjectly evil.

What follows has to be one of the craziest stories I have in my repertoire. At this point I have no recollection where it came from, but it is way too good for me to have made up.

A man and his date for the evening go through a KFC drive-thru just before closing. The manager had put the day's cash proceeds in a KFC bag. The attendant working the window grabbed the wrong bag and handed it to the man instead of his order of chicken. When the man and woman pulled over to eat their meal, they found nothing in the bag but $800 in cash. (That had to be disappointing.) They immediately returned to the drive-thru to give back the money. (Apparently once you start craving fried chicken, there is no way to get it out of your mind.)

The man received a hero's welcome from the manager. "I'm going to call the newspaper," he exclaimed. "Your picture is going to be on the front page if I have anything to say about it. You're one of the most honest men I've ever heard of!"

The man shot back in a muffled voice, "No, no don't do that! You see… this woman… she's, uh, somebody else's wife."

How could someone be so honest on one hand, and such a scoundrel on the other? Nobody is 100% good or 100% bad. This guy rated a solid 50% on the moral-o-meter.

There is an old story about an elderly Catholic priest who was tired of hearing confessions about the townsfolk's adulterous affairs. He started to preach on sexual purity, which made everyone uncomfortable. This less-than-upright group of parishioners came up with a code word for adultery, and when they went to confession they would simply say, "I tripped and fell." After hearing this multiple times, the priest visited the town's mayor and told him to fix the sidewalks, as everyone in town was tripping and falling. The mayor started snickering, realizing the priest had misunderstood. The priest, not impressed said, "What are you laughing about? Your wife has tripped and fallen three times!"

Cleveland Stroud served twenty-eight years as a City Councillor in Conyers, Georgia, but he is best known for "losing" the 1987 Georgia State championship as the coach of the Rockdale High School boys basketball team. Cleveland, now in his seventies, has been a devout Baptist his entire life. In his hometown of Conyers, he is known to everyone only as "Coach." For years he taught in the local high school and was the coach of the boys basketball team. In 1987 they had a banner year and went twenty-one wins and only five losses.

Landing the tiny high school in the state finals was a huge triumph in and of itself. The arena was packed that night and the Rockdale boys came from behind to win the championship. The whole town celebrated, and a few days later the trophy was safely tucked away in the school glass case.

That day, a memo arrived from the county school board to advise them that one of the players was scholastically ineligible. The ineligible player had only played forty-five seconds in one of the playoff games and had not been a factor in one way or another. Only Stroud saw the memo, but he made it known to all and gave the trophy back. Some people said it out loud, and everybody thought it: "If you had just kept quiet, nobody would have known."

Cleveland didn't care. He answered, "You've got to do what's honest and right and what the rules say. I told my team that people forget the scores of basketball games; they don't ever forget what you're made of."[11] His simple act of integrity earned him multiple state, national and international honours, including the International Olympic Committee award. Numerous articles covered the story, including the *New York Times* and *Sports Illustrated*.

When people ask, he says, "I am more than basketball," adding, "If a kid can't get anything out of a coach other than a win—that coach is a failure. He doesn't deserve to be a coach, because coaching is so much more than that."[12]

GREATER PERSPECTIVE LIVING MEANS DOING THE RIGHT THING EVEN IF IT IS THE HARDER THING

When I was in high school, I had a math teacher named Mr. Hersak. He taught us a lot of things, like when Campbell's said their soup contained seven different vegetables, they meant it had one pea, one bean, etc. But every once in a while, he actually taught us something that could be used in real life, like the shortest distance between two points is a straight line. He must have made quite the impression on me because whenever I travelled as a young adult, I always looked at a map and then plotted the straightest route.

It took me a few years to recognize that Mr. Hersak's mathematical rule did not always work in real life. On one occasion, driving through the night and trying to make good time, me and my buddy Mike ended up on a road that got narrower and narrower until it disappeared entirely, eventually going through a barbed wire fence and into a cow pasture. We did not make good time that night.

Most sane people will instinctively choose a wide, comfortable passageway over a narrow difficult one any day of the week. That is why they drive on smoothly paved Interstate highways and not dirt roads through cow pastures. It is why they build big grand entrances to shopping malls and not narrow dangerous staircases coming up from the back alley. It is why luxurious hotels have grand, inviting entrances. Nobody enjoys being confined to constricting doorways, narrow hallways, or back lanes when they have the choice to easily breeze through.

So why would Jesus want us to choose the narrow and difficult? Most of the time, if there is something meaningful on the other side there is usually no easy way to get there. For instance, the children of Israel had a wonderful Promised Land awaiting them, but there was an overflowing river to cross and giants to fight in order to get it.

Along the Atlantic and Gulf of Mexico coasts of the United States there is a popular navigational channel called the Intracoastal Waterway. It is 4,800 km long and runs from Boston, Massachusetts, to Brownsville, Texas. If you travel this route, there are places where you have no choice but to venture into the Atlantic Ocean on the east or into the Gulf of Mexico on the gulf side. However, for much of the journey, you can navigate the more tranquil waters of the Intracoastal Waterway. On the east coast of Florida, much of it is highly protected from the pounding surf of the Atlantic by barrier islands like Miami Beach and Hollywood beach and others as you travel northward. There are some nice wide and natural inlets at the ends of these barrier islands.

Miami Beach is a good example. On the south end, the passageway is wide and fairly easily navigated, irrespective of the tide and incoming surf. However, on the north end of Miami Beach, the US Army Corps cut a manmade inlet to allow vessels an egress out to the Atlantic so they would not have to travel additional miles to the natural openings at the south. It is called Haulover Inlet and it is both narrow and difficult. In recent years it has become famous for the multiple YouTube videos of boaters recklessly attempting the strait without understanding the dangers.

On a calm day one could take a kayak through without incident, but when the winds are howling from the east, which they often are, all bets are off. The confluence of the waves coming into the restrictive inlet with the tide going out creates enormous rolling waves that are disproportionate to how rough the seas are once you clear the inlet. Smaller boats can capsize or take on water over the bow and sink in seconds. Even larger craft get into trouble as the bow rises high into the air and then crashes down under the next wave. It is generally the novice pilots who get themselves in the most trouble, as they go too fast or too slow, or they attempt to turn around, only to be broadsided by a wave and imperilled. On a busy weekend, boaters are determined to get through the Haulover and get out to the Atlantic. Some will take multiple cracks at it, and some will quickly turn about and call it a day.

Jesus reminds us that kingdom living is often like this. If we desire everything He has for us, we will need to take some risks. We will need to be prepared for a difficult passage.

Consider how we all came into this world. For anyone who has ever been in the birthing room (and I would argue you have all been there), it is nothing short of traumatic. There is no wide and broad way, only a narrow difficult one. There is blood, sweat and tears, wailing and gnashing of teeth… and I understand it is uncomfortable for the mother and baby as well.

It is the curse of the fall: *"I will greatly multiply your sorrow and your conception; In pain you shall bring forth children"* (Genesis 3:16). The mother has to push a baby the size of a watermelon through an opening that seems better suited to a golf ball. The baby is subjected to massive contractions that take their perfectly formed round head and make it look more like flesh-coloured zucchini. When the baby finally splooshes out, it is covered in blood and guts and a slimy goo of some sort. (I am, of course, using the medical terms here. I am sure there are slang terms for all of this as well.)

I literally cried when all three of our kids were being born, and all I really did was watch. These days, they have introduced the concept of giving birth under water; apparently it is less stressful for both the mother and the baby. However, I would think it must be terrifying for the other swimmers in the pool at the time.

We are introduced into life in this inglorious way primarily because it is preparing us for the rest of life. Everything meaningful comes to us through pain, discomfort or difficulty.

Doing the right thing is almost always the harder thing. On the night before Jesus was betrayed, He was praying in the Garden of Gethsemane. He knew what lay ahead for Him, and He faced it with a sense of dread. *"And He said, "Abba, Father, all things are possible for You. Take this cup away from Me; nevertheless, not what I will, but what You will"* (Mark 14:36). Going to the cross was the difficult way to resolve the sin problem of mankind.

On this side of heaven, we will never likely fully appreciate the price Jesus paid on the cross. He bore in His body all the sin, sickness and death of every man, woman and child in history. Hanging there on the cross, He cried out with a loud voice, *"My God, My God, why have you forsaken Me!"* (Mark 15:34). Why would He say such a thing? Because it was true. When He died, He was separated from God the Father for three days and went into the bowels of hades. That was the narrow and ever-so-difficult way necessary to pay the price for man's indiscretions.

Even though He knew what the eternal outcome would be, the earthly outworking of the crucifixion was more than even Christ wanted to bear. He begged God to take this path away if there was any other way to accomplish the goal. But there were no other options, so in the end He did the right thing, the harder thing, the most painful and difficult way possible.

When I was thirty years old, I was invited to pastor my first church. It was called Abundant Strife… uh, I mean… Abundant Life (I always get that mixed up). This little church was made up of mostly people twice my age. I only had two years of experience in ministry and had much to learn. I will be the first to admit that I made mistakes. For one, I did not appreciate the older generation's need to approach change more slowly.

After only about a month, there was an emergency board meeting called at noon right after the Sunday service. I thought, "How exciting, I wonder what the emergency is?" Much to my surprise, it was me.

The usual spokesman for the group got right to the point and asked, "What was that woman doing on stage this morning?"

Naively, I answered, "Singing?" We then got into an animated discussion about how women could lead worship, but only if there were no men in the congregation. They pointed to Moses' sister, Miriam, only leading the women in song after the crossing of the Red Sea (Exodus 15:20). I was so green, I didn't even know that. More importantly, this was my first indication that I was in big trouble at this church.

As the months wore on, we had more and more minor conflicts of this nature. This group did not like the progressive way I was leading the church. Nevertheless, the church grew, and their influence began to wane. I was respectful but believed I was called to lead, and that was what I was going to do. Within six months, ten of the original twelve who had hired me left the church. A few months later, they changed their strategy and decided that I should leave, not them.

The situation escalated—first they just wanted me gone, then they wanted me defrocked of my ordination, then they wanted me humiliated, and finally, they decided I deserved to be in jail. They hired a lawyer and accused me of stealing $235 from the church. Trying to resolve this situation, I met with the group one Saturday morning. I produced the evidence of the "missing funds" and it was a cheque *they had given to me* as a Christmas gift, with one of their signatures on the cheque. It was almost laughable. I should never have said this, but I told them, "If I am going to embezzle money from the church and compromise my integrity, it is going to have to be for a lot more than $235… like maybe $500, minimum!" (It is not easy going through life as a smart aleck.)

In the end, I asked them what they wanted from me, and they said, "We want our church back." I asked them what that meant, and they explained it was the name and the bank account. I am not sure they had a clear understanding of what a church was, but I made the decision that I was not going to let these people drag me into court and, in the process, destroy the real essence of the church, which was the people. So, I agreed and turned all the church records, bank account, etc., over to them. Then this group of people made me a verbal commitment that they were going to ruin my reputation and see to it that my days in ministry were over.

At this point I had to figure out what tack to take. I now had these people mad at me, and everybody else as well. Even some of the people who were on my side were angry at me for giving away "their" money. They had a point.

I began with what I always do, which is to forgive everybody all the time. This in itself will solve ninety percent of all conflicts. Then I prayed, asking the Lord what I should do to protect my reputation. I felt like He said, "Nothing." The remarkable thing about when Jesus was betrayed was how He chose the narrow and difficult way and never defended Himself.

> *And the chief priests accused Him of many things, but He answered nothing. Then Pilate asked Him again, saying, "Do You answer nothing? See how many things they testify against You!" But Jesus still answered nothing, so that Pilate marvelled.*
>
> —Mark 15:3–5

Deuteronomy 20:4 promises us, *"For the LORD your God is he who goes with you to fight for you against your enemies, to give you the victory"* (ESV). It is a much longer story, but as these people proceeded to make the circuit of bad mouthing me to my friends, peers and fellow city pastors, every one of them came to my defense. Many of them literally said, "I don't believe you. I have known Mark for years. I know his character. You can take your accusations elsewhere." Within a few short weeks, my critics were shut down, we planted Church of the Rock, and it has literally grown every single year since 1987. It turns out my days in ministry were not over.

Doing the right thing is almost always the harder thing, but it is still the right thing. As *greater perspective* Christians, we are called to live "off broad way."

Chapter Fifteen

Knock, Knock! Who's There?

Knock. Pound on heaven's door if you have to, but don't give up. God hears all sincere prayers.

—Toni Sorenson

MUCH OF THE Sermon on the Mount is about taking a lowly path in life—the last shall be first, the way up is down, backward is forward—and letting God elevate us. The exception is when it comes to the subject of prayer. God still does the elevating, but He expects us to adopt an assertive posture and knock on heaven's door.

> *Ask, and it will be given to you; seek, and you will find; knock, and it will be opened to you. For everyone who asks receives, and he who seeks finds, and to him who knocks it will be opened. Or what man is there among you who, if his son asks for bread, will give him a stone? Or if he asks for a fish, will he give him a serpent? If you then, being evil, know how to give good gifts to your children, how much more will your Father who is in heaven give good things to those who ask Him!*
>
> —Matthew 7:7–11 ▲

The single greatest key to a successful Christian life is prayer. Eighteenth-century preacher John Wesley was famous for saying, "God does nothing except in response to believing prayer." Jesus is emphatic that our prayers should be bold and confident. Time and again, He reminds us that we should be storming the gates of heaven with our requests. In Luke 18, He told us that we *"ought to always pray and not lose heart"* (Luke 18:1).

The parable Jesus shares to illustrate this imperative is known as The Importunate Widow (Luke 18:2–8). A widow is in a dire predicament, being unfairly treated by an adversary. The judge in town was an unjust man who regarded neither God nor his fellow man. At first, he tried to ignore this woman's plea, but because she was so importunate (persistent), he wearied of her continually coming back. The judge gives in to her request, if for no other reason than just to get rid of her.

God, of course, is not reluctant or unjust. Jesus is merely explaining that our persistence in prayer works the exact same way. He punctuates the parable with a rhetorical question: *"Shall God not avenge His own elect who cry out day and night to Him, though He bears long with them?"* (Luke 18:7). The secret to answered prayer is persistence—to keep asking, to keep seeking and to keep knocking. These are the kind of prayers God responds to. It is not that He is deaf and cannot hear us the first time; our determination is what demonstrates that we believe that He will do as He has promised in His Word.

It is like the story of the boy who was praying at the top of his lungs in his room for a new Xbox gaming device for Christmas. Annoyed, his mother came into the room and said, "Brady, you don't have to shout when you pray, God's not deaf!"

To which he replied, "I know… but Grandma is."

George Müller was arguably one of the greatest prayer warriors in history. He was a German born pastor who moved to Bristol, England, in 1832 to pastor the Bethesda Chapel. It was there that he established the Ashley Down orphanage and became one of the founders of the Plymouth Brethren movement. He cared for over 10,000 orphans during his lifetime, established 117 schools and educated more than 120,000 children. He is known for never once appealing to others to meet the significant financial needs of these endeavors. Instead, he diligently made specific requests in prayer for the ongoing needs of the ministry. He fastidiously kept a prayer notebook, in which he recorded his requests on one page and the answer to each of those petitions on the facing page. By this means he persevered in praying until he received answers to thousands of specific requests.

Müller recorded this remarkable personal story in his prayer journal:

> In November, 1844, I began to pray for the conversion of five individuals. I prayed every day without a single intermission, whether sick or in health, on the land or on the sea, and whatever the pressure of my engagements might be. Eighteen months elapsed before the first of the five was converted. I thanked God and prayed on for the others. Five years elapsed, and then the second was converted. I thanked God for the second, and prayed on for the other three. Day by day I continued to pray for them, and six years passed before the third was converted. I thanked God for the three, and went on praying for the other two.
>
> These two remain unconverted. The man to whom God in the riches of His grace has given tens of thousands of answers to prayer in the self-same hour or day in which they were offered has been praying day by day for nearly thirty-six years for the conversion of these individuals, and yet they remain unconverted. But I hope in God, I pray on, and look yet for the answer. They are not converted yet, *but they will be.*[1]

Müller continued to pray for fifty-two years for the two remaining men, who were sons of one of his friends from his youth. When he died in 1897, these two now grown men remained as non-Christians. Shortly after his passing, both men gave their lives to Christ. It is a great example of persistent prayer. For over half a century Müller kept asking, knocking and seeking, and even after his death God answered that prayer.

Nowhere do we learn more about prayer than in the Sermon on the Mount. Jesus instructs us that prayer is not a demonstration sport but a private communication with God. When it is done in secret it is rewarded openly (Matthew 6:6 ▲). And though prayer is to be continual, it is not a matter of repeating ourselves over and over again endlessly (Matthew 6:7 ▲) because God already knows our needs before we ask.

Jesus also gives us the unique (and sometimes misunderstood) model of prayer that we know most commonly as the Lord's Prayer (Matthew 6:8–15 ▲). Although it may not be wrong to merely recite the prayer, like my generation did in school[2] decades ago, the words are meant to be a framework or outline of how to pray, not a prayer itself. Hence, it begins with these words, *"In this <u>manner</u>, therefore pray."* Not once did Jesus intimate that what followed was to be repeated as a prayer in and of itself.

The Luke 11 record of the Lord's Prayer includes that it was shared in response to the disciples requesting Jesus to teach them how to pray. A key step in developing *a greater perspective* is to learn the art of supplication from the Lord's Prayer which can revolutionize one's prayer life and, consequently, transform every part of one's life. Entire books can and have been written on this one prayer motif alone, so to cover the Lord's Prayer in a single chapter will require more of a "crash course" approach. Here we will review it in a simple point by point manner, in order to accentuate the practical applications of what Jesus teaches.

> *In this manner, therefore, pray:*
> *Our Father in heaven,*
> *Hallowed be Your name.*
> *Your kingdom come.*
> *Your will be done*
> *On earth as it is in heaven.*
> *Give us this day our daily bread.*
> *And forgive us our debts,*
> *As we forgive our debtors.*
> *And do not lead us into temptation,*
> *But deliver us from the evil one.*
> *For Yours is the kingdom and the power and the glory forever.*
>   *Amen.*
>
>   —Matthew 6:9–13

WHEN YOU PRAY, SAY

Luke's version of the Lord's Prayer begins with, *"When you pray, say…"* (11:2). Many of us were brought up in environs where prayer was something that was done quietly, if not silently. It is not as if God can't hear a silent prayer—of course He can—but if we only pray silently we miss out on the power of vocalization. When we pray out loud, not only does heaven hear it but so does the earth. When God interacted with creation, He thundered from the heavens (Psalm 18:13). *"Let there be light,"* He shouted, *"And there was light"* (Genesis 1:3). Jesus, too, spoke to inanimate objects… and they obeyed. To the empty fig tree He said, *"Let no one eat fruit from you ever again. And His disciples heard it"* (Mark 11:14). Apparently the tree heard it too, as it was dried up from the roots by the next day. Why does the passage state so explicitly that the disciples heard Him say it? Because he was talking to a TREE! (Generally, we have homes for people who do things like that.) Jesus knew the power of audible prayer.

Jesus did not limit Himself to talking to trees—he also talked to the wind, invisible demons, and dead people. When He was with His disciples in a boat in the midst of a storm, *"He arose and rebuked the wind, and said to the sea, 'Peace, be still!' And the wind ceased and there was a great calm"* (Mark 4:39). After His good friend Lazarus was both dead and buried, Jesus spoke to him to walk out of that grave—*"He cried with a loud voice, "Lazarus, come forth!"* (John 11:43)—and he obeyed! Lazarus had been dead for four long days. Rigor mortis would have already set in. After four days, he was good and dead, not just "mostly dead," like Westley in the movie *The Princess Bride*.[3]

> Inigo Montoya: He's dead. He can't talk.
>
> Miracle Max: Whoo-hoo-hoo, look who knows so much. It just so happens that your friend here is only MOSTLY dead. There's a big difference between mostly dead and all dead. Mostly dead is slightly alive. With all dead, well, with all dead there's usually only one thing you can do.
>
> Inigo Montoya: What's that?
>
> Miracle Max: Go through his clothes and look for loose change.[4]

Lazarus was "all dead" and yet somehow, he still heard the command from Jesus and came hopping out of the tomb (as he was still wrapped in grave cloths). Would it have worked if Jesus had just thought to Himself, "Boy, wouldn't that be great if Lazarus wasn't so dead?" Do we ever see Jesus mumbling prayers to Himself? No, He repeatedly made bold and often impossible proclamations.

We can access the power of heaven the same way. In one of the most impossible prayers in the entire Bible, Joshua commanded the sun to stand still, and God performed it on his behalf.

> *So the sun stood still,*
> *And the moon stopped,*
> *Till the people had revenge*
> *Upon their enemies.*
>
> *Is this not written in the Book of Jasher? So the sun stood still in the midst of heaven, and did not hasten to go down for about a whole day. And there has been no day like that, before it or after it, that the LORD heeded the voice of a man; for the LORD fought for Israel.*
>
> —Joshua 10:13–14

You almost get the impression that even the Lord wasn't sure about doing that one. At the very least, He had no intention of ever doing it again, so don't even bother trying! What would have happened if Joshua had only given thought to the sun standing still? Nothing! Or maybe if he just silently prayed in his head? Nada!

When Jesus cast out demons, without exception He did it verbally.

> *When evening had come, they brought to Him many who were demon-possessed. And He cast out the spirits with a word...*
>
> —Matthew 8:16

The Devil, his demons, or even God's angels are not omniscient! They do not and cannot hear our thoughts. If we have any hope of engaging angels or evicting demons, we must pray aloud. If we will simply extend our prayers from silent to vocal, that one key alone will supercharge our prayer lives. I have countless stories where I casually prayed something out loud, only to be surprised with extraordinary results.

One year we did a family vacation in the Florida Keys. The place we stayed had a small but lovely beach that was punctuated with a stand of palm trees. There were hammocks between the palms, and we spent a couple of afternoons lounging on them. I asked the staff where the hammocks came from, and they informed us they had bought them at the Home Depot in Homestead, Florida. Since it was on the way home, I told the family I was stopping in to buy one for next summer. Walking into the store I said out loud, "Lord, I pray they have one in stock." Sure enough, hanging on the wall was a display of the exact hammock we had enjoyed all week. After enquiring, the clerk informed me they did not stock them in the winter. "Winter?" I said, "What would you know about winter here?" I pointed at the one on the wall and emphatically said, "I want that one right there. Why don't you just sell me that one right there." After asking his manager, he agreed to sell me the hammock and went up the ladder to retrieve it for me. Now, are you ready for this? Then I asked for a discount because it was a display model. They gave me 10% off. We still have the hammock today, and whenever we string it up between two pines my kids will mock me and say, "I want that hammock. That one right there!"

APPROACH THE HEAVENLY FATHER IN A REVERENTIAL MANNER

The second point in the Lord's Prayer model addresses to whom we pray. Just before Jesus raises Lazarus, He speaks to His Father in heaven: *"And Jesus lifted up His eyes and said, 'Father, I thank You that You have heard Me'"* (John 11:41). This was precisely what He taught his disciples to do. *"Our Father in heaven, Hallowed be Your name"* (Matthew 6:9 ▲▲). It shouldn't surprise us, but He did follow His own model. We need to be acutely aware that prayer isn't merely about walking around speaking to trees, storms, dead people or hammocks and expecting results. There is much more to it than that. We need to have a keen understanding that it is our God in heaven who brings the results.

Judeo/Christianity is the only religion that relates to God as a father. Even in Islam, which requires dutiful prayer five times daily, there is not a single reference to Allah being father. It is fascinating that in the Qur'an there are ninety-nine names or descriptions for Allah, some of them similar to the Bible—provider, merciful, defender. But not father.[5] It is worth noting that Mohamed called himself "the slave of Allah," whereas Jesus called Himself "the Son of God." This ability to have a personal relationship with the living God is what distinguishes Christianity from all the rest.

Imagine for a moment that you were Prince William (we won't talk about the estranged Harry). You would have certain privileges that none of the royal staff would ever have. Because your father is the King of England, you have use of virtually everything he has. You could hang out at Windsor Castle, Buckingham Palace, Kensington Palace or any one of twenty-three other royal residences. If you wanted to go for a spin in the royal Bentley, you would have access to the keys. (You may not get the Aston Martin, though, because King Charles reserves that for himself. I guess he fancies himself as something of a 007. And he recently had it converted to burn biofuel and now claims it runs on wine and cheese.[6])

When describing our access to heaven, the Bible uses the same royal metaphors:

> *Let us therefore come boldly to the throne of grace, that we may obtain mercy and find grace to help in time of need.*
>
> —Hebrews 4:16

We can come so boldly to God in prayer only because we are considered family. To take this one step further, most scholars agree that Jesus would have used the Aramaic word *Abba*[7] in addressing the

Father. The New Testament is written in Koine Greek, but Jesus would have spoken in the common language of Aramaic. The term Abba, more literally translated, would be "Papa" or "Daddy"—a more intimate and familiar term for father. Scripture puts our relationship with the Father on the same level of intimacy. *"Because you are sons, God has sent forth the Spirit of His Son into your hearts, crying out, 'Abba, Father!'"* (Galatians 4:6). Because we are sons, we can approach Him as our daddy. Because this is about relationship, not formula, the actual terminology we used can be personalized.

We have a staff member who oversees our audio team, named Isaac. He has a deep and meaningful relationship with God, as he was miraculously saved out of a broken past, and he always carries an open gratitude for it in his prayer life. He is a joy to watch as he conversationally refers to the Father as "Dad" in his prayers. I suspect there are other people who do the same—but I don't know any of them. I grew up in a house where grace sounded more like this: "Rub a dub, dub, thanks for the grub, Yeah God!"

As irreverent as that sounds, it does segue nicely into the second part of how we should address the Father, which is seen in the phrase *"Hallowed be Your name."* Immediately, He affirms the need for reverence of His name. Historically, the Jewish scribes were extremely diligent to avoid disrespecting the name of Jehovah. They would not utter it or even write it out. Consequently, we are not even sure if "Jehovah" is a correct transcription. In the Hebrew language it would be "Yahweh," but even that is a guess, since what the scribes recorded was merely the four consonants, YHWH. Contrast that today with how TV, movies and pop culture denigrate the name of Christ and use it in various forms of vulgarity. It might be one of the most offensive things about modern culture, yet most people don't even notice it anymore. On at least some level, it is a violation of the third commandment, *"You shall not take the name of the LORD your God in vain"* (Exodus 20:7).

Prayer is an act of worship. We begin by honouring and revering who God is. He is not our buddy, our bubba, our home boy or the man upstairs—He is the Creator of heaven and earth. It the reason why people bow their heads, fold their hands and even kneel down to pray.

The first time I ever set foot in an evangelical church, I came looking for things to criticize. The pastor got down on one knee and I thought, "That's pathetic. At best he will only get half his prayers answered." Today I understand how important the posture of prayer is. He has a name above every name that is named and at the name of Jesus every knee will bow and every tongue confess that Jesus is Lord. Let's not forget that.

> *Therefore God also has highly exalted Him and given Him the name which is above every name, that at the name of Jesus every knee should bow, of those in heaven, and of those on earth, and of those under the earth, and that every tongue should confess that Jesus Christ is Lord, to the glory of God the Father.*
>
> —Philippians 2:9–11

INVOKE HEAVEN'S RESOURCES TO MEET EARTH'S NEEDS

One of the most extraordinary things in the Bible is that our access to God's throne (Hebrews 4:16) affords us the privilege of invoking heaven's resources to meet earth's needs. The Lord's Prayer declares, *"Your kingdom come. / Your will be done / On earth as it is in heaven"* (Matthew 6:10 ▲). We can call the kingdom of heaven to come to bear on earth, asking the Father for His will to be done on earth in a like fashion to the way it is in heaven. This is a bit mind-blowing when you consider that His will in heaven is divine health, abundance in all things, impeccable relationships, pure peace, unrequited love, endless joy and so much more.

When John the Baptist rolled into town, he was an unlikely messenger. Dressed in camel's skin and chowing down on locusts and wild honey, he was a better candidate for the nut house. But his message struck a chord with thousands: *"Repent, for the kingdom of heaven is at hand!"* (Matthew 3:2). The people had been living under the tyranny and the oppression of the Romans for far too long, and now, finally, a hope—the kingdom of heaven was coming to earth. They were not sure what that meant exactly, until Jesus finally appeared. When John was sent off to prison to await his execution, he sent two of his own disciples to Jesus just to double check and make sure they had the right Messiah.

> *"Are You the Coming One, or do we look for another?" Jesus answered and said to them, "Go and tell John the things which you hear and see: The blind see and the lame walk; the lepers are cleansed and the deaf hear; the dead are raised up and the poor have the gospel preached to them."*
>
> —Matthew 11:3–5

In other words, His Kingdom had come, His will was being done on earth as it is in heaven. The examples are myriad. When the multitude following Him was without food in the wilderness, He LOOKED UP TO HEAVEN and prayed and 5,000 men plus women and children were fed with five loaves and the two fish (Matthew 14:19). When the deaf mute was brought to Him, *"<u>Looking up to heaven</u>, He sighed, and said to him, 'Ephphatha,' that is, 'Be opened.' Immediately his ears were opened, and the impediment of his tongue was loosed, and he spoke plainly"* (Mark 7:34–35, emphasis added). There was no earthly solution to these problems, but heaven had a ready answer. We are to take inspiration from these stories. They were precisely what Jesus had in mind when He was teaching His disciples (and subsequently us) to pray.

Honestly, the muddle we find ourselves in is that we are afraid to ask too big, so we instead ask way too small. The nineteenth-century revivalist Charles Finney used to pray, "I come with Thy faithful promises in my hand, and I cannot be denied."[8] Few of us have the nerve (faith?) to pray that boldly. But maybe we should.

A few years back, I started playing tennis with a bunch of cranky old men. I was new to the game and thought I would be able to handily defeat them. It turned out that most of them had been playing for fifty years, and even with their artificial knees, hips and shoulders, they still managed to beat me. The class clown was Brian. (Every group of men has one. Jesus had Peter.) He was a riot and had a smart remark for everyone and everything. When he found out I was a preacher—and a televangelist no less—he began to mock me mercilessly. "You probably own a jet, like all televangelists?" He charged.

Never one to take guff from anybody, I shot back, "Don't be ridiculous. The church owns the jet, not me. I don't even own the mansion."

He pressed on, undeterred, "Are your blind followers required to give you all their money?"

Staying on point, I countered, "Oh no, that would be greedy. I only ask them for 10%."

This line of inappropriate questioning went on for several weeks. I didn't care; he was giving me ample opportunity to share the gospel with him, even if he didn't realize it. Then one week he showed up very distressed. He had gone deaf in one ear and the doctors were not able to tell him why, let alone cure it. Brian threw out an angry challenge: "Why don't you lay hands on me and heal my ear?" I told him I would lay hands on him and that although I couldn't heal him, I knew someone who could. At that, we were interrupted by the start of the match.

As we were getting ready to leave the court, he said it again, "I thought you said you were going to heal my ear!"

I said, "You bet." When I started praying for him, the other players gathered around and bowed their heads. There was no instant change, but he thanked me for praying.

That was the last game of the season, and I did not see him again until the next year. When he saw me he came running up, shouting, "Praise the Lord!" (in a slightly mocking fashion) and announced to the whole group that his deaf ear was healed when I prayed for him.

A new player asked, "Are you a minister of some sort?"

Brian jumped in and responded emphatically. "Are you kidding? He's the real deal! He's the only guy who prayed for me and I got healed. He's not like all those phonies on TV."

I marvelled at how God used a sort of ridiculous situation to show His power to a group of old coots by healing one of them in a very public way. I have often thought about that day and wondered what would have happened if I had chickened out and not accepted the public challenge to pray. That day God's Kingdom came and His will was done on earth as it is in heaven.

It was a much better result than when a rough-looking stranger came up to me one Sunday and said, "Pastor can you pray for my hearing?"

Which I immediately did, and then asked him, "How's your hearing?"

To which he replied in a confused manner, "How would I know? It's not until Wednesday."

MAKE PRAYER A DAILY DISCIPLINE

The next line in the Lord's Prayer is *"Give us this day our daily bread"* (Matthew 6:11). In simple terms, God is not interested in stockpile prayers, like "Lord, give me $1 million and I will see you next year." He is not interested in turning us into trust fund brats who only show up when they need Daddy's money. We all understand this—none of us want children who only talk to us when they want something from us. "I want a new bike, I want a new cell phone, I want a new laptop…" I can hear some of you right now, saying, "That pretty much sums it up!" Conversely, if our children love us, respect us and are interested in our company, there is not much we wouldn't do for them. Probably every parent reading this has at some time gone to extraordinary lengths to help out their offspring when a need arose. The Lord is no different. *"Do not fear, little flock, for it is your Father's good pleasure to give you the kingdom"* (Luke 12:32).

God's desire is for daily communication as well as to care for us on a daily basis. We see a powerful allusion to this in the book of Exodus. God provided daily bread for His children every single day for forty years. If they tried to stockpile it, it was rotten by the next day. God was teaching them utter reliance.

Humorously, the meaning of the word "manna" is "What is it?" Every morning for years and years, the children of Israel woke up and said, "What is it?" The Psalmist Asaph seemed to know what it was. Psalm 78 describes that God *"Had rained down manna upon them to eat, / And given them of the bread of heaven. / Men ate angels' food"* (Psalm 78:24–25a). It was daily bread, fresh baked by the angels in heaven every morning.

Prayer can seem counterintuitive, just like the rest of the Sermon on the Mount. From birth, we train our children to be self-reliant and self-sufficient. "Learn to make your way in life. If you don't take care of yourself nobody else will." But God calls us to a life of complete dependence on Him.

> *For after all these things the Gentiles seek. For your heavenly Father knows that you need all these things. But seek first the kingdom of God and His righteousness, and all these things shall be added to you.*
>
> —Matthew 6:32–33 ⛰

Jesus' disciples were hardworking fisherman. Some of them owned their own boats and ran their own businesses. He asked them to leave it all behind, and for the rest of their lives, they literally lived day by day as God provided. Before Jesus left the earth for heaven, *"He said to them, 'When I sent you without money bag, knapsack, and sandals, did you lack anything?' So they said, 'Nothing'"* (Luke 22:35).

This is not to say that we should quit our jobs or refuse to work, for theirs was a unique calling. It does, however, illustrate the fact that God is interested in daily conversation with us and wants to participate in ensuring we have everything we need on a daily basis.

There is something more important than the bread here. Twice, in one tiny verse, it mentions the current day. THIS DAY our DAILY bread. He is telling us we need to pray every single day, looking for a daily conversation. At the same time, He does, of course, warn us of it being formulaic or mechanical. *"And when you pray, do not use vain repetitions as the heathen do. For they think that they will be heard for their many words"* (Matthew 6:7 ⛰). He was referring to pagan religions where prayer is nothing more than chanting or repeating a mantra, which is still true of many world religions today. They memorize prayers, sometimes in languages they do not speak, and repeat them over and over. Jesus tells us not to be like them. Why? Because prayer is about relationship and communication.

Imagine if I spoke to my wife like this: "Dear Kathy, thou dost know that I love thee. I come to you in deep contrition and recompense for my transgressions. I humbly beseech thee this day that thou may grant me eight dollars for my daily pilgrimage to the temple of Starbucks on my vocational recess." That's not how we talk to people, so why would we talk to God like that?

Prayer is just talking to God in a personal and normal way. The more we get used to communicating with Him on this level, the more we will enjoy praying. One more aspect to remember is that every relationship requires two-way conversation. We would do well to pause and listen once in a while during prayer. He might just answer back.

We probably all have one of those friends who just does not know how to stop talking. Likely, they are the friend we try to avoid. I recall sitting in the airport one day, waiting for a flight, unable to avoid overhearing a woman's cell phone conversation. It still amazes me that, years after the advent of the smart phone, so many people have no concept of cell phone etiquette. I was subjected to a one-sided conversation as the woman across from me talked in her outdoor voice without taking a single breath. It went something like this:

> "So how was your day? Well, let me tell you what my day was like. I was in the line at grocery store and the woman in front of me was buying Pop-Tarts. Can you imagine? What kind of mother is that, who buys her kids Pop-Tarts for breakfast? You know, when I go to the Pancake House I always order the giant apple pancake because I will always have enough left over for breakfast the next day. I just think that's smart! What do you like for breakfast? You probably eat bacon. You know, I tried the keto diet and it didn't work for me. I gained twenty pounds in two weeks. Blah, blah, blah…"

There was no chance for the person on the other end to answer any of the questions. And there was nothing any of us in the gate lounge could do but sit there and think to ourselves, "Would you just shut up!" I remember wondering that day if my prayer life didn't sometimes sound just like that to God. He is going to love me anyway, but I still don't want to be that annoying.

The one thing that God wants from us in prayer, more than anything else, is fellowship. That is why we were created. I often think how heartbreaking it must be for God, to have created billions of people and then have the majority of them completely ignore Him or, worse yet, deny His existence.

It reminds me of the story of the two widowers out playing golf. Sam hit his tee shot into a water trap. Upon retrieving his ball, a frog jumps out of the water and says, "If you kiss me I will turn into a beautiful princess." Sam picks up the frog and puts it in his pocket.

George asks, "Aren't you going to kiss it?"

Sam calmly responds, "Are you kidding? At my age I would rather have a talking frog."

FORGIVE EVERYBODY ALL THE TIME

We covered this is detail in Chapter Eleven, so we will not retrace our steps, except to ask this question: Why is this particular aspect of the Sermon on the Mount specifically included in the Lord's Prayer? Because it is that critical! It is incumbent upon us to keep our accounts short with others. We can't expect for a minute that God will answer our prayers if we will not forgive one another. The Psalmist wrote, *"If I regard iniquity in my heart, / The LORD will not hear"* (Psalm 66:18). Wow, once again, that is far too high a price to pay to carry bitterness in our heart. Unforgiveness, offence, bitterness—they are all iniquities.

In old translations, such as the one used in the Book of Common Prayer, the Lord's Prayer reads, *"And forgive us our trespasses, as we forgive them that trespass against us."*[9] But my favourite is eight-year-old Bethany's version, "And forgive us our trash baskets as we forgive those who put trash in our baskets." That almost says it better than any scholarly translation. Every one of us has a trash basket full of garbage in our life. People put trash in our baskets, and we put trash in their baskets. God wants us to empty the trash basket.

We are all familiar with the junk mail that comes into the inbox on our computer. We can delete it, but it only goes into the "recycle bin." That means we can still retrieve it if we want to. That is exactly what we do when we half-heartedly forgive someone. The moment an irritation arises, we hit the "restore" button and are offended once again. We must make sure that the "recycle bin" is emptied (deleted) as well.

I had an old pair of steel toe work boots that I used for mowing the lawn. They we so ratty that Kathy didn't want them in the house anymore, so she threw them in the trash. I noticed them sitting at the top of bin and went and retrieved them. The next day Kathy said, "What are these doing here? I threw them out."

I replied, "I know—it was a lucky thing that I saw them and pulled them out!"

I won't bore you with the details, but I lost that battle and the boots went back into the trash bin. The next day I watched as the sanitation truck emptied our bin and then continued down the street. NOW they were officially discarded! We have got to learn to let our offences go in their entirety, never to be picked up again.

Troy had forgotten to take out the garbage the night before pickup. When his wife, Brenda, saw the garbage truck coming down the street, she ran to the curb wearing her old ratty house coat and curlers in her hair. Chasing after the garbage truck with the trash bag in her hand, she shouted, "Do you have room for one more?"

Without missing a beat, the driver answered, "Sure, lady, hop in!"

One of the great little-known secrets of answered prayer is to forgive everybody all the time.

REQUEST HELP TO DEAL WITH TEMPTATION

One of the more confusing aspects of the Lord's Prayer is that we are instructed to pray, *"Lead us not into temptation"* (Matthew 6:13 ▲). Why would God be leading us into temptation? At first glance, it seems to imply that if we don't specifically ask Him not to, He might lead us right into it! It is a bit more complex than that. I have heard preachers explain that it really means we should be praying that God will keep us from being tempted. No, that is far too facile of an answer. In fact, that is actually a prayer God will refuse to answer, for the only way He could answer that would be to make you die and go to heaven. If you live in this world, you will be subject to worldly temptations. It goes with the territory.

Jesus Himself was tempted multiple times. On the mount of temptation, it was three times in one day, and catch this, it specifically says, *"Jesus was <u>led up by the Spirit</u> into the wilderness <u>to be tempted by the devil</u>"* (Matthew 4:1, emphasis added). The Holy Spirit led him into temptation. Hebrews 4:15 takes our understanding to a whole new level: *"For we do not have a High Priest who cannot sympathize with our weaknesses, but was <u>in all points tempted</u> as we are, yet without sin."* Jesus Himself was tempted in *all points* on earth, just as we are. Are you ready for this, men? Jesus was tempted sexually, just like you are! Jesus had to guard his heart against lust, just like you do! Jesus had to resist the temptations of greed, gluttony, envy, pride, and, and, and… "Say it ain't so, preacher!" It's so! The Bible says it is so. Most of us cannot even imagine Jesus struggling with these things. However, He would not have been human if He didn't.

Even with God leading us through life, we will pass by many temptations. But if we pray, God will guide our steps so that we do not fall into those temptations. Imagine a guide leading a group of hikers along a treacherous mountain path. There is danger on every side. But if you follow the guide's instruction, it will keep you from falling off the edge.

Our son, Jay, and one of his friends went to Peru to do the Inca Trail. It is a high-altitude three-day trek to Machu Picchu. Built in the fifteenth century and later abandoned, this Incan citadel is set high in the Andes Mountains of South America. Most tourists will take a bus tour up to the site and enjoy the awe-inspiring handiwork of this ancient civilization. However, my son and his friend were young and wanted the full experience, so they did the trek and camping trip.

Upon hearing about the skill and experience of their guide, it was clear that they could not have done this trek unassisted. Some of the areas they encountered sounded nothing short of spectacular, but it wasn't until we saw the pictures that we really began to appreciate why millions make the pilgrimage to Machu Picchu. The Inca Bridge was the most terrifying. This staircase/bridge traverses along the side of a mountain. It has no railing and is less than a metre wide. There is a section of the bridge with a 6-metre gap, which at one time had a couple of logs across it, over a 600-metre drop. It is now closed to the public, of course.[10] (You will really need to take a brief break from reading here to go look up the links in the footnotes to see the pictures, which are much better than a thousand words.)

Then there is the Huayna Picchu, also known as "the stairs of death," which climbs 183 metres up a rock face. To navigate the stairs, tourists must use both hands to hold the wall. Apparently, no one has died on the stairs of death… yet.[11] Still, every year someone loses their life elsewhere on the Inca trail for various reasons. And yes, some have fallen to their death.[12] But nobody needs to die—they just need to heed the instructions of their guide, which will lead them *near* temptation but not *into* it.

Because temptation surrounds us in the twenty-first century more than any other time in history, we had better be praying that the Lord will lead us through it. Oscar Wilde's Lord Darlingford said it best, "I couldn't help it. I can resist everything except temptation."[13] Jesus has a better solution.

> *Watch and pray, lest you enter into temptation. The spirit indeed is willing, but the flesh is weak.*
>
> —Matthew 26:41

> *Watch and pray, lest you enter into temptation. The spirit indeed is willing, but the flesh is weak.*
>
> —Mark 14:38

> *When He came to the place, He said to them, "Pray that you may not enter into temptation."*
>
> —Luke 22:40

> *Then He said to them, "Why do you sleep? Rise and pray, lest you enter into temptation."*
>
> —Luke 22:46

I wonder what He was driving at. Maybe that the key to avoiding bad behaviour is to replace it with good behaviour? Maybe that if we would pray when we are tempted, we would not enter temptation? Maybe if we prayed more like this: "Lord, lead me in such a way that I do not succumb to my own pathetic temptations and end up becoming my own worst enemy. Help save me from my weaknesses and instead lead me into your perfect will for my life," we would be getting better results. A prayer like that puts the blame on us and the protection on Him.

USE THE AUTHORITY OF JESUS' NAME
TO DEFEAT THE DEVIL

The last line in the Lord's Prayer closes in a triumphal invocation: *"But deliver us from the evil one. For Yours is the kingdom and the power and the glory forever. Amen"* (Matthew 6:13 ▲).

Jesus did not shy away from talking about the Devil. He mentions him by name thirty-two times in the Gospels. We don't talk much about Satan today. He is more of a footnote in biblical history as someone or "something" that existed is Jesus' time. We are too sophisticated to entertain mystical explanations to medical and psychological conditions. Yet, as we peer into the New Testament, we observe Jesus solving earthly problems by engaging in a spiritual battle. *"For this purpose the Son of God was manifested, that He might destroy the works of the devil"* (1 John 3:8b).

One of the greatest deceptions Satan has perpetrated upon our generation is that he doesn't even exist. Consequently, he can move about freely, wreaking havoc in people's lives, since we will just come up with some scientific, medical or psychological explanation. "I have a hormone imbalance in my dipthoid gland." (I made the word up so as not to unnecessarily offend anybody with an imbalance in their dipthoid gland.) This is not to say that there are not medical abnormalities. Of course, there are. But the Devil and his demons can easily involve themselves in such matters.

> *Then His fame went throughout all Syria; and they brought to Him all sick people who were afflicted with various diseases*

and torments, and those who were demon-possessed, epileptics, and paralytics; and He healed them.

—Matthew 4:24

… God anointed Jesus of Nazareth with the Holy Spirit and with power, who went about doing good and healing all who were oppressed by the devil, for God was with Him.

—Acts 10:38

Jesus seemed to lump it all together as one big spiritual problem. Disease, torment, oppression, demon-possession—He merely used His authority to heal it all. The Lord's Prayer reminds us that He still possesses all authority in heaven and earth; therefore, we should be invoking His power for deliverance from the evil one.

The apostle Peter also reminds us that we are in the same spiritual battle. *"Be sober, be vigilant; because your adversary the devil walks about like a roaring lion, seeking whom he may devour"* (1 Peter 5:8). The Devil is no longer God's adversary; he is ours. He is seeking out those whom he MAY devour—only those who will let him! Our ignorance of his devices is the deficiency that allows him such access to our lives.

If you ever go to Banff National Park in Alberta, you may be intimidated by the signs everywhere that say Be Bear Aware. They list practical suggestions to avoid getting devoured by a bear. You might get the impression that 25–30% of all hikers get eaten. The reality is that it is only the careless hikers that get devoured; 99.99% of people can easily avoid an encounter with a bear. Be one of these sober and vigilant ones.

Every autumn, we have a bear that visits our summer place to look for an easy snack. She has broken into our family cottage several times and made quite a mess. One year she hibernated under the cottage and woke up cranky and hungry. She tore the siding right off the cottage to get into the kitchen. There was no food to speak of in there, so she ate an entire can of coffee beans. (Apparently, even bears need their caffeine fix when they first wake up.) She must have had a buzz going for a week after that much coffee.

You may have noticed I keep referring to the bear as "she." That is because I have seen her on a few occasions with cubs, and admittedly, one time I acted carelessly. We had seen her coming down the path and I decided I would try to chase her away. I loaded a single shell into the shotgun and went after her. I had no intention of killing her, only scaring her off. When I encountered the bear, I shot over her head. Fortunately, she did run away. Later I realized that, had she decided to charge me, I did not even have a second shell with me. What on earth was I thinking? It could have been a very dangerous mistake.

Many of us live carelessly everyday when it comes to the Devil. We walk too close to the line regarding bad behaviour and then we wonder why he eats our lunch… or worse yet, eats us!

> One of the greatest deceptions Satan has perpetrated upon our generation is that he doesn't even exist.

It is hard to resist throwing this important story in here. Two bears escaped from a zoo. After two months, they met up and one was plump and healthy while the other was skinny and anemic.

The skinny one said, "Freedom went alright at first, but then I ate a human and they have been hunting me ever since. I've been hiding in a park and all I have had to eat are insects and mice."

The healthy bear said, "I have been doing great. I broke into a government office building and have been eating a department manager every single day—and nobody has even noticed."

If we are going to take on the enemy, we need to be really clear about the weapons of our warfare and how to use them. In 25% of Jesus' healings He actually cast out a demon. With the level of mental illness, depression, anxiety, sickness in the world today, we need to at least entertain the possibility that some of it is demonic. Even within our relationships, we make the mistake of thinking that the people involved are our enemies—our boss, our banker or our mother-in-law. Especially our mother-in-law! As pastors we see marriages in trouble all the time. Nine times out of ten, the spouses see each other as the enemy.

One evening I had a couple in my office for over an hour, and they were at each other's throats. We were getting nowhere. To be honest, even I didn't see much hope for the situation. Finally, I stopped them and said, "Can't you see how the Devil has brought strife between you? You are fighting the wrong enemy!" Without asking for permission, I prayed very aggressively and invoked the name of Jesus to take authority over the enemy that was destroying their marriage. After several minutes, they both began to weep and the hatred in the room began to melt. The reality was they still loved each other. They had just allowed the enemy to get between them and devour their relationship. The marriage wasn't healed instantly, but it was a turning point and eventually this couple ended up as leaders of the marriage ministry in our church.

Sometimes we forget that we have access to Jesus' authority to fight our spiritual battles. In Matthew 10, Jesus sent out His disciples with this command: *"Heal the sick, cleanse the lepers, raise the dead, cast out demons. Freely you have received, freely give"* (Matthew 10:8). They must have not expected it to work, because they came back rejoicing, saying, *"Lord, even the demons are subject to us in Your name"* (Luke 10:17). Jesus explained why.

> *I saw Satan fall like lightning from heaven. Behold, I give you the authority to trample on serpents and scorpions, and over all the power of the enemy, and nothing shall by any means hurt you. Nevertheless do not rejoice in this, that the spirits are subject to you, but rather rejoice because your names are written in heaven.*
>
> —Luke 10:18–20

Notice that it does not say that we are somehow more powerful than the demons. Rather, Jesus has given us "authority" over their "power."

Here is my favourite way to illustrate this. An 80,000-pound 650-hp Kenworth W900 semi-trailer is rolling down the highway. A highway patrolman catches him on the radar doing 30 km over the posted limit. The 210-pound officer steps out of the patrol car and raises his hand for the driver to pull over. In that moment, who has more power? Clearly the truck. But the trucker dutifully pulls to the side of the road. Why? Because he respects the authority of the police officer. He knows that that authority is backed up by another power (like the cop's partners, Smith and Wesson, for example).

The same thing is true with us. We in ourselves are not that powerful, but the work of the cross has granted authority to all whose names are written in heaven. We access heaven's resources because we are known there, and our Lord possesses all the authority in heaven and on earth (Matthew 28:18).

Prayer is an enormous topic and has been the subject of countless books. But even a cursory understanding of the Lord's Prayer, like this one, can go a long way toward revolutionizing our prayer lives. If we will be diligent in prayer, there is not a single problem we can encounter in life in which God will not intervene and remedy in some fashion. If God is for us, who can be against us?

Chapter Sixteen

Rock around the Clock

And so castles made of sand, melts into the sea eventually.
—Jimi Hendrix

In 1996, a group of pastors from our city travelled together to Pensacola, Florida. We went to investigate what would be best described as a Pentecostal revival. Beginning on Father's Day in 1994 at Brownsville Assembly, meetings were held every single night for almost five years. We had never seen anything like it. People lined up outside the church for four or five hours in order to get into the evening services. It is estimated 2.5 million people went through the doors and 200,000 made commitments for Christ.

An evangelist named Steve Hill preached a fire and brimstone sermon to the crowd and basically told everybody they were going straight to hell. He was very good at it. At the end of the service, I actually raised my hand (perhaps I misunderstood the question) and was immediately ushered into a new converts room. When I explained to them that I had already been a pastor for twenty years, they said, undeterred, "Praise God! We have had dozens of pastors coming to Christ." I didn't want to spoil anybody's fun and so said thank you and took the new Christian packet. Even still, it was a unique and educational experience and I think I learned a lot about how God can do mighty things even when we are taking ourselves too seriously.

I am not sure why God chose this unlikely location for this revival, awakening or whatever it might actually have been. Pensacola is in the Florida Panhandle, which is far more similar to Alabama than it is to Florida. In the previous year it had been hit by not one, but two Gulf of Mexico hurricanes—Erin and then Opal.

One morning, when we weren't waiting in line to go to church, I suggested to my pastor friends that I wanted to run out to Santa Rosa Island and survey the aftermath of Hurricane Opal. They call it an island, but it looked like a sandbar to me. It is a 64-km long Gulf Coast barrier island consisting entirely of sand. There are no natural trees and it is only several hundred metres wide. There is a single paved road that runs right down the middle of the sandbar… er, I mean island. Most of the beach houses were built on stilts and elevated. When the Category 4 Opal went through, some of the houses managed to remain standing (most were destroyed) but the "island" itself moved to the other side of the road. The houses were standing out in the Gulf of Mexico on their stilts but all the sand had gone north for the summer.

I spotted a homeowner repairing his siding and went over to talk to him. "What are you going to do with the house?" I asked.

"Rebuild it… just like I have done twice before. This is my home. I am not leaving," he stated emphatically.

"Yeah, but what about the beach? It's gone." I queried.

Without hesitation, he replied, "It's not gone, it just moved. It's over there (pointing north). I will hire someone to haul it back for me."

Trying not to laugh because I knew he wasn't joking, I pointed to a For Sale sign in the water beside his home, representing nothing but a few piles poking up out of the Gulf. "How much is that one listed for?"

"$400,000," he calmly replied, "and that is a steal of a deal. I think it's worth twice that."

As impactful as the Pensacola revival was, and it truly was an enlightening experience, it was the trip to the beach that got etched into my memory. Why would anyone build so close to the water—on a sandbar in hurricane alley—again and again? It made no sense to me. No view of the ocean is worth that grief. All I could think of that day were the immortal words of Jesus from the Sermon on the Mount.

> *Therefore whoever hears these sayings of Mine, and does them, I will liken him to a wise man who built his house on the rock: and the rain descended, the floods came, and the winds blew and beat on that house; and it did not fall, for it was founded on the rock. But everyone who hears these sayings of Mine, and does not do them, will be like a foolish man who built his house on the sand: and the rain descended, the floods came, and the winds blew and beat on that house; and it fell. And great was its fall.*
>
> —Matthew 7:24–27 ⛰

Notice He doesn't say, "IF the rain and wind and floods come," but, "WHEN." I am sure Santa Rosa is a very beautiful location when the winds are calm and the sun is shining. But the people on that beach are smart enough to know that another hurricane is coming. They will always come. A hurricane makes landfall in the Panhandle on an average of every six years. Still, these wealthy and otherwise intelligent people continue to build in harm's way. They can build their houses stronger and better, which they do, but they can do nothing to stop the storm from coming and the "island" from moving somewhere else. And so, "Castles made of sand / Melts into the sea, eventually."[1]

As far as Jesus is concerned, there are only two kinds of people—sand dwellers and rock dwellers. Sand dwellers have heard the teachings of Christ but disregard them or fail to act on them. They don't think they need God's help in navigating planet earth. It is called the "pride of life" in Scripture (1 John 2:16). It was the original sin of Adam and Eve. They heard the word from God not to eat of the tree in the midst of the garden, but they ate anyway. In their eyes, it was *"good for food… pleasant to the eyes, and… desirable to make one wise"* (Genesis 3:6). They thought they knew better than their Creator, and their house (Eden) came crashing down. They were ejected from a place far more beautiful than Santa Rosa Island.

The sand dwellers of today make the same mistake. They have heard what Jesus has to say but they disregard it, as they have had some level of success in life without needing any divine intervention. Maybe they have a wonderful spouse and some good kids. Maybe life has worked out pretty well without having to get bogged down in all those ridiculously difficult life lessons of Jesus. Then one day, cancer comes a-calling, COVID-19 comes a-calling, calamity comes a-calling. The winds and the waves pound on their house, but it has no secure foundation because it was built on the shifting sands of secular humanism and worldly values.

Rock dwellers discover that the more difficult way is often the better way. The winds and the waves still beat on these people too, but they dig deep and remember who they are in Christ.

It is not that rock dwellers are smarter than sand dwellers, it is just that they are more humble. They do not pretend to be able to bear up against all of life's greatest challenges on their own strength, so they take the challenging lessons of the Sermon on the Mount literally and put them into practice. And, as counterintuitive as they are, Jesus' principles of life actually work. Rock dwellers discover that the more difficult way is often the better way. The winds and the waves still beat on these people too, but they dig deep and remember who they are in Christ. They know that God holds them securely in the palm of His hand, and there is nothing in this world that can change that.

When Peter and Petra Rockwall moved into their new home on Stoney Plains Drive, they were excited about meeting all their new neighbours and being part of a community. Their house had been meticulously maintained, but the one behind them, on Sandstone Place, needed a bit of love, to say the least. The fence was in disrepair, and the house needed new paint and shingles. The dandelions were in full bloom and it looked like it was going to be a bumper crop this year. With the west wind blowing, there was a very good chance the Rockwalls would be sporting the same beautiful yellow flowers the next spring.

After a few days, they still had not met the people on the other side of the fence, so they headed over with a box of Tim Hortons donuts to say hello. Adam and Eva Sandberg were interesting people. Adam was sporting the requisite white sleeveless t-shirt, also indelicately known as "the wife beater." It appeared as if it also doubled as a dinner napkin. Eva was larger than life, literally, and looked like the poster girl for the local cosmetic surgery clinic. She had it all going on and would fit in nicely on Hollywood Boulevard any day of the week. Nevertheless, they were demonstratively friendly and outgoing. And they both used "colourful language" that Peter and Petra rarely got to hear down at their Pentecostal church. Still, they felt there was no reason they could not be their new best friends. After all, people are people, right?

On Friday night, the Rockwalls invited the Sandbergs over to play bridge, as they had claimed they played the game all the time. Unfortunately, Adam and Eva misunderstood and were expecting the somewhat unrelated game, Across the Bridge. It was also a card game, but in their version you down a shot every time you turn over a face card. Peter didn't have shot glasses or Tequila, so they settled on playing Texas Hold-em poker instead. Still, the couples got to know each other as they both shared a love of travel. Peter and Petra shared about their short-term missions trip to Honduras. Adam and Eva, completely tracking, told them about bar hopping and parasailing in Cancun.

The following week, Adam took Peter to the bowling alley to meet all his buddies. Peter learned some new expletives that he didn't know existed, as he had never heard them on *Jeopardy*. At the end of the evening, as they were putting their street shoes back on, one of Adam's buddies, Tom, was lacing up Peter's brand new Nikes. When confronted, Tom pointed to a tired old pair of the same shoes and said, "Those are yours over there. Mine are brand new." Peter was more than a little perplexed. Was he in the twilight zone here? It was completely bizarre. He insisted that they were, in fact, his and that he had just bought them the week before. But Tom wasn't budging. Peter didn't know what to do. It was clearly "not" an honest mistake, but it wasn't as if he had written his name on the shoes either. So, he had no way to prove it. What should he do? Call him a liar? Call him out into the parking lot and duke it out? Call the police?

When he looked at Adam, he just shrugged and did not offer to arbitrate, which would have been the right thing to do. Peter could make a scene, but how would that affect his new friendship with Adam? He still had to live behind the dude.

Trying to decide how to proceed, Peter could hear the words of Jesus swirling in his head, *"If anyone wants to sue you and take away your Nikes, let him have your Reeboks also"* (Matthew 5:40 ⛰).[2] Fortunately for Peter, his Reeboks were at home, so he didn't have to give up two pairs of runners. In the end, he laced up the older Nikes and headed home. At least they were nicely broken in. The first thing he did when got home was to spray them down with Lysol.

As he lay in bed that night, he realized his friendship with Adam was not going to be easy. That night, Peter determined in his heart that he was going to choose to be Christlike no matter the cost. Little did he know what he had just committed to.

Over the following months, the Rockwalls had their resolve tested time and again. Adam would borrow tools and forget to return them, or if he did bring them back, they often were no longer working. Petra, trying to relate with her new worldly neighbour, made the mistake of sharing a secret with Eva, confiding that she had not always been the goody-two-shoes Christian that she appeared. She told her that, before she met Peter, she had been a promiscuous teen. Not only did Eva not keep the secret, she embellished on it and told the other ladies on the cul-de-sac that Petra had been "quite the slut" before she was married. She was devastated when it got back to her. She sobbed as she shared what had happened with Peter, swearing that she could never forgive Eva. But a few days later, God spoke to Petra's heart as she was praying. "Lord, how often shall I have to forgive Eva? Up to seven times?" She knew the answer was, *"I do not say to you, up to seven times, but up to seventy times seven"* (Matthew 18:21–22).

The next day Petra went over with a bundt cake. Eva appeared oblivious to her transgression. So, very gently, Petra shared how hurt she had been that her confidence had been breached. But she quickly added that she had let it go and was not going to let it interfere with their friendship. Eva was clearly embarrassed, but she didn't exactly offer an apology. Petra knew how these things sometimes work, that you don't always get the outcome you hope for. At the end of the day, she remembered that you have to forgive everybody all the time.

The two couples still managed to develop a great friendship. As it turned out, both Adam and Eva had some very good qualities. They were always hospitable and included the Rockwalls in their social events. Adam was a great mechanic and, on several occasions, saved Peter some big bucks on car repairs. Peter also helped him fix his fence and roof. Despite Eva's rough edges, she had a kind heart and congenial nature that really shone through one Christmas when they went caroling at the seniors home.

A couple of years later, the Sandbergs faced a serious tragedy. Their college-aged son, Abel, was killed by a drunken driver in an automobile accident. They were inconsolable and had no real way to deal with a calamity of this magnitude. Peter and Petra sprang into action. They made sure they had meals at the ready and ran interference when the Sandbergs became overwhelmed with the details of it all.

The Rockwalls were no strangers to adversity themselves. Petra had developed stage four breast cancer and spent three years in surgery, chemo and radiation. By the grace of God, she managed to keep a good attitude the entire time and eventually emerged cancer free. The Rockwalls referred to it as the biggest storm of their lives, and they could not imagine how they would have handled it had they not "built their house on the Rock."

Peter and Petra were able to share with Adam and Eva how God's grace had sustained them and that they had never felt abandoned. The Sandbergs could see that the Rockwalls' faith was not some religious crutch but something rooted in a real relationship with a living God. One evening, they admitted, "Whatever it is that you guys have, we need it." That night the Sandbergs gave their hearts to Christ and began their own journey of faith.

This tale may sound suspiciously like the friendship of Ned Flanders and Homer Simpson ("Hi-Diddly-Ho, Neighbour!"), but it is actually an amalgam of real-life stories that I have witnessed in my years as a pastor. I have woven them together into a single narrative, with the intent of painting a picture of what it looks like when we live by the *greater perspective.* Yes, it is counterintuitive! Yes, it sounds unrealistic! Yes, it is contrary to our very human nature, but it is, in fact, how the Sermon on the Mount instructs us to live.

Although there is a significant short-term price when we take Jesus' imperatives at face value and apply them to real life, the resulting payoff is immense. Not only do these truths have the power to change our lives and make us better people, they have the power to change the people around us and make our world a better place.

Conclusion

Light in Darkness
(and a Pinch of Salt in a Sour World)

I WAS TRAVELLING solo to a speaking engagement by plane one day and was sitting next to a middle-aged couple. We got into the requisite, "Where you heading? Do you have family there? What do you do back in Winnipeg?" conversation. When I answered that I pastored a church, my answer clearly struck a nerve. (I have become accustomed to this reaction.) The husband very proudly informed me that he no longer attended any church because they were all full of hypocrites. To which I assured him, "That shouldn't stop you; there's always room for one more!" He did not think that was the least bit funny and he literally started shouting insults at me. I was a bit surprised. I spent the next ten minutes explaining to him why it was funny. That didn't help either. And then the stewardess came and told him if he didn't calm down he would be asked to get off the plane. We were at 30,000 feet. He didn't think that was funny either. I thought it was hilarious.

We sometimes forget that we are responsible for God's reputation on earth; the only experience most unchurched people will have with Him is vicariously through us. It is a daunting level of responsibility. While the salt and light metaphors were employed near the beginning of the Sermon on the Mount, the rest of the discourse is really just an elaboration of what it means to be salt and light to our world.

> *You are the salt of the earth; but if the salt loses its flavor, how shall it be seasoned? It is then good for nothing but to be thrown out and trampled underfoot by men.*
>
> *You are the light of the world. A city that is set on a hill cannot be hidden. Nor do they light a lamp and put it under a basket, but on a lampstand, and it gives light to all who are in the house. Let your light so shine before men, that they may see your good works and glorify your Father in heaven.*
>
> —Matthew 5:13–16 ▲

Notice it doesn't say we will be *like* salt and light; it says we *are* the salt and we *are* the light. Again, we are often the only encounter unbelieving people will have with the Christian faith. It is, at least in part, why Jesus seemed so interested in us gaining the *greater perspective*. It is His reputation on the line, not ours. This should frighten all of us at least a little bit. Some will contend, "Well, people shouldn't judge God based on what they see His followers do!" But what choice do they have?

There are many beautiful things and wonderful people in God's creation, but the level of darkness, despair, violence, hatred, abuse, oppression, hurt and brokenness is ubiquitous. History has proven, time and again, that when the human race is left to its own devices the world degenerates into a very dark place. Where was the salt and light when Germany went down the dark and deadly path of Nazism? Where was the salt and light when Mussolini went down the path of fascism? Where was the salt and light when Russia went down the path of Marxist communism? Our text asks the pivotal question, "once the salt loses its flavor, how will the world be seasoned?" Salt is meant to penetrate and preserve.

Pure salt cannot actually lose its flavor. Jesus, of course, would have been aware of that. However, in that area of the world, salt came from the Dead Sea. At 1,400 feet below sea level, it is the lowest place on earth. Runoff water has nowhere else to go, so it evaporates and leaves behind massive amounts of salt. The Dead Sea itself, which is really a lake, is 9.6 times saltier than sea water. It is, of course, not pure sodium chloride but made up of dozens of different elements. When it is stockpiled, the sodium is the first thing to be dissolved and leached out by rainwater. The mounds of white crystals left behind are no longer salty. To dispose of it, they would throw the crystals on the road to control the growth of weeds, and it was literally trampled underfoot by men.

(Canadians, of all people, understand the metaphor all too well. Our streets and sidewalks are covered with salt all winter long.)

When we lose our saltiness, our message, our morals and our meaning get trampled underfoot. We are experiencing this firsthand in the twenty-first century. If we are the moral modulators of our day, we are not doing a very good job. We have lost every single cultural battle over abortion, the definition of marriage, the definition of gender, public decency, pornography, honouring the Sabbath, medically assisted suicide, etc. How far can a culture fall? It may be just a matter of time before churches like ours lose their charitable status. That is not hypothetical; it is very much part of the political discussion.[1] I wonder how long it will be before pastors are imprisoned because their message is deemed illegal.

It was a bitter disappointment as we watched a Canadian pastor imprisoned for life in North Korea in 2015.[2] I never imagined that we would be jailing pastors in Canada just five years later.[3] The fact that the latter were COVID-19 related incidents is not the point. When they start putting pastors in jail for their convictions, it is a sign of how far we have tumbled in disregarding the religious liberty and autonomy of the church. Irrespective of one's political views on lockdowns, masks, vaccines and vaccine mandates, we should all be very concerned about the loss of the freedom of religion and the freedom of speech.

On the upside, maybe being arrested for one's faith is not the end of the world. The Apostle Paul seemed to regard it as a badge of honour, or at least an indication of devotion to the cause. He commended himself as a minister of the gospel based on his patience in in the midst of tribulations, distresses, beatings, imprisonments, tumults, etc. (1 Corinthians 6:4–10). Shamefully, I am sometimes glad that I am not quite that devoted.

Someone once asked the question, "If you were arrested for being a Christian, would they have enough evidence to convict you?" Anecdotally, it would appear the answer would be "No." Most of us have become far more worldly than the Christians of previous generations. Many church folks would be hard-pressed to be identified as believers by their neighbours. We just don't act, live or conduct ourselves in ways that distinguish us from the people around us. The fact that we drive off to church at 9 AM Sunday morning doesn't mean anything. For all they know, we are taking our kids to hockey or soccer practice, which is what many Christian families now find themselves doing on weekends. Then we wonder why a shocking two-thirds of young people drop out of church before adulthood.[4] Coincidence? I doubt it. None of this is new, of course. For thousands of years, God's people have experienced cycles of spiritual decline and renewal. The latter only happens when God's people get serious about being salt and light again.

But enough of the bad news. This is exactly the reason why the Sermon on the Mount was preached—so that God's people would gain a *greater perspective* on what it is to *"seek first the kingdom of God"* (Matthew 6:33 ⛰). We are called to live out our faith in such extraordinary ways that those who look at us will say, "I want to party with them." (That is a paraphrase, of course.) Jesus said it like this:

"Let your light so shine before men, that they may see your good works and glorify your Father in heaven" (Matthew 5:16 ▲).

The Industrial Revolution was one of those periods of spiritual decline (1760–1840). The social structure of the Western world was irrevocably disrupted. Men left the farm and went off to work in the factories of the big cities. Sons were no longer being apprenticed by their fathers. Mass migration from rural areas to the city occurred. Not only did the family suffer but so did faith, as people found themselves physically removed from their churches and their faith communities.

In 1842, twenty-year-old George Williams moved from the family farm to the big city of London to get a job in a drapery factory. He was appalled by the working conditions and conduct of the employees. They worked ten to twelve hours a day, six days a week. They slept crowded into rooms over the company's shop, a location thought to be safer than the city's tenements. The streets of London in those days were characterized by open sewers, pickpockets, prostitutes, thieves, beggars, drunks, and orphans roaming the streets by the thousands. The only options the young workers had for entertainment usually involved a bar or a bordello. George decided he was going to live out his faith in such a way that London would become the hardest place to NOT be a Christian.

It was an audacious goal. On June 6, 1844, he found twelve other young men and they met in his bedroom and formed a little group he called the Young Men's Christian Association,[5] or YMCA for short. They would rent halls to provide lectures on faith, and to provide a place for some physical exercise and amusement. By 1851, there were twenty-four YMCAs in Great Britain, with a membership of 2,700. The first YMCA in North America was established in Montreal, Canada in that same year.[6] Apparently the world took notice of his *"good works,"* and in 1884, Queen Victoria knighted

George Williams for his distinguished contribution to humanity.[7] When he died in 1905, the membership of the YMCA was 150,000 in England and 500,000 in North America. Today, the Y has 11 million members in 10,000 chapters in 120 countries around the world.[8] The mission statement of the YMCA to this day remains "To put Christian principles into practice through programs that build healthy spirit, mind and body for all."[9] However, it is doubtful that many people think of the Y as a center of spirituality today.

In 1989, I was in Hyderabad, India. Our host was the director of the YMCA and he put us up in the facility. I do not want to seem ungrateful, but for a Westerner the conditions were difficult. We slept on a concrete floor with dusty old blankets. I remember because I sneezed all night. One of our young team members was overcome with the conditions and became quite upset. I guess he had never stayed anywhere more rustic than the Holiday Inn Express, so I suggested we sing to him to cheer him up. I began and everyone joined in.

> "Young man, there's no need to feel down.
> I said, young man, pick yourself off the ground.
> I said, young man, 'cause you're in a new town…
> it's fun to stay at the YMCA, it's fun to stay at the YMCA…"[10]

We all spelled out Y-M-C-A with our arms and, by the time we were done, he was smiling from ear to ear and ready to live for another day.

The important part of the story is this: the director of the YMCA had invited us to India to conduct gospel outreach. At that time, the C still stood for Christian in India. We put on an outdoor gospel "festival" (we did not use the term "crusade," which would be quite inflammatory in an Eastern culture), and by the last night there were at least 20,000 people in attendance. Thousands of people came to Christ. It was not the thing most people think of when they think of the YMCA, but that is exactly what it was founded for in the first place almost 300 years ago. I have been a member of the Y locally for many years and that is not what we do here. I remember when I joined, the membership application asked, "How did you hear about us?" I checked the "other" box and wrote in "The Village People."

George Williams was a *greater perspective* follower of Christ. He knew what it meant to be salt and light. There are countless ways we, too, can be salt and light. And like Williams, we do not have to travel across the world to some distant mission field to do so. We usually only need to cross the street. The key is to merely live out the Sermon on the Mount right where we already are. Our job is not to rail against all the impiety and transgressions of the world. That has done little to convince infidels that Jesus is the answer. No, we answer the folly of our fallen world with a life well lived. As salt and light, we quietly penetrate and illuminate the culture around us.

C. S. Lewis once said, "What we want is not more little books about Christianity, but more little books by Christians on other subjects—with their Christianity latent."[11] He was not insulting Christian literature but encouraging us to take our faith into the marketplace, to write books about everything but to use them as a vehicle to espouse our biblical worldview.

Francis Collins became something of a household name during the COVID-19 pandemic as the director of the National Institute of Health. He was Dr. Anthony Fauci's boss, but he is more famous for sequencing the human genome. He headed the Human Genome project from 1993 until its completion in 2003. They decoded all 3.1 billion base pairs of the human DNA. Without his work, we would not have *CSI: Miami,* and every murder in Florida would go unsolved. Most significantly for us, however, is that the next thing

Collins did after the project was complete was to write a book called, *The Language of God: A Scientist Presents Evidence for Belief.*[12]

As a medical student in the 1970s, Collins was an avowed atheist. Once he began to practice medicine, he began to have face to face encounters with life and death. Patients would ask him awkward questions about the afterlife like, "What do you believe, doctor?" The science he loved so much was powerless to answer their questions. Conversely, he began to observe how some of his patients were able to rely implicitly on their faith as a source of strength in circumstances that were unbearable. "They had terrible diseases from which they were probably not going to escape, and yet instead of railing at God, they seemed to lean on their faith as a source of great comfort and reassurance."[13] These encounters precipitated his own crisis of faith. He started asking questions he had never even contemplated before. "If the universe had a beginning, who created it?" "Why are the physical constants in the universe so finely tuned to allow the possibility of complex life forms?" "Why do humans have a moral sense?" "What happens after we die?" "What is the meaning of life?" "Why am I here?" "Why does mathematics work, anyway?"[14]

He went to speak to a Methodist minister he had become acquainted with. The pastor said, "You know, your story reminds me a little bit of somebody else who has written about his experience—that Oxford scholar, C. S. Lewis."[15] He gave him a copy of Lewis' book *Mere Christianity*. After reading it, he began to devour other works by C. S. Lewis, and after about a year he reluctantly concluded that he needed to become a Christian. Here is how he explained the transformation in his own words:

> Lewis argues that if you are looking for evidence of a God who cares about us as individuals, where could you more likely look than within your own heart at this very simple

> concept of what's right and what's wrong. And there it is. Not only does it tell you something about the fact that there is a spiritual nature that is somehow written within our hearts, but it also tells you something about the nature of God himself, which is that he is a good and holy God. What we have there is a glimpse of what he stands for….
>
> If I'm walking down the riverbank, and a man is drowning, even if I don't know how to swim very well, I feel this urge that the right thing to do is to try to save that person. Evolution would tell me exactly the opposite: preserve your DNA. Who cares about the guy who's drowning? He's one of the weaker ones, let him go. It's your DNA that needs to survive. And yet that's not what's written within me.[16]

Collins found Lewis' arguments irrefutable, and it caused him to accept the fact that we are all more than just a sequence of chemical base pairs. We were created in the image of a personal and remarkably intelligent God.

Thirty years later, the idea of Collins' book was to try to convince other men and women of science that their understanding of the cosmos could still coexist with a faith in a personal God. Somewhat ironically, his publisher described the book as "the best argument for the integration of faith and logic since C. S. Lewis' *Mere Christianity*."[17] Collins exemplified precisely how Lewis contended we could be salt and light in the world of literature.

I have observed over the years that there has been an unspoken ethic within evangelical Christian communities as to what it means to give our lives in the service of the Lord. We have given the impression that a career path as a pastor or missionary is clearly the most significant way a Christian can serve God and make a difference in the world. Obviously, I would place high value on a young person accepting the call to ministry, but I would by no means agree that other career pursuits are inferior. C. S. Lewis got it right when he encouraged authors to write about other subjects from the context of their latent Christianity. The same holds true for every profession. To even entertain the idea that only pastors and missionaries are the best examples of salt and light is to completely misinterpret the intent of the Sermon on the Mount.

We all are the salt; we all are the light. The call is to every one of us to penetrate our world—not just with the gospel, but with a biblical worldview. We need to encourage our young people to become the next generation of Christian politicians, Christian professors, Christian scientists… journalists, actors, authors, movie producers, musicians, engineers, architects, accountants, doctors, lawyers, Indian chiefs, butchers, bakers and candlestick makers. (Well, I am not too sure about that last one.) If we are not satisfied with the direction of our world, it is our responsibility to get a seat around the table and make a difference. We cannot merely complain that our world is going to hell in a handbasket and do nothing about it.

The call to be salt and light is simple—take your faith into the public arena with whatever it is that you do and let your light shine. That is what it means to live a life characterized by *a greater perspective.*

NOTES

INTRODUCTION

[1] *Seinfeld*, Season 5, episode 22, "The Opposite," written by Larry David, Jerry Seinfeld, and Andy Cowan, directed by Tom Cherones, aired May 19, 1994, on NBC.

[2] Francis X. Clooney, S. J., "The Sermon on the Mount: A Hindu Reading, Part 1," *America: The Jesuit Review* (America Press Inc., January 29, 2011), https://www.americamagazine.org/content/all-things/sermon-mount-hindu-reading-part-1.

[3] P. T. Subrahmanyan, "Mahatma Gandhi and the Sermon on the Mount," Comprehensive Gandhi website by Gandhian Institutions (Bombay Sarvodaya Mandal & Gandhi Research Foundation), accessed October 26, 2022, https://www.mkgandhi.org/articles/mahatma-gandhi-and-sermon-on-the-mount.html.

[4] As Robin R. Meyers writes, "Consider this: there is not a single word in the Sermon on the Mount about what to believe, only words about what to do. It is a behavioral manifesto, not a propositional one. Yet three centuries later, when the Nicene Creed became the official oath of Christendom, there was not a single word in it about what to do, only words about what to believe!" Meyers, *Saving Jesus from the Church: How to Stop Worshiping Christ and Start Following Jesus* (HarperCollins, 2010), 14.

CHAPTER ONE

[1] "The Ladder of Divine Ascent," OrthodoxWiki, accessed October 25, 2022, https://orthodoxwiki.org/The_Ladder_of_Divine_Ascent.

[2] Shane Claiborne, *Irresistible Revolution: Living as an Ordinary Radical* (Zondervan, 2016), 201.

[3] "Stairway to Heaven by Led Zeppelin - Songfacts," Song Meanings at Songfacts (Songfacts, LLC), accessed October 14, 2022, https://www.songfacts.com/facts/led-zeppelin/stairway-to-heaven.

[4] Ibid.

[5] Adam Gold, "What Is the Meaning behind Led Zeppelin, 'Stairway to Heaven'?," American Songwriter (American Songwriter, October 1, 2019), https://americansongwriter.com/stairway-to-heaven-led-zeppelin-behind-the-song.

[6] author's paraphrase

[7] "Kevin O'Leary," Shark Tank Blog, December 28, 2012, https://www.sharktankblog.com/the-sharks/kevin-oleary.

[8] Dianne Buckner, "Kevin O'Leary, Canada's Own Scrooge," CBC news (CBC/Radio Canada, December 21, 2011), https://www.cbc.ca/news/business/kevin-o-leary-canada-s-own-scrooge-1.1104462.

CHAPTER TWO

[1] "The Declaration of Independence," ushistory.org (Independence Hall Association), accessed October 25, 2022, https://www.ushistory.org/declaration/document.

[2] Alexandra Sifferlin, "Here's How Happy Americans Are Right Now," *Time* (Time USA, July 26, 2017), https://time.com/4871720/how-happy-are-americans.

[3] Author unknown.

[4] C. S. Lewis, *The Problem of Pain*, sixteenth printing (London: Geoffrey Bles, The Centenary Press, 1946), chap 6, Project Gutenberg Canada ebook, posted June 24, 2014 at https://gutenberg.ca/ebooks/lewiscs-problemofpain/lewiscs-problemofpain-00-h.html.

[5] Marvin E. Goldberg and Gerald J. Gorn, "Some Unintended Consequences of TV Advertising to Children," *Journal of Consumer Research* 5, no. 1 (June 1978): pp. 22–29, https://doi.org/10.1086/208710.

[6] Sam Carr, "How Many Ads Do We See a Day? 2021 Daily AD Exposure Revealed," Lunio, May 18, 2022, https://ppcprotect.com/blog/strategy/how-many-ads-do-we-see-a-day.

[7] A. Guttmann, "North America Ad Spend 2024," Statista, July 1, 2022, https://www.statista.com/statistics/429036/advertising-expenditure-in-north-america.

[8] Johann Hari, "Op-Ed: We Know Junk Food Makes Us Sick. Are 'Junk Values' Making Us Depressed?" *Los Angeles Times* (Los Angeles Times,

January 21, 2018), https://www.latimes.com/opinion/op-ed/la-oe-hari-kasser-junk-values-20180121-story.html.

[9] Douglas Goldstein, "Tim Kasser–The High Price of Materialism–interview–Goldstein on Gelt," Mar 7, 2016, YouTube video, https://www.youtube.com/watch?v=bJSO3Wc0Mcw, 1:53–3:45.

[10] Ibid., 1:10–1:45.

[11] Martin Luther King, Jr., "Beyond Vietnam —A Time to Break Silence" (speech) Delivered 4 April 1967, Riverside Church, New York City, https://www.americanrhetoric.com/speeches/mlkatimetobreaksilence.htm.

[12] Mark Hughes, *A Greater Purpose: Finding Your Place in God's Great Big Space* (Winnipeg, MB: Mark Hughes, 2015), 20.

[13] 1 Peter 1:6–8

[14] According to Strong's Concordance, *makarios* is a prolonged form of the poetical *makar* – blessed, happy, happier (James Strong, Strong's Expanded Exhaustive Concordance of the Bible (Nashville: Thomas Nelson, 2009), s.v. "makarios.")

[15] Tim Kasser and Richard M. Ryan, "Be Careful What You Wish for: Optimal Functioning and the Relative Attainment of Intrinsic and Extrinsic Goals," in *Life Goals and Well-Being: Towards a Positive Psychology of Human Striving*, ed. Peter Schmuck and Kennon M. Sheldon (Seattle, WA: Hogrefe and Huber, 2001), 116–131. Accessed online at https://psycnet.apa.org/record/2001-01629-007.

[16] Orville E. Kelly, *Make Today Count* (Delacorte, 1977).

[17] Phil Callaway, *Tricks My Dog Taught Me* (Eugene, OR: Harvest House Publishers, 2015), 147.

CHAPTER THREE

[1] Barry Cohen and Michael Record, "Don't Worry, Be Happy 5.4 Project," Composition I: The online home of ENC 1101 with Dr. Record, December 11, 2013, https://enc1101.edublogs.org/2013/12/11/dont-worry-be-happy-5-4-project.

[2] George Carlin, *Napalm & Silly Putty* (Waterville, ME: G. K. Hall, 2001), 240.

[3] "Run for Your Life! It's the 50 Worst Songs Ever!," *Blender*, May 2004.

4 Marc Bekoff, "Do Animals Worry and Lose Sleep When They're Troubled?," *Psychology Today* (Sussex Publishers, April 24, 2013), https://www.psychologytoday.com/us/blog/animal-emotions/201304/do-animals-worry-and-lose-sleep-when-theyre-troubled.

5 Low German expression used by local Mennonites to refer to their afternoon nap.

6 Nan Robertson, "At the Movies," *New York Times* (The New York Times, September 27, 1985), https://www.nytimes.com/1985/09/27/movies/at-the-movies.html.

7 Robert K. Merton, "The Self-Fulfilling Prophecy," *The Antioch Review*, Vol 8 No 2 (Summer 1948), 193–210, accessed at https://www.jstor.org/stable/4609267?origin=crossref.

8 Jake Rossen, "Wiped out: When Johnny Carson Helped Cause a Toilet Paper Shortage in 1973," Mental Floss (Mental Floss, April 23, 2020), https://www.mentalfloss.com/article/623271/when-johnny-carson-caused-a-toilet-paper-shortage-1973.

9 ABC7 Staff, "The Tragic History of the Wallendas," https://www.mysuncoast.com, June 23, 2019, https://www.mysuncoast.com/2019/06/24/tragic-history-wallendas.

10 Harvey Mackay, "Fear Factor Can Create Positives from the Negatives," *Times Union* (Hearst, August 29, 2016), https://www.timesunion.com/business/article/Fear-factor-can-create-positives-from-the-9191525.php.

11 Henry Ford Health Staff, "Worry and Anxiety: Do You Know the Difference?" Henry Ford Health, August 21, 2020, https://www.henryford.com/blog/2020/08/the-difference-between-worry-and-anxiety.

12 Jordan Peterson, "The Reason for Almost All Mental Illnesses," YouTube video posted August 7, 2027, on Jordan Peterson Fan Channel, https://www.youtube.com/watch?v=OW_zpi2hmI4.

13 Richard Carlson, Don't Sweat the Small Stuff … and It's All Small Stuff: Simple Ways to Keep Little Things from Taking over Your Life (Hyperion: New York, 1997).

14 Don Joseph Goewey, "85 Percent of What We Worry about Never Happens," HuffPost (BuzzFeed, Inc. , December 6, 2017), https://www.huffpost.com/entry/85-of-what-we-worry-about_b_8028368.

15 Will Yakowicz, "U.S. Cannabis Sales Hit Record $17.5 Billion as Americans Consume More Marijuana than Ever Before," Forbes (March 3, 2021), https://www.forbes.com/sites/willyakowicz/2021/03/03/us-cannabis-sales-hit-record-175-billion-as-americans-consume-more-marijuana-than-ever-before/?sh=65c2edc32bcf.

16 Nicole Lyn Pesce, "Anti-Anxiety Medication Prescriptions Have Spiked 34% during the Coronavirus Pandemic," MarketWatch (MarketWatch, Inc., May 26, 2020), https://www.marketwatch.com/story/anti-anxiety-medication-prescriptions-have-spiked-34-during-the-coronavirus-pandemic-2020-04-16.

CHAPTER FOUR

1 See Judges 6:15.

2 Joseph was a slave in Egypt, Daniel was a captive in Babylon and Mordecai lived in Persia.

3 Meek —mildness of disposition, gentleness of spirit. "In the OT, the meek are those wholly relying on God rather than their own strength to defend them against injustice…. meekness is the opposite to self-assertiveness and self-interest. It stems from trust in God's goodness and control over the situation." (Online Bible Greek Lexicon) "G4239 - praus - Strong's Greek Lexicon (esv)." Blue Letter Bible. Accessed 27 Oct, 2022. https://www.blueletterbible.org/lexicon/g4239/esv/mgnt/0-1.

4 James Strong, Strong's Exhaustive Concordance of the Bible (Peabody, MA: Hendrickson Publishers, 988) s.v. meek (Cognate: 4239 *praýs*). It should be noted that *praýs* means more than "meek." Biblical meekness is not weakness but rather refers to exercising God's strength under His control – i.e. demonstrating power without undue harshness.

5 *"Donuts" - Jim Gaffigan Stand up Compilation, YouTube* (jimgaffigan, 2020), https://www.youtube.com/watch?v=Iz346Sb9vMs, 2:29–3:13.

6 Joel 2:12

7 C. S. Lewis, *Mere Christianity* (London: Geoffrey Bles, 1952), 74.

CHAPTER FIVE

[1] Alan Abrahamson, NBC Olympics, "Bolt Wins 200, Declares He's a 'Legend,'" nbcolympics.com, August 10, 2012, https://web.archive.org/web/20120810070845/http://www.nbcolympics.com/news-blogs/track-and-field/bolt-wins-200-declares-hes-a-legend.html.

[2] Jonathan Brown, "I'm a Legend, Says Usain Bolt. No You're Not, Says IOC Chairman Jacques Rogge," *Independent* (Independent Digital News and Media, August 11, 2012), https://www.independent.co.uk/sport/olympics/athletics/im-a-legend-says-usain-bolt-no-youre-not-says-ioc-chairman-jacques-rogge-8031962.html.

[3] Mark Hughes, *A Greater Purpose: Finding Your Place in God's Great Big Space* (Winnipeg, MB: Mark Hughes, 2015).

[4] Mark Hughes, "Chapter 16: In Search of Excellence," in *A Greater Passion: Lessons on Living Large in Life and Love* (Winnipeg, MB: Mark Hughes, 2020), 163–171.

[5] Jordan B. Peterson, Van Ethan Sciver, and Norman Doidge, *12 Rules for Life: An Antidote to Chaos* (Toronto: Vintage Canada, 2020) 74.

[6] "Roster #85 Milt Stegall," CFL.ca, accessed October 17, 2022, https://web.archive.org/web/20081016231136/http://www.cfl.ca/index.php/roster/show/id/13.

[7] David Plotz, "Charles Colson: How a Watergate Crook Became America's Greatest Christian Conservative," Slate Magazine (The Slate Group, March 11, 2000), https://slate.com/news-and-politics/2000/03/charles-colson.html.

[8] Dylan Matthews, "9 Questions about Watergate You Were Too Embarrassed to Ask," Vox (Vox Media, November 25, 2019), https://www.vox.com/2014/8/7/5970967/what-was-watergate-scandal-nixon.

[9] Bill Marsh, "Ideas & Trends – When Criminal Charges Reach the White House," *New York Times* (October 30, 2005), https://www.nytimes.com/2005/10/30/weekinreview/ideas-trends-when-criminal-charges-reach-the-white-house.html.

CHAPTER SIX

[1] *Inside Out*, directed by Pete Doctor & Ronnie Del Carmen (California, Disney/Pixar, 2015).

[2] Temple and religious prostitution were rites consisting of paid intercourse performed in the context of religious worship, possibly as a form of fertility rite or divine marriage. Wikipedia contributors, "Sacred prostitution," *Wikipedia, The Free Encyclopedia,* https://en.wikipedia.org/w/index.php?title=Sacred_prostitution&oldid=1116700845 (accessed October 26, 2022).

[3] See Romans 8:11–29

[4] David R. Wilkerson et al., *David Wilkerson's the Cross and the Switchblade* (Old Tappan, NJ: F. H. Revell, 1972).

[5] "Following up with Graduates of Minnesota Teen Challenge," Wilder Research (Wilder Foundation), accessed October 26, 2022, https://www.wilder.org/sites/default/files/imports/MN_TeenChallenge Follow-up_Sum2-pg_1-11.pdf.

[6] There are dozens of iterations of this progression attributed to various people over the years from Buddha to Ralph Waldo Emerson. (Garson O'Toole, "Watch Your Thoughts, They Become Words; Watch Your Words, They Become Actions," Quote Investigator®, January 10, 2013, https://quoteinvestigator.com/2013/01/10/watch-your-thoughts). The closest to my version would be Mahatma Gandhi's "Your beliefs become your thoughts, Your thoughts become your words, Your words become your actions, Your actions become your habits, Your habits become your values, Your values become your destiny." (Judy Schindler, "Your Thoughts Become Your Destiny," Stan Greenspon Holocaust and Social Justice Education Center, December 21, 2018, https://www.stangreensponcenter.org/2018/12/19/your-thoughts-become-your-destiny.) I have simplified it to make it follow more closely with how the Bible would most clearly teach it.

[7] Gary Smith, "Coming Into Focus," SI.com (Sports Illustrated Vault | SI.com, July 17, 2006), https://vault.si.com/vault/2006/07/17/coming-into-focus.

8 The Career Grand Slam recognizes a player who wins all four Grand Slam tennis tournaments during their career: The Australian Open, French Open, Wimbledon and US Open.

9 The Career Super Slam is reserved for a player who wins all four Grand Slam tournaments plus the Olympic gold medal and the year-end championship during their career.

10 "Igor Sikorsky the Aviation Pioneer Speaks," Igor Sikorsky Historical Archives, September 11, 2013, https://www.sikorskyarchives.com/igor-sikorsky-speaks.php.

11 Aaron Sorkin, *A Few Good Men*, accessed online at The Internet Movie Script Database, July 15, 1991, https://imsdb.com/scripts/A-Few-Good-Men.html.

CHAPTER SEVEN

1 *A History of the World: Part 1* (20th Century Fox Film Corporation, Brooks Films, 1981).

2 John 1:14

3 *Raca* is just an Aramaic word for "fool."

4 In Matthew 23:17 Jesus called the Pharisees the Greek word *moros*, which is considered more harsh than *raca*.

5 1 Samuel 16:7 illustrates the priority God places on the heart: *"But the LORD said to Samuel, 'Do not look at his appearance or at his physical stature, because I have refused him. For the LORD does not see as man sees; for man looks at the outward appearance, but the LORD looks at the heart.'"*

6 Harvey Mackay, "In Life and in Business, a Sense of Humor Shines," *Star Tribune* (Star Tribune, April 12, 2020), https://www.startribune.com/mackay-in-life-and-in-business-a-sense-of-humor-shines/569552642/#:~:text=Ford%2C%20the%20founder%20of%20Ford,Stick%20to%20one%20model.%E2%80%9D.

7 "The Model T," Ford Corporate (Ford Motor Company), accessed October 21, 2022, https://corporate.ford.com/articles/history/the-model-t.html.

8 Kris Manty, "A Misprint in a Bible from 1631 Endorses Hanky-Panky," Antique Trader (Antique Trader, July 11, 2021),

https://www.antiquetrader.com/collectibles/misprint-in-wicked-bible-endorses-hanky-panky.

9 Bev Shea was a Canadian musician who travelled with Billy Graham for sixty-six years. I met him over lunch in Ottawa one day when he was 100 years old. He was a class act. He died at 104.

10 Numbers 30:2

11 Leviticus 19:12

12 See Matthew 2:24, 27; 23:23, 25–26.

13 C. S. Lewis, *Mere Christianity* (London: Geoffrey Bles, 1952), 102.

14 "Nommensen, Ingwer Ludwig (1834-1918)," Nommensen, Ingwer Ludwig (1834-1918) Pioneer missionary to the Batak in Sumatra (BU School of Theology History of Missiology), accessed October 21, 2022, http://www.bu.edu/missiology/missionary-biography/n-o-p-q/nommensen-ingwer-ludwig-1834-1918.

15 See Romans 8:2–5.

CHAPTER EIGHT

1 David Von Drehle, "Lincoln's Reluctant War: How Abolitionists Leaned on the President," *The Atlantic* (Atlantic Media Company, October 26, 2012), https://www.theatlantic.com/national/archive/2012/10/lincolns-reluctant-war-how-abolitionists-leaned-on-the-president/264125.

2 Michael Youssef, The Leadership Style of Jesus: How to Make a Lasting Impact (Eugene, OR: Harvest House Publishers, 2013), 92.

3 Lincoln stated, "In regard to this Great Book, I have but to say, it is the best gift God has given to man. All the good the Savior gave to the world was communicated through this book. But for it, we could not know right from wrong. All things most desirable for man's welfare, here and hereafter, are to be found portrayed in it." Stephen Flurry, "Lincoln and the Bible," theTrumpet.com (Philadelphia Church of God, August 12, 2019), https://www.thetrumpet.com/21110-lincoln.

4 David Neff, "Jesus through Jewish Eyes," ChristianityToday.com (Christianity Today, April 1, 2012), https://www.christianitytoday.com/ct/2012/april/jesus-through-jewish-eyes.html.

[5] Jennifer Otto, "Were the Early Christians Pacifists? Does It Matter?" *The Conrad Grebel Review* 35, no. 3 (Fall 2017), accessed at https://uwaterloo.ca/grebel/publications/conrad-grebel-review/issues/fall-2017/were-early-christians-pacifists-does-it-matter.

[6] Joseph Cardinal Bernadin, accessed October 18, 2022, https://stmarych.com/documents/2015/10/Cardinal%20Bernadin%20SEAMLESS%20GARMENT.pdf.

[7] Ryan P. Burge, "(Almost) No One in the United States Believes in a Consistent Ethic of Life," Religion in Public, September 13, 2017, https://religioninpublic.blog/2017/09/13/almost-no-one-in-the-united-states-believes-in-a-consistent-ethic-of-life.

[8] John 8:3–11

[9] Anthony A. Braga and Philip J. Cook, "Guns Do Kill People," The Regulatory Review (University of Pennsylvania Law School, November 5, 2018), https://www.theregreview.org/2018/11/05/braga-cook-guns-do-kill-people/#:~:text=%E2%80%9CGuns%20don't%20kill%20people,case%20for%20their%20deregulation%20agenda.

[10] Sarah Hutchinson, "Just-War Theory," Guilford County Schools, December 17, 2018, https://www.gcsnc.com/cms/lib/NC01910393/Centricity/Domain/5418/Just-War%20Theory.pdf. This is merely a summary. His specific writings on the subject are found in *Contra Faustum Manichaeum* book 22 sections 69–76.

[11] Hiram Erb Steinmetz, "Peter Miller and Michael Witman: a Revolutionary Episode," *Journal of the Lancaster County Historical Society* 6, no. no. 3 & 4 (1901), accessed at https://www.lancasterhistory.org/images/stories/JournalArticles/vol6nos3&4pp46_49_118632.pdf.

[12] Christopher Hitchens, *The Missionary Position: Mother Teresa in Theory and Practice* (London: Atlantic Books, 2021).

[13] Nikhil Kumar, "Indian Leaders Prepare for Mother Teresa's Canonization," *Time* (Time, September 2, 2016), https://time.com/4477267/indian-leaders-head-to-the-vatican-for-mother-teresas-canonization.

[14] Joyce Hackel, "A Pastor and an Imam 'Programmed to Hate One Another' Bridge a Religious Divide," The World (The World from PRX, December 10, 2015), https://www.pri.org/stories/2015-12-10/pastor-and-imam-programmed-hate-one-another-bridge-religious-divide.

[15] Martin Luther King, Jr., "'Loving Your Enemies," Sermon Delivered at Dexter Avenue Baptist Church," The Martin Luther King, Jr. Research and Education Institute (Stanford University, November 17, 1957), https://kinginstitute.stanford.edu/king-papers/documents/loving-your-enemies-sermon-delivered-dexter-avenue-baptist-church.

[16] Details about the movie can be found online at https://en.wikipedia.org/wiki/Friday_the_13th_(franchise).

CHAPTER NINE

[1] Anthony J. Alessandra and Michael J. O'Connor, The Platinum Rule: Discover the Four Basic Business Personalities and How They Can Lead You to Success (New York: Grand Central Publishing, 1998), 6.

[2] Tony Alessandra, "The Platinum Rule," The Official Site of Dr. Tony Alessandra, accessed October 22, 2022, https://www.alessandra.com/abouttony/aboutpr.asp, emphasis added.

[3] "Titanium Rule 'Do Unto Others As Christ Has Done Unto You.' Trademark Information," Trademark of Sweet, Leonard I., jr, Dr. Serial Number: 75771852, Trademarkia Trademarks, accessed October 25, 2022, https://trademark.trademarkia.com/titanium-rule-do-unto-others-as-christ-has-done-unto-you-75771852.html.

[4] Nicholas Mancall-Bitel, "How to Drink, According to Frank Sinatra," Thrillist, September 14, 2016, https://www.thrillist.com/culture/frank-sinatra-quotes-on-drinking.

[5] G. K. Chesterton, Illustrated London News, July 16, 1910. Quoted section accessed online at http://platitudesundone.blogspot.com/2010/06/bible-tells-us-to-love-our-neighbours.html.

CHAPTER TEN

[1] 1 Peter 2:9 *"But you are a chosen generation, a royal priesthood…"*

[2] "Maximilian Kolbe (1894 - 1941)," Jewish Virtual Library (American-Israeli Cooperative Enterprise), accessed October 19, 2022, https://www.jewishvirtuallibrary.org/maximilian-kolbe.

[3] Ibid.

4 "Saint Maximilian Kolbe," Saints.SQPN.com, May 1, 2010, https://web.archive.org/web/20120201110545/http://saints.sqpn.com/saint-maximilian-kolbe.

CHAPTER ELEVEN

1 Taylor Lambert, "Father of Taber School Shooting Victim Remembers Pain of Tragedy ...," *Calgary Herald* (Postmedia Network Inc., January 22, 2016), https://calgaryherald.com/news/crime/father-of-taber-school-shooting-victim-remembers-pain-of-tragedy.

2 Author unknown, often attributed to be an African proverb.

3 John 12:6

4 John 13:26

5 Lewis B. Smedes, *Forgive and Forget - Healing the Hurts We Dont Deserve* (San Francisco: Harper & Row, 1984) 133.

6 "The 1973 Pulitzer Prize Winner in Spot News Photography" The Pulitzer Prizes, accessed October 22, 2022, https://www.pulitzer.org/winners/huynh-cong-ut.

7 "1973 Photo Contest, World Press Photo of the Year," World Press Photo (World Press Photo Foundation), accessed October 22, 2022, https://www.worldpressphoto.org/collection/photo-contest/1973/nick-ut/1.

8 Courtney Greenberg, "'Napalm girl' Kim Phuc has come a long way since she was photographed 50 years ago today," *National Post* (Postmedia Network Inc, June 8, 2022), https://nationalpost.com/news/canada/napalm-girl-kim-phuc-has-come-a-long-way-since-she-was-photographed-50-years-ago-today.

9 Kathy Sheridan, "Kim Phuc, the Napalm Girl: 'Love Is More Powerful than Any Weapon'," *Irish Times* (The Irish Times, May 28, 2016), https://www.irishtimes.com/life-and-style/people/kim-phuc-the-napalm-girl-love-is-more-powerful-than-any-weapon-1.2661740.

10 Johann Christoph Arnold, *The Lost Art of Forgiving: Stories of Healing from the Cancer of Bitterness* (Walden, NY: Plough Publishing House, 1998).

11 Sheridan, "Kim Phuc, the Napalm Girl…" *Irish Times*. (see n.9)

CHAPTER TWELVE

[1] Aja Romano, "A History of 'Wokeness,'" Vox (Vox, October 9, 2020), https://www.vox.com/culture/21437879/stay-woke-wokeness-history-origin-evolution-controversy.

[2] *Merriam-Webster*, s.v. "woke (*adj.*)," accessed October 22, 2022, https://www.merriam-webster.com/dictionary/woke

[3] Kara Brown, "In the Aftermath of Ferguson, Stay Angry and Stay Woke," Jezebel (Jezebel, August 15, 2014), https://jezebel.com/in-the-aftermath-of-ferguson-stay-angry-and-stay-woke-1622364931

[4] Ryan Bort, "Obama Calls out Online Call-out Culture: 'That's Not Activism'," *Rolling Stone* (Penske Business Media, LLC, October 30, 2019), https://www.rollingstone.com/politics/politics-news/obama-calls-out-call-out-culture-not-activism-905600.

[5] National Post Staff, "Don Cherry Fired by Sportsnet Over 'You People' Rant on Coach's Corner," *National Post* (Postmedia Network Inc., November 11, 2019), https://nationalpost.com/news/canada/don-cherry-fired.

[6] Andrea Park, "'Megyn Kelly Today' Canceled after Blackface Comments," CBS News (CBS Interactive, October 26, 2018), https://www.cbsnews.com/news/megyn-kelly-today-canceled-after-blackface-comments.

[7] Wilson Wong and Diana Dasrath, "Chris Harrison Exits 'the Bachelor' Franchise after Defending Former Contestant's Racist Behavior," NBCNews.com (NBC Universal News Group, June 8, 2021), https://www.nbcnews.com/news/us-news/chris-harrison-exits-bachelor-franchise-after-defending-former-contestant-s-n1269960.

[8] Robertas Lisickis and Saulė Tolstych, "30 Celebs Who Were Canceled but Didn't Deserve It, According to People Online," Bored Panda, October 5, 2021, https://www.boredpanda.com/celebrities-never-been-cancelled-reddit/?utm_source=google&utm_medium=organic&utm_campaign=organic.

[9] Emmy Wallin, "The 20 Richest Authors in the World," Wealthy Gorilla, October 6, 2022, https://wealthygorilla.com/richest-authors-world.

10 Abby Gardner, "A Complete Breakdown of the J.K. Rowling Transgender-Comments Controversy," *Glamour* (Condé Nast, October 14, 2022), https://www.glamour.com/story/a-complete-breakdown-of-the-jk-rowling-transgender-comments-controversy.

11 Rowling's concerns are that, as a culture under the influence of trans-activism, the importance of biological sex (the physical sex characteristics we are all born with) is disappearing. She argues that if anyone can suddenly call themselves a woman, then the rights and protections of women as a group no longer mean anything. She uses the example of trans-men being allowed to use the ladies room or women's shelters simply because they "feel" they are women. As a former victim of sexual abuse, she feels this poses a threat to vulnerable women.

12 Alan McEwen, "JK Rowling Wades into New Trans Controversy after US Gender Poll Released," *Daily Record* (Scottish Daily Record and Sunday Mail Ltd, December 29, 2021), https://www.dailyrecord.co.uk/news/scottish-news/jk-rowling-new-trans-row-25810816.

13 Nick Romano, "Why J.K. Rowling Didn't Join the New 'Harry Potter' Reunion Special," EW.com (Meredith Corporation, December 30, 2021), https://ew.com/movies/why-j-k-rowling-didnt-join-harry-potter-reunion-special-return-to-hogwarts.

14 Isobel Lewis, "Which Harry Potter Stars Have Criticised JK Rowling's Transgender Comments?," The Independent (Independent Digital News and Media, June 12, 2020), https://www.independent.co.uk/arts-entertainment/books/news/jk-rowling-trans-harry-potter-rupert-grint-daniel-racliffe-emma-watson-bonnie-wright-a9560376.html.

15 J. K. Rowling, "J.K. Rowling Writes about Her Reasons for Speaking out on Sex and Gender Issues," J.K. Rowling, June 10, 2020, https://www.jkrowling.com/opinions/j-k-rowling-writes-about-her-reasons-for-speaking-out-on-sex-and-gender-issues.

16 "The Overton Window®," Mackinac Center for Public Policy, accessed October 22, 2022, https://www.mackinac.org/OvertonWindow.

17 Joseph G. Lehman, "Glenn Beck Highlights Mackinac Center's 'Overton Window,'" Mackinac Center for Public Policy, November 23, 2009, http://www.mackinac.org/11398.

18 Maggie Astor, "How the Politically Unthinkable Can Become Mainstream," *New York Times*, February 26, 2019, https://

[19] www.nytimes.com/2019/02/26/us/politics/overton-window-democrats.html.

[19] Jackie Dunham, "Unvaccinated? Here are some of the things that are off-limits to you in Canada," CTV News (BellMedia, August 19, 2021, updated September 2, 2021), https://www.ctvnews.ca/health/coronavirus/unvaccinated-here-are-some-of-the-things-that-are-off-limits-to-you-in-canada-1.5553655.

[20] Owen Dyer, "Covid-19: Quebec to Tax the Unvaccinated as Vaccine Mandates Spread in Europe," The BMJ (British Medical Journal Publishing Group, January 14, 2022), https://www.bmj.com/content/376/bmj.o112.

[21] I fully understood the need to manage the pandemic to create a safe environment for people and to keep the hospitals from overflowing, I just disagreed with doing it by completely disregarding the Charter of Rights and treating otherwise conscientious people with such contempt. Jesus saved His greatest compassion for the outcasts: lepers, publicans and Samaritans. We could have done the same.

[22] Mike Davis, "Big Tech Censorship of COVID Information Leads to Vaccine Hesitancy," Newsweek, November 2, 2021, https://www.newsweek.com/big-tech-censorship-covid-information-leads-vaccine-hesitancy-opinion-1644051.

[23] Ron Johnson, "YouTube Cancels the U.S. Senate," WSJ Opinion (Dow Jones & Company, Inc, February 2, 2021), https://www.wsj.com/articles/youtube-cancels-the-u-s-senate-11612288061.

[24] Tristin Hopper, "First Reading: So, the Truckers Didn't Convince Trudeau to Lift the ...," *National Post* (Postmedia Network Inc., January 31, 2022), https://nationalpost.com/news/canada/first-reading-so-the-truckers-didnt-convince-trudeau-to-lift-the-mandates.

[25] Nick Andrews et al., "Covid-19 Vaccine Effectiveness against the Omicron (B.1.1.529) Variant," New England Journal of Medicine, March 2, 2022, https://www.nejm.org/doi/full/10.1056/NEJMoa2119451.

[26] Andrea Woo and James Bradshaw, "Trinity Western's Law-School Bid Gets Provincial Approval despite Same-Sex Intimacy Ban," *The Globe and Mail*, December 18, 2013, https://www.theglobeandmail.com

/news/british-columbia/trinity-westerns-law-school-bid-gets-provincial-approval-despite-same-sex-intimacy-ban/article16034139.

27 The Canadian Press, "Trinity Western Wins Victory in Fight to Open Christian Law School, Limits on Accrediting Called 'Unreasonable'," *National Post,* (Postmedia Network Inc., November 1, 2016), https://nationalpost.com/news/canada/trinity-western-wins-legal-victory-in-fight-to-open-christian-law-school-limits-on-accrediting-future-lawyers-called-unreasonable.

28 Kathleen Harris, "Trinity Western Loses Fight for Christian Law School as Court Rules Limits on Religious Freedom 'Reasonable'," CBC NEWS (CBC/Radio-Canada, June 15, 2018), https://www.cbc.ca/news/politics/trinity-western-supreme-court-decision-1.4707240.

29 Morgan Lee, "Christian College Drops Sex Standards in Law School Bid," *Christianity Today,* August 16, 2018, https://www.christianitytoday.com/news/2018/august/trinity-western-community-covenant-canada-law-school-twu.html.

CHAPTER THIRTEEN

1 See Chapter 11 "The F-Bomb."

2 In Matthew 16:23, Jesus did say Peter acted in an offensive manner, but it was clear from the context of the story that He was not personally offended.

3 Peter J. Pitts, "Outside View: New York's 'Little Flower'," UPI (United Press International, Inc., October 7, 2002), https://www.upi.com/Archives/2002/10/07/Outside-View-New-Yorks-Little-Flower/6781033963200.

CHAPTER FOURTEEN

1 Jesse Lawrence, "'Hamilton' Is Broadway's Most Expensive Show-Ever," Daily Beast (The Daily Beast Company LLC, July 12, 2017), https://www.thedailybeast.com/hamilton-is-broadways-most-expensive-showever.

2 "The Unknown Story of Broadway Street," MetroFocus (WNET, October 20, 2015), https://www.thirteen.org/metrofocus/2015/10/the-

unknown-story-of-broadway-street/#:~:text=It%20became%20one%20of%20the,and%20farms%20of%20New%20Amsterdam.

3. Norma Robertson, "Herod's Temple Courts, with Josephus Text," Location of Herod and Solomon Temples on the Temple Mount Jerusalem, accessed October 23, 2022, http://templemountlocation.com/herodTempleCourts.html.

4. For example, see Luke 6:22 and John 7:7.

5. "Quotes from "*The Simpsons*: Bart the Murderer,'" IMDb.com, accessed October 23, 2022, https://www.imdb.com/title/tt0701060/quotes/?ref_=tt_trv_qu. Excerpt is from "Bart the Murderer," Written by John Swartzwelder, Directed by Rich Moore, *The Simpsons* (FOX, October 10, 1991).

6. Nicole Darrah, "Alexandria Ocasio-Cortez Says NYC Crime Surge Due to People 'Stealing Bread to Feed Their Children'," *The U.S. Sun*, July 13, 2020, https://www.the-sun.com/news/1129423/alexandria-ocasio-cortez-nyc-surge-crime-coronavirus.

7. "When You Come to a Fork in the Road, Take It," Quote Investigator, July 25, 2013, https://quoteinvestigator.com/2013/07/25/fork-road.

8. "Integrity," Cambridge Dictionary (Cambridge University Press 2022), accessed October 26, 2022, https://dictionary.cambridge.org/dictionary/english/integrity.

9. Adapted from "Mark Twain's Melon," *Star*, September 23, 1899, Issue 6598 edition, p. 3, https://paperspast.natlib.govt.nz/newspapers/TS18990923.2.15. This is the longer original version of the story. Apparently he was known for telling abbreviated versions in speeches.

10. "Pablo Escobar - Evil Kingpin or Robin Hood?," Crime+Investigation UK (AETN UK), accessed October 23, 2022, https://www.crimeandinvestigation.co.uk/article/pablo-escobar-evil-kingpin-or-robin-hood.

11. Kysa Daniels, "Coach Cleveland Stroud," *Covington News*, October 19, 2015, https://www.covnews.com/news/coach-cleveland-stroud.

12. Ibid.

CHAPTER FIFTEEN

[1] Vance Christie, "The Half-Century Prayer Request of George Muller," VanceChristie.com, May 7, 2020, http://vancechristie.com/2020/05/07/the-half-century-prayer-request-of-george-muller.

[2] I always remind those who lament the end of school prayer that as long as there are still exams, there will always be prayer in schools.

[3] *The Princess Bride* (Twentieth Century Fox, 1987) Directed by Rob Reiner, Written by William Goldman.

[4] "The Princess Bride (1987) Billy Crystal: Miracle Max - Quotes," IMDb.com, accessed October 23, 2022, https://www.imdb.com/title/tt0093779/characters/nm0000345.

[5] "Is Allah Called 'Father'? How Can We Know God as Our Father?" CompellingTruth.org (Got Questions Ministries), accessed October 23, 2022, https://www.compellingtruth.org/Allah-Father.html.

[6] Joanna Whitehead, "Prince Charles' Beloved Aston Martin Now Runs on Wine and Cheese," *The Independent* (Independent Digital News and Media, October 12, 2021), https://www.independent.co.uk/life-style/royal-family/prince-charles-car-runs-wine-cheese-b1935985.html.

[7] Not to be confused with the annoying Swedish pop band that sings in falsetto.

[8] Charles G. Finney, "Short Life of Charles G. Finney," ed. William Allen, The Gospel Truth (Gospel Truth Ministries), accessed October 23, 2022, https://www.gospeltruth.net/finney-101/shortlifetxt/shortlifepg.htm.

[9] "The Book of Common Prayer," The General Synod of the Anglican Church of Canada 1962, (Toronto, Anglican Book Centre, 962) 123, accessed online at https://www.anglican.ca/wp-content/uploads/BCP.pdf.

[10] Tony Dunnel, "The Little-Known Backdoor to Machu Picchu," Atlas Obscura, December 27, 2017, https://www.atlasobscura.com/places/inca-bridge.

[11] "Huayna Picchu: The Stairs of Death," Ticket Machu Picchu (Machupicchu Terra S.R.L.), accessed October 25, 2022, https://www.ticketmachupicchu.com/huayna-picchu-stairs-death.

Notes

[12] Norman, "Huayna Picchu Death Toll – Facts & Myths," Années de Pèlerinage, March 5, 2016, https://www.annees-de-pelerinage.com/huayna-picchu-death-toll-and-accidents.

[13] *Project Gutenberg eBook of Lady Windermere's Fan, by Oscar Wilde*, eBook #790, released January 25, 1997, updated June 7, 2021 [eBook #790] Act One, Scene One, https://www.gutenberg.org/files/790/790-h/790-h.htm

CHAPTER SIXTEEN

[1] The Jimi Hendrix Experience, "Castles Made of Sand," by Jimi Hendrix, released December 1, 1967, track 2 on side on *Axis: Bold as Love*, Track Records, vinyl LP.

[2] Author's paraphrase

CONCLUSION

[1] John Longhurst, "Should Religious Organizations Maintain Their Charitable Status?," *The Free Press* (Winnipeg Free Press, May 22, 2021), https://www.winnipegfreepress.com/arts-and-life/life/faith/should-religious-organizations-maintain-their-charitable-status-574474232.html.

[2] "N Korea Sentences Canada Pastor to Life in Jail," BBC News (bbc.co.uk, December 16, 2015), https://www.bbc.com/news/world-asia-35109452.

[3] Adam Lachacz, "U.S. Senator Pushes to Place Canada on Religious Freedoms Watch List for Alberta Pastors Arrests," CTV News Edmonton (BellMedia, June 25, 2021), https://edmonton.ctvnews.ca/u-s-senator-pushes-to-place-canada-on-religious-freedoms-watch-list-for-alberta-pastors-arrests-1.5486231.

[4] "Church Dropouts Have Risen to 64%-but What about Those Who Stay?" Barna (Barna Group Inc., September 4, 2019), https://www.barna.com/research/resilient-disciples.

[5] Mark Stevens, "Spotlight on the History of the YMCA," Mark Stevens Charity, October 14, 2020, https://www.stevensdonation.org/news/spotlight-on-the-history-of-the-ymca.

[6] Ibid.

[7] "Our History - A Brief History of the YMCA Movement," Marshfield Clinic Health System YMCA, accessed October 24, 2022, http://www.mfldymca.org/about_us/history_national.php.

[8] "Welcome to the Y," The Y (YMCA of the USA), accessed October 24, 2022, https://www.ymca.org.

[9] Ibid.

[10] "Y.M.C.A." written by Henri Belolo, Jacques Morali, and Victor Edward Willis, 1978, Sony/ATV Music Publishing LLC.

[11] William OFlaherty, "(CCSLQ-18) Christian Literature," Essential C.S. Lewis, January 16, 2016, https://essentialcslewis.com/2016/01/16/ccslq-18-christian-literature.

[12] Francis S. Collins, *The Language of God: A Scientist Presents Evidence for Belief* (New York: Free Press, 2007).

[13] "An Interview with Francis Collins," The Question of God (PBS.org) (WGBH Interactive, 2004), https://www.pbs.org/wgbh/questionofgod/voices/collins.html.

[14] Ibid.

[15] Ibid.

[16] Ibid.

[17] "The Language of God - About the Book," Simon & Schuster (Simon & Schuster, Inc.), accessed October 24, 2022, https://www.simonandschuster.com/books/The-Language-of-God/Francis-S-Collins/9781416542742.

Also in the "Greater" Series by Mark Hughes

A GREATER PURPOSE
Finding Your Place in God's Great Big Space

This book seeks to answer the big questions in life: Why am I here? What are the purposes that make life truly worth living? Is there a divine destiny that is specific to me alone?

Life is often hard and sometimes doesn't make sense, but God, in His omniscience, has placed us in the midst of it all to discover our greater purpose.

The only real joy we experience in life is when our plans begin to align with God's plan for our lives. *A Greater Purpose* is all about finding your place in God's great big space.

A GREATER PASSION
Lessons on Living Large in Life and Love

Passion is the fuel for life—all great achievement and advancement comes from passionate people.

Reaching our full potential will ultimately come down to our willingness to align our passions with God's unique plan for our lives.

A Greater Passion is based on the life and teachings of King Solomon, the world's most passionate man. What would our immediate world look like if we became passionate to love our spouse, raise our kids, help our friends, excel in our careers, serve our church and bring change to our communities?

Available in both trade paperback and eBook formats.

Manufactured by Amazon.ca
Acheson, AB